Shakespeare's Golden Ages

Edinburgh Critical Studies in Renaissance Culture

Series Editors: Lorna Hutson, Katherine Ibbett, Joe Moshenska and Kathryn Murphy

Titles available in the series

Open Subjects: English Renaissance Republicans, Modern Selfhoods and the Virtue of Vulnerability
James Kuzner

The Phantom of Chance: From Fortune to Randomness in Seventeenth-Century French Literature
John D. Lyons

Don Quixote in the Archives: Madness and Literature in Early Modern Spain
Dale Shuger

Untutored Lines: The Making of the English Epyllion
William P. Weaver

The Girlhood of Shakespeare's Sisters: Gender, Transgression, Adolescence
Jennifer Higginbotham

Friendship's Shadows: Women's Friendship and the Politics of Betrayal in England, 1640–1705
Penelope Anderson

Inventions of the Skin: The Painted Body in Early English Drama, 1400–1642
Andrea Ria Stevens

Performing Economic Thought: English Drama and Mercantile Writing, 1600–1642
Bradley D. Ryner

Forgetting Differences: Tragedy, Historiography and the French Wars of Religion
Andrea Frisch

Listening for Theatrical Form in Early Modern England
Allison Deutermann

Theatrical Milton: Politics and Poetics of the Staged Body
Brendan Prawdzik

Legal Reform in English Renaissance Literature
Virginia Lee Strain

The Origins of English Revenge Tragedy
George Oppitz-Trotman

Crime and Consequence in Early Modern Literature and Law
Judith Hudson

Shakespeare's Golden Ages: Resisting Nostalgia in Elizabethan Drama
Kristine Johanson

Visit the Edinburgh Critical Studies in Renaissance Culture website at www.edinburghuniversitypress.com/series/ECSRC

Shakespeare's Golden Ages

Resisting Nostalgia in Elizabethan Drama

Kristine Johanson

EDINBURGH
University Press

Edinburgh University Press is one of the leading university presses in the UK. We publish academic books and journals in our selected subject areas across the humanities and social sciences, combining cutting-edge scholarship with high editorial and production values to produce academic works of lasting importance. For more information visit our website: edinburghuniversitypress.com

© Kristine Johanson 2022, 2024

Edinburgh University Press Ltd
The Tun – Holyrood Road
12(2f) Jackson's Entry
Edinburgh EH8 8PJ

First published in hardback by Edinburgh University Press 2022

Typeset in 10.5/13 Adobe Sabon LT Pro by
by Cheshire Typesetting Ltd, Cuddington, Cheshire,
Croydon, CR0 4YY

A CIP record for this book is available from the British Library

ISBN 978 1 4744 9354 3 (hardback)
ISBN 978 1 4744 9355(paperback)
ISBN 978 1 4744 9356 7 (webready PDF)
ISBN 978 1 4744 9357 4 (epub)

The right of Kristine Johanson to be identified as the author of this work has been asserted in accordance with the Copyright, Designs and Patents Act 1988, and the Copyright and Related Rights Regulations 2003
(SI No. 2498).

Contents

Series Editors' Preface	vii
Prologue	x
Note on Citation	xiv
Introduction: Rethinking Nostalgia	1
1. Against Nostalgia: Looking Forward to the Future in the Queen's Men's Plays and Marlowe's *Tamburlaine*	35
2. What Merry World in England? Nostalgic *Paroemia* and *The Second Part of Henry VI*	68
3. In the Mean Season: *Richard II*'s Absent Hospitality	96
4. The Lessons of Nostalgia in *Julius Caesar* and *Sejanus*	132
Conclusion: Resisting Nostalgia	165
Bibliography	172
Index	201

For my parents

Series Editors' Preface

Edinburgh Critical Studies in Renaissance Culture may, as a series title, provoke some surprise. On the one hand, the choice of the word 'culture' (rather than, say, 'literature') suggests that writers in this series subscribe to the now widespread assumption that the 'literary' is not isolable, as a mode of signifying, from other signifying practices that make up what we call 'culture'. On the other hand, most of the critical work in English literary studies of the period 1500–1700 which endorses this idea has rejected the older identification of the period as 'the Renaissance', with its implicit homage to the myth of essential and universal Man coming to stand (in all his sovereign individuality) at the centre of a new world picture. In other words, the term 'culture' in the place of 'literature' leads us to expect the words 'early modern' in the place of 'Renaissance'. Why, then, 'Edinburgh Critical Studies in *Renaissance Culture*'?

The answer to that question lies at the heart of what distinguishes this critical series and defines its parameters. As Terence Cave has argued, the term 'early modern', though admirably egalitarian in conception, has had the unfortunate effect of essentialising the modern, that is, of positing 'the advent of a once-and-for-all modernity' which is the deictic 'here and now' from which we look back.[1] The phrase 'early modern', that is to say, forecloses the possibility of other modernities, other futures that might have arisen, narrowing the scope of what we may learn from the past by construing it as a narrative leading inevitably to Western modernity, to 'us'. *Edinburgh Critical Studies in Renaissance Culture* aims rather to shift the emphasis from a story of progress – early modern to modern – to a series of critical encounters and conversations with the past, which may reveal to us some surprising alternatives buried within texts familiarly construed as episodes on the way to certain identifying features of our endlessly fascinating modernity. In keeping with one aspect of the etymology of 'Renaissance' or 'Rinascimento' as 'rebirth', moreover, this series features books that explore and interpret anew elements of the critical encounter between writers of the period 1500–1700 and texts of Greco-Roman literature, rhetoric, politics, law, oeconomics, *eros* and friendship.

The term 'culture', then, indicates a license to study and scrutinise objects other than literary ones, and to be more inclusive about both the forms and the material and political stakes of making meaning both in the past and in the present. 'Culture' permits a realisation of the benefits to be reaped after two decades of interdisciplinary enrichment in the arts. No longer are historians naïve about textual criticism, about rhetoric, literary theory or about readerships; likewise, literary critics trained in close reading now also turn easily to court archives, to legal texts, and to the historians' debates about the languages of political and religious thought. Social historians look at printed pamphlets with an eye for narrative structure; literary critics look at court records with awareness of the problems of authority, mediation and institutional procedure. Within these developments, modes of research that became unfashionable and discredited in the 1980s – for example, studies in classical or vernacular 'source texts', or studies of literary 'influence' across linguistic, confessional and geographical boundaries – have acquired a new critical edge and relevance as the convergence of the disciplines enables the unfolding of new cultural histories (that is to say, what was once studied merely as 'literary influence' may now be studied as a fraught cultural encounter). The term 'Renaissance' thus retains the relevance of the idea of consciousness and critique within these textual engagements of past and present, and, while it foregrounds the Western European experience, is intended to provoke comparativist study of wider global perspectives rather than to promote the 'universality' of a local, if far-reaching, historical phenomenon. Finally, as traditional pedagogic boundaries between 'Medieval' and 'Renaissance' are being called into question by cross disciplinary work emphasising the 'reformation' of social and cultural forms, so this series, while foregrounding the encounter with the classical past, is self-conscious about the ways in which that past is assimilated to the projects of Reformation and Counter-Reformation, spiritual, political and domestic, that finally transformed Christendom into Europe.

Individual books in this series vary in methodology and approach, sometimes blending the sensitivity of close literary analysis with incisive, informed and urgent theoretical argument, at other times offering critiques of grand narratives of the period by their work in manuscript transmission, or in the archives of legal, social and architectural history, or by social histories of gender and childhood. What all these books have in common, however, is the capacity to offer compelling, well-documented and lucidly written critical accounts of how writers and thinkers in the period 1500–1700 reshaped, transformed and critiqued the texts and practices of their world, prompting new perspectives on what we think we have learned from them.

Lorna Hutson, Katherine Ibbett, Joe Moshenska and Kathryn Murphy

Note

1. Terence Cave, 'Locating the Early Modern', Paragraph, 29:1 (2006) 12–26, 14.

Prologue

'Are you homesick?' a witty colleague asked me years ago, as I summarised my PhD project on nostalgia and rhetoric at an annual Shakespeare Association of America conference. Not only did his question reference nostalgia's origins in *Heimweh*, the disease of homesickness; it also asked me, an American studying in Scotland, if my research was driven by my own subconscious concerns. I said no. Perhaps my ego lied: who wants to be nostalgic? In contemporary usage, to be nostalgic is to be banal, unimaginative, conservative in policy and politics, retrograde in one's desires (to long to be in Denmark rather than Wittenberg). It is to commodify history, to be open to the commercial exploitation of your memory and the seemingly inevitable longing attached to objects from one's youth. To be nostalgic is to be lured by the aesthetics and moments of cultural recognition manufactured by *Mad Men* and *Stranger Things*. But as I argue below, such aesthetic manipulation of personal desires is just one way to understand the elusive shape-shifter that is nostalgia.

This book examines William Shakespeare's use of nostalgia as a political rhetoric that is contingent not strictly on a desire for the past, but on a longing for the future. From the perspective of 2022, such future-oriented nostalgia may no longer seem extraordinary. The COVID-19 pandemic created a rupture in real time and, consequently, longings for pre- and post-virus life as well as an eventual 'lockdown nostalgia' in those countries beginning to ease restrictions. In 2016, political campaigns across the United States and Europe in particular demonstrated just how potent the idealised past could be as a convincing blueprint for the imagined future. Donald Trump's enduring and successful reprise of Ronald Reagan's 1980 'Let's Make America Great Again'; Brexit Leave campaigners' discourse of Britain's past glories as reclaimable only by leaving the EU; Geert Wilders's use of the iconography of seventeenth-century admiral Michiel de Ruyter to demand

'*Nederland terugveroveren*', 'Reconquer the Netherlands'. The success of these politicians and campaigns exemplified after the fact the power of such rhetoric.

The origins of *Shakespeare's Golden Ages* predate these developments, but as I argue it is precisely the suasive force of nostalgia that Shakespeare stages by coupling it to moments of historical crisis which depend on a future vision for their success. I make this connection between the present and the past not to insist on nostalgia's transhistoricity – indeed, this book argues that nostalgia is influenced by historically- and culturally-specific ideas. In staging nostalgic rhetoric's consistent ability to persuade, Shakespeare offers a dramatic innovation that requires his audience to evaluate just what the desire for the past and its presence in the future can achieve.

It has been a long journey to get to this page, and the debts I have are many. The Amsterdam School of Historical Studies has funded vital research and conference trips. I am grateful to audiences in Amsterdam, Belfast, Berlin, New York, Cambridge, London, Split and York, and to SAA seminar colleagues – particularly Chris Crosbie – at locations across North America for questions, comments and ideas that have influenced this book. For funding to attend the 'Pasts of Early Modern Britain' weekend seminar with Daniel Woolf in 2017 and the 'Shakespeare and Political Thought' spring seminar with Conal Condren in 2007, I am happily indebted to the Folger Shakespeare Library and thankful to those seminars' excellent leaders and participants. My thanks to Conal for his friendship and support over the ensuing fifteen years. The Folger is an invaluable scholarly refuge, and Owen Williams and the library staff have my sincere thanks for their hospitality and help. The Huntington Library has my sincere appreciation for a short-term fellowship that enabled me to do research on time and on Burton's *Anatomy*. For their enthusiasm for this project, my thanks to Michelle Houston at EUP and series editors Lorna Hutson, Joe Moshenska, Katherine Ibbett and Kathryn Murphy. I am grateful to anonymous readers at Edinburgh and Cambridge for their serious, generous attention to my work.

The journey has also been long in a literal sense, from the US to Scotland to the US to the Netherlands, my adopted home. A conversation about Juliet and a Shakespeare class with Joan Holmer at Georgetown University effectively changed the course of my life, and I am grateful for her encouragement and enthusiasm then and since. Maya Roth at Georgetown likewise has my deep appreciation for her support across the years. The School of English at the University of St Andrews provided an intellectually challenging and generous postgraduate environment, and the early modern cohort in particular – Alex

Davis, Eric Langley, Andy Murphy, the late Barbara Murray, Neil Rhodes and Lorna Hutson – played a crucial role in my development as a scholar. Alex and Philip Schwyzer provided important suggestions that found their way into various chapters here, and I am sincerely grateful for their careful and critical reading. Lorna supervised the PhD that has become this book, and she deserves my lasting appreciation for her stewardship and support over the years, and for modelling how to be a generous scholar and teacher.

At the University of Amsterdam, I am deeply appreciative of my colleagues in the English Department and across the Faculty of Humanities and fortunate that so many of these colleagues have become dear friends. The collegiality of Nick Carr, Rudolph Glitz and Ben Moore warrants particular mention. Thank you Manon Parry and Astrid Bracke for constant and generous friendship. I remain astounded by the luck I had that Tara MacDonald and Jane Lewty were at the UvA when I arrived in 2012; I am grateful for their willingness to be sounding boards, bastions of support and careful readers. My conference comrade Sarah Lewis has my sincere thanks for her friendship and smart critiques.

I am lucky in my family and friends. In good and bad times, Jen, Elizabeth and Alan Gordon, Donovan McAbee, Sally Crumplin, Peter Kushner, Kate McGladdery, Tara Quinn and Chris Jones offered laughter and warmth in Fife. I am grateful to my Amsterdam gang, Tamara van Kessel, Toni Pape, Mark Vicente and Simon Tindemans for good talks, walks, dinners; for so much. Without Rob Carson and Bronnie Johnston, my (academic) life would have less joy and wit in it. I am grateful to Rob for his abiding friendship, intelligence and support in the many years since our fortuitous meeting in Conal's seminar. Bronnie has been overwhelmingly generous with her time, her critical eye and her encouragement, and I am thankful for her. Aisling O'Suilleabhain's three decades of friendship and love keep me steady. Finally, I am sincerely grateful for the kindness and spirit of my *schoonfamilie*, particularly Paul De Jong, Barbara de Vries and Dirk De Jong. Thank you to my brother, Erik Johanson, for being in the world. The incomparable Wouter De Jong has six years of my thank yous behind him and a lifetime of them ahead for all of his gifts, but most especially his humour, his patience and his love. Finally, I dedicate this book to my parents, Patti and Tim, as a small gesture of gratitude for their unwavering support and love across all the miles and all the years.

Whatever the faults of this book, they are my own.

An early version of Chapter 2 appeared in *Representations of Elizabeth I in Early Modern Culture*, ed. Alexandra Petrina and Laura Tosi

(Basingstoke: Palgrave Macmillan, 2011); some material from the Introduction and a version of Chapter 3 were published in my 'Approaches to Early Modern Nostalgia' special issue of *Parergon* (33:2).

Note on Citation

When citing early modern sources, I have retained their spelling but have expanded contractions and silently modernised i/j, long-s/s, u/v, and vv/w.

Introduction: Rethinking Nostalgia

CANTERBURY [. . .] At that very moment,
  Consideration like an angel came
  And whipped the offending Adam out of him,
  Leaving his body as a paradise[.][1]

Every nostalgia needs an origin point: a time to return to, a moment of rupture and creation. In *Henry V* (1599), Shakespeare's eponymous king seems himself to represent just such an origin, as he no longer possesses 'the offending Adam' that marks his post-lapsarian state. The moment of Consideration's appearance and of 'whipping' rewrites historical decline as progress; Henry's body, remade as 'a paradise', implicitly negates any longing for Eden. From the play's start, then, the Bishops of Ely and Canterbury illustrate how Henry 'is full of grace and fair regard', 'a true lover of the holy Church' whose dramatic, unlooked-for change can only be understood as a consequence of time's passing, since 'miracles are ceased' (1.1.22, 23, 67). In Henry Shakespeare appears to fashion an ideal ruler upon whom disgruntled Elizabethans could focus their desires and fantasies for a youthful, male monarch, the play seeming to offer a paean to a legendary king, a synecdochal image of an imperial England leading a united Britain.[2] Consistently made to contrast the French nobles' feminine-coded vanity, plain Henry rejects 'idol ceremony', casts himself with his soldiers as 'warriors for the working-day', and can only speak 'plain soldier' to Princess Katherine (4.1.237, 4.3.109, 5.2.150). Alongside this 'mirror of all Christian kings', the play consistently praises ancient Rome and likens England to its ideal (2.0.6). Henry is like 'the Roman Brutus, / Covering discretion with a coat of folly'; Fluellen lauds those like Captain Jamy who have 'the Roman disciplines' and laments Gower's ignorance of Pompey the Great (2.4.37–8, 3.2.73, 79, 4.1.69–72). England itself seems a new Rome, as upon the king's return to London, 'The Mayor and all his brethren in best sort,

/ Like to the senators of th'antique Rome [...] / Go forth and fetch their conquering Caesar in' (5.0.25–6, 28). But the play also intimates an ambivalence about Rome's influence, as 'Caesar' carries implicitly the idea of 'tyrant', and elsewhere the idealisation of Rome is made ridiculous. Fluellen's interest in the 'disciplines', for example, becomes part of his comedic character. Most strikingly, the Dauphin's histrionic post-battle declaration, 'Let's stab ourselves' (4.5.7), works simultaneously both to mock the French and to cast doubt on the entire practice of playing the noble Roman (which Shakespeare depicts in earnest in *Julius Caesar*, produced the same year).

As Shakespeare offers subjects to idealise, and as he collapses time and space to make England proximate and like to Rome, he turns the seemingly black-and-white process of idealising the past into a grey area. While that grey area was a result of the Renaissance's own complicated approach to the past, this book argues that Shakespeare's staging of nostalgia as an undoubtedly potent, ambivalent and suspect rhetoric was his own dramatic innovation. *Henry V* emphasises the political convenience of an idealised past by evoking it at key policy-making moments which require immediate action. During Ely and Canterbury's campaign to persuade the king to war, Henry asks probingly, 'May I with right and conscience make this claim?', and to convince him Canterbury offers a glorified version of Henry's personal history (1.2.96). 'Look back into your mighty ancestors', he advises; Edward III and the Black Prince are the heroes of a 'tragedy' (for the French) (1.2.102, 106). But Ely suggests that looking back into the past is not enough: Henry must repeat his forefathers' deeds, 'renew their feats', and he suggests that the time to act is now, as Henry, 'in the very May-morn of his youth', is 'Ripe for exploits and mighty enterprises' (1.2.116, 120, 121). When the king attempts to correct the historic record of Edward III and the Black Prince by recalling Scotland's invasion of England, Canterbury rejects this narrative, arguing that Edward's fame was 'fill[ed]' by the consequent capture of 'prisoner kings' (1.2.162). At this vital, early moment in a play whose outcome we already know, the incorporation of the idealised past as an essential part of the bishops' persuasive discourse tellingly underlines its rhetorical power and its centrality to the play's political manoeuvring.

This book is about nostalgia as a dramatic rhetoric, as a language which idealises the past and which is crafted to persuade on-stage auditors to political action in service of an imagined future. Shakespeare stages nostalgia as rhetoric, as a means of persuasion, and in the first decade of his career his Elizabethan histories perform nostalgic rhetoric's power as a political tool. While nostalgia suggests an inability to see the (imperfect) present in the (perfect) past, its discursive function indicates the desire to recognise that past in the present, to register the sense both of historical contiguity and of rupture that characterises early modern attitudes to the past. By attending both to how nostalgia is put to work in dramaturgy as well as to the extra-dramatic valences nostalgic rhetoric obtains in Elizabethan England, *Shakespeare's Golden Ages* argues that Shakespeare's English and Roman history plays innovate in their use of a future-focused nostalgia. I place this innovation in its immediate dramatic context by examining those dramatists most influential to Shakespeare as he wrote his history plays: the Queen's Men playwrights and Christopher Marlowe. Their respective plays, I argue in Chapter 1, establish dramatic trends critical for Shakespeare – most notably by making temporal consciousness political and by attaching an ethics to the act of retrospection. Shakespeare's particular model of nostalgic rhetoric offers a departure from a dramatic trend that insistently focused on the present and future, even in the staged past of the history play. In the succeeding chapters I turn to three plays which rely on nostalgia as a catalyst for political action: *2 Henry VI*, *Richard II* and *Julius Caesar*. These plays use the rhetoric of an idealised past and a lost, but reclaimable, political inheritance as the impetus for rebellion. By situating the dramas' respective nostalgic discourses – laments for merry England, for a lost hospitality, or for a republican past – in their dramatic and sociopolitical contexts, I demonstrate how Shakespeare draws on the early modern ambivalence attached to nostalgia to undermine the notion of a perfect past. Shakespeare exposes that nostalgia to be a rhetoric: not an exclusively, or even predominantly, memorial practice, but a potent political tactic.[3]

But what is nostalgia? Is it an emotion? A physical disease? A 'social disease'? A 'time-strategy'? The 'mutant form' of history?[4] Nostalgia is a structure of longing, an orientation of desire in time. That orientation is unfixed, as it can look both forward and back: while dissatisfied nostalgics turn initially towards a past they idealise, they do not necessarily remain fixed there. The future, in this construction, is not an inevitably imperfect state, and the nostalgia I examine depends upon it as an ideal *in potentia*. In Shakespeare's use in particular, nostalgia always has an end that exceeds, that is not limited to, the past. As my title implies, the histories I examine articulate multiple nostalgias, and such staging both insists on the irresistibility of idealising rhetoric and suggests that it can have only violent outcomes.

In its particular focus on the Elizabethan history play, and on rhetoric and dramaturgy in that genre, *Shakespeare's Golden Ages* concentrates on nostalgia's power and that power's political effects. In doing so it departs from the traditional pastoral and romance modes associated with nostalgia, which respectively create a 'golden age' ideal and enact a return.[5] Likewise, this book corrects an imbalance in scholarship on Stuart nostalgia for Elizabeth which has come to dominate studies of nostalgia in early modern English literature. Analyses of the discourse of 'Good Queen Bess' and discussions of Stuart England's nostalgia for Elizabeth suggest a general critical consensus about the certainty of pre-1688 nostalgia and its exclusive orientation towards the past. These studies are often concerned with the memory of Elizabeth: how she was remembered, the uses of her memory and the politics of such use.[6] By exploring nostalgia's rhetorical and dramaturgical uses, this book turns away from familiar critical approaches that locate early modern nostalgia in memory studies. In its necessary act of exalting the past – calling up its perfections, omitting its defects – nostalgia has been interpreted as a process of remembering and forgetting whose significance is restricted to that process. That is, literary and cultural meaning is extracted from what a nostalgic statement includes and excludes. Jonathan Baldo and Isabel Karremann's respective works, for example, have argued powerfully for the importance of oblivion in constructing memory.[7] But where these and other scholars necessarily attend to acts of nostalgia as primarily acts of remembrance, or as a memorialising practice, I examine acts of nostalgia as rhetorical moves. To do so is not to analyse rhetoric at the exclusion of memory, but to expand the horizon with which scholars study nostalgia. Attending to nostalgia as an act of persuasion enables a consideration of nostalgia's relationship to the civic imaginary and Shakespeare's dramatic interest in its ability to destabilise, rather than inevitably reinscribe, particular historical narratives.

As I show, such destabilisation relies on Shakespeare's use of nostalgic discourses familiar to his Elizabethan audiences. Social, economic and political realities therefore form important contexts for this book's case studies, and the influence of New Historicism is evident in my reading of religious, governmental and historical texts alongside Shakespeare's plays. Such contexts often reveal nostalgia's potential for topicality, particularly present in history plays which by nature are invested in the comparison of past to present and consequently create topicality. As if confronting an infinity mirror, Elizabethan audiences would have seen and heard their own concerns articulated in the past as they watched representatives of a bygone era longing for a more perfect future – the Elizabethans' present. This process both denies the audience any security in a knowledge of a preferable past and demands a re-evaluation of their present. In that sense, topicality is always present under the surface of dramatic nostalgic rhetoric. However, New Historicist readings – invested in such topicality and a given work's contexts – tend to lose sight of literature's and drama's own power both to influence how we read context and indeed to create context itself. Recent critical developments such as historical formalism have sought to address that perceived loss, and in that vein I analyse Shakespeare's use of the idealised past in its particular dramatic and literary contexts.[8] Such analysis demonstrates how Shakespeare theatrically shaped nostalgic discourse in the Elizabethan era.

Shakespeare's Golden Ages intervenes in nostalgia scholarship both by harnessing a rhetorical and dramaturgical approach to investigate early modern attitudes to nostalgia and by recognising the crucial role the future can play in how those attitudes are formed.[9] This intervention resists trends in twentieth- and twenty-first-century nostalgia studies which articulate a universal nostalgia, rendering it uniform across time; which understand it predominantly as the commodification and fetishisation of history; and which tend to associate the nostalgic exclusively with a past-oriented political conservatism. In what follows, I establish why we need to historicise and expand how we look at nostalgia in the early modern period. First tracing nostalgia's historical use and its modern definitions, I then turn to early modern rhetoric and politics and conceptions of rupture and continuity to set up this Introduction's final section, which outlines how Shakespeare's dramaturgy stages nostalgia.

Historicising Nostalgia

Since 2000 alone, numerous monographs, journal articles, special issues and book chapters have been dedicated to thinking through what nostalgia is, to diagnosing it, to considering its historical development and its relationship to literatures across time.[10] With few exceptions, these texts begin their analyses with Johannes Hofer's 1688 dissertation on nostalgia, implicitly or explicitly following Jean Starobinski's injunction that 'No facet of an emotion can be traced before it is named, before it is designated and expressed. It is not, then, the emotion itself which comes before us; only that part which has passed into a given form of expression can be of interest to the historian.'[11] Starobinski's influential insistence on the primacy of naming as the only means of understanding and 'tracing' emotion allows him to exclude the possibility of diverse discourses expressing similar sentiments, which we can eventually identify with nostalgia. His argument has enabled a critical neglect of nostalgia's long pre-history and a critical insistence on nostalgia's modernity, and its accordingly parasitic, pathological or rapacious qualities. However, characterising nostalgia as modern because it depends, for example, upon 'historical process as the continual production of the new', cannot account for the cyclicality it depends on in Shakespeare's drama.[12] Etymologically what is 'modern' is what is *now*, at this ephemeral moment. Nostalgia is inherently and always modern, regardless of its use or aim, because nostalgia is always reacting to the present – to its now. Ironically, even while the present is perpetually in flux, that nostalgia can represent a shared response to time across time consequently obscures its nuances, its inherent differences or registers. Nostalgia has arguably always been because change has always been, but the 'now' that changes is never the same, and the possibility remains that nostalgia never is, either.

Critical attention to nostalgia's modernity has obfuscated its early modern nuances, particularly its ambivalence. Throughout his *Survey of London*, for example, John Stow uses the phrase 'old time' as he charts the changes that London has undergone. In the 'old time' people were responsible for the upkeep of bridges; in the present, lewd people and a weak building have replaced a postern that used to house men 'of good credite'. Reflecting on the Tower of London's origins, Stow doubts the stories that Caesar was involved in its construction: 'nor had hee in his head any such matter, but onely to dispatch a conquest of this barbarous Countrey, and to proceede to greater matters'.[13] In his *Survey*, Stow can acknowledge his country's 'barbarous' past, bemoan the state of London's ditches and what has happened to his father's house, and report urban improvements such as a conduit to bring water into houses.[14] Rather than producing a project that fixates solely on an idealised past, Stow writes London as a palimpsest. He identifies temporal change and makes it present, his ambivalent approach to the past requiring his reader to reflect on what it is to live continuously with that past, rather than insisting on it as always or inevitably desirous.[15]

Johannes Hofer's 1688 *Dissertatio Medica de Nostalgia, oder Heimwehe* itself unwittingly attaches ambivalence to nostalgia. In his medical dissertation, the Swiss doctor defines 'nostalgia' as a 'wasting disease' of homesickness, as *Heimweh*, and Hofer's title alone reveals how the author was both creating something new and locating that new disease within a contemporary – even past – context.[16] His titular use of the vernacular *Heimweh* demonstrates that this idea was already circulating prior to the work's publication, as *Heimweh* was current in the Swiss German dialect for over a century before 1688, its use traceable to 1569.[17] *Heimweh* (*heim*, home/abode; *weh*, pain) articulates its own particularity of place; Hofer's neo-Greek mash-up 'nostalgia' expresses the 'weh' of *Heimweh*, as it joins the Greek 'nostos' (νόστος, 'a return homeward') with 'algia' (αλγία, from ἄλγος, pain). 'Nostos' itself comes from '*neomai*, "to go back, return safely home", whose root in the active voice means "to save"', and the home implied in nostalgia's return represents restoration and even renewal.[18] Nevertheless, Greek compounds identify where the *algia* is situated in the body; nostalgia 'could never be a Greek word' because it refuses to indicate its pain's nature and location.[19] While *Heimweh* represents a local, culturally-specific disease, *nostalgia* offers a literal resistance to specificity and locality, hinting at home but binding nostalgia's source firmly to fantasy.

For Hofer, nostalgia was both a physical and a mental disease, in particular 'one sympathetic of an afflicted imagination', and it was as this disease that it became known across Europe and introduced into English in the eighteenth century.[20] Nostalgia's victims 'grieve, either because they are abandoned by the pleasant breeze of their Native Land or because at some time they picture themselves enjoying this more'.[21] The mind's power to cultivate the disease is matched by the body's power to reinscribe it: by constantly thinking on the 'Fatherland', the traces of its image(s) in the brain's 'middle fibers' are strengthened and 'impressed more vigorously'. Furthermore, the body could 'excite the mind again to seek ideas of the Fatherland'.[22] Attending to the anxieties of the mind, writ large on the body, can cure nostalgia; the diseased must be convinced that she is returning home and then actually returned. Temporal imagination, then, plays a vital role in both the illness and the cure, as the past remembrance of the *Patria* precipitates nostalgia and the future promise of return, its relief. Hofer's medical nostalgia is therefore concerned not only with place; it is also contingent on the past-ness of that place for its existence, and consequently Hofer's nostalgic longs for both.[23] This temporal-spatial understanding rewrites the critical narrative that nostalgia changes from a spatial understanding to a temporal understanding, each excluding the other.

In the decades succeeding Hofer's diagnosis, nostalgia represented not the emotional yearning with which it has come to be associated, but rather the potentially fatal disease of homesickness. As it became pathologised and introduced into late eighteenth-century nosologies, some scholars recognised it as a distinct disease; Ralph Augustus Vogel labelled it 'a subspecies of melancholy'.[24] Robert Burton's 1621 *Anatomy of Melancholy* describes an emotion that anticipates Vogel's classification. He writes of a nostalgia *avant la lettre* under 'banishment', recognising the sense of displacement inherent in articulations of nostalgia, a displacement made clear in Hofer's and Joseph Banks's respective reflections on transient groups (soldiers and sailors).[25] Burton argues: ''Tis a childish humour to hone after home, to be discontent at that which others seek; to prefer, as base Icelanders and Norwegians do, their own ragged island before Italy or Greece, the gardens of the world.' This desire is inherently foolish, for 'All places are distant from heaven alike [. . .] to a wise man there is no difference of climes.'[26] Burton's reasoning echoes the counsel that John of Gaunt offers his son after King Richard sentences the latter to exile. Gaunt instructs Bolingbroke that 'All places that the eye of heaven visits / Are to a wise man ports and happy havens.'[27] Through Gaunt, Shakespeare offers the same counterargument to homesickness that Burton does: all places are equal because God looks upon them, and it is a sign of wisdom to understand that equality.

Moreover, Gaunt argues how central fantasy is to experiencing the sorrow of 'an enforced pilgrimage', as Bolingbroke names his exile (1.3.264). In an early version of Coriolanus's famous banishment of the Romans, Gaunt counsels that thought will enable Bolingbroke to reverse his position: 'Think not the King did banish thee, / But thou the King' (1.3.279–80). But the mind cannot overpower sensual experience:

> O, who can hold a fire in his hand
> By thinking on the frosty Caucasus,
> Or cloy the hungry edge of appetite
> By bare imagination of a feast,
> Or wallow naked in December snow
> By thinking on fantastic summer's heat? (1.3.294–9)

Bolingbroke rejects the possibility that the fantasy of an alternate reality can ease an insufferable present; imagination alone cannot mediate desire or need. However, as I discuss in Chapter 3, *Richard II* stages the power of the idealised past when coupled with the promise of the future, inciting action in the present. Shakespeare and Burton both reflect on the (enforced) displacement that creates longing, although Shakespeare is not interested in substituting one place for another, which is Burton's advice. Rather, through Bolingbroke's melancholy, Shakespeare explores the dynamics of longing for a place and, through Gaunt, ultimately frames longing as mediated by hope. Return is possible.

Burton consistently links melancholy with an inactivity and an idleness which anticipates Hofer's disease, and which is absent in Shakespeare's historic nostalgics. For Burton, political bodies, like human ones, may be melancholy, and the mark of the healthy, sanguine state is industry.[28] Melancholy emerges from the physical consequences of sorrow, which 'contracts the Heart, macerates the Soule, subverts the good estate of the body, hindering all the operations of it, causing Melancholy, and many times death itself'.[29] Burton does not list the symptoms of 'hon[ing] after home', but its inclusion in the *Anatomy* strongly suggests that the homesick and the sorrowful would share the same symptoms of passivity. In contrast, Shakespeare's successful nostalgics are a decidedly active and industrious bunch. Jack Cade, Lord Northumberland, Cassius, Antony: these men have political aims, and their nostalgic rhetoric manifests not exclusively from a deep-rooted sorrow, but rather from a deeply rooted desire for power and change. Considering the close relationship between melancholy and nostalgia, and melancholy's associations with femininity and with age in the early modern humoral model and early modern ideas of physiology, we might expect some of Shakespeare's nostalgics to be women or the elderly. As this book shows, however, Shakespeare's nostalgics are men in their prime driven by ambition and political conviction. I highlight these discrepancies not to exclude melancholy from any understanding of nostalgia, but to expand how nostalgia has been, and can be, conceived: as a complex of emotions that includes desire and sanguinity alongside sorrow.

My point here is that the longing for an idealised past can be shaped by culturally-specific ideas. It is precisely nostalgia's cultural specificity that this book explores, and in so doing nuances claims for nostalgia's transhistorical nature. Such claims are grounded in confident observations by influential critics – for Raymond Williams 'nostalgia [. . .] is universal and persistent' – and in compelling evidence of nostalgic literary *topoi* from Homer to Ali Smith via Virgil, Ovid and the *ubi sunt* tradition.[30] Such continuity in Western literature does not signify that longing and homesickness are the same across time; nostalgia's diagnosis as a product of Western, secular societies with a linear concept of time has further narrowed where and how critics identify the desire that fosters nostalgia.[31] While scholars of early modern nostalgia accept its existence prior to Hofer's dissertation, they have done so without much apparent anxiety about what that assumption of transhistoricity implies. Even as critical work in this field expands and scholars suggest early modern nostalgia's ambivalence or Shakespeare's suspicion of it, early modern scholarship on nostalgia has largely ignored the ways that early modern ideas themselves might shape the understanding, experience and representation of nostalgia.[32]

For example, Katherine Eggert's analysis of 'supernostalgia' in *Henry V* argues that it is the play's insistence on the past's ability to return that defines its nostalgia in this superlative way. However compelling her argument is, this neologism and its characterisation as 'irrational' deny the possibility of a specifically early modern nostalgia: one shaped by discourses of cyclical time and Queen Elizabeth's political self-fashioning as the goddess Astraea and the embodiment of the return of the Golden Age.[33] Although cultural histories of nostalgia have produced narratives of its fundamental semantic shift, critical discussions have not attended to the possibility of historical differences in nostalgia before 1688, or even during this shift. Given that one of New Historicism's promised legacies, recently re-articulated by historical formalists, calls for 'our attention to the constructedness of our historical narratives', then part of that critical work must be to attend to how we universalise certain ideas.[34] Alex Davis aptly summarises the consequences of this universalising process: 'by positioning premodern nostalgia as the predecessor to its modern descendants, such formulae deploy a nostalgia of their own, flattening the specificity of the past into a simple template which can then be used as a benchmark against which to measure off present complexities'.[35] One of this book's aims is to destabilise the assumptions that accompany how critics read and identify nostalgia by closely reading and analysing the way Elizabethan drama, and Shakespeare's plays in particular, construct, stage and frame nostalgic rhetoric. Doing so requires serious attention not only to early modern notions of temporality and history, but to contradictory discourses concerning what it meant to idealise the past and to make temporal comparisons in early modern England.

In rethinking and historicising nostalgia, I question the dominant readings of nostalgia that have emerged from Marxism's influence on literary theory. In *The Eighteenth Brumaire of Louis Bonaparte* (1852), Marx denounces the past as 'less just' and declares that 'The social revolution of the nineteenth century cannot take its poetry from the past but only from the future'; the past, the place of 'obsolete social arrangements', cannot be viewed as a site of social justice, and in its longing for such a past and its refusal to look towards the future, nostalgia becomes a symptom of injustice.[36] This suspicion of idealising the past and its anti-revolutionary position inevitably informs contemporary nostalgia scholarship, as Marx's statement 'transformed nostalgia into a sort of political crime'.[37] Nostalgia is a site of repression, fuelling capitalism; it commodifies and fetishises history; it participates in obliterating class struggle and perpetuating the consumerist desires that prolong that struggle. As Fred Davis asks, 'what more powerful antidote to revolutionary fervour than nostalgia's penchant for believing that the future can only be worse than the past?'[38] His rhetorical question articulates the structure of longing characteristic of the modern nostalgic: the nostalgic looks to the present, then to the future, and, anticipating only decay, desires the past. This positioning has been expressed most influentially by Susan Stewart, for whom the direction of the nostalgic's 'desiring narrative [. . .] is always a future-past, a deferment of experience in the direction of origin and thus eschaton, the point where narrative begins/ends'.[39] This construction, in which the future's inevitable decline (and the consequent wish to 'defer experience') urges a turn to the past, eliminates the possibility of a future-fulfilling nostalgia, one which orients itself from what was to what is to come and which is active in early modernity. Rather, for Stewart's nostalgic the future is a void, and it remains so because what is longed for cannot be attained. As her oft-cited definition states: 'nostalgia is the desire for desire'.[40] The nostalgic longs for longing, reminding us of the absence at the root of desire. In its inability to be satiated, nostalgia's utopic narrative operates for Stewart as the site where consumerist, materialist impulses begin.

Such argumentation interprets nostalgia as a negative desire which reifies the past and translates it into a product for consumption. The crystallised past becomes an anodyne object that seemingly enables history to be relived through the production of a simulacrum. Consequently, the fractured experience of the past is ignored and streamlined, idealised through the material object. This account has been influential for early modern scholarship. Drawing on Renée Trilling's claim that nostalgia represents 'the manipulation of material events into aesthetic objects [which] turns the present into history', Lucy Munro has argued for nostalgia's almost parasitic nature.[41] Here I find myself uncharacteristically at odds with Munro when she claims that where the early modern archaist 'seek[s] to recreate and reshape', the nostalgic is inclined 'simply to remember or fantasise'.[42] In this account, nostalgia is idle, a paradoxically passive producer of fantasy worlds lacking agency and which, unlike archaism, can neither 'transform' nor 'reinvigorate'. Similarly, Natasha Korda's idea of nostalgia in *The Shoemaker's Holiday* relies on the assumptions rehearsed above; nostalgia fetishises an object (here, the individually produced shoe) and it is always backwards facing, a retrograde emotion that scorns present practice.[43] The history play itself – or perhaps, our historical appreciation of the history play's popularity – could represent an early modern equivalent of this commodification. Indeed, Harriet Phillips's important work has recently argued that the markets for cheap print and performance drove the creation of mirth (as the 'merry world') and invented a collaborative, 'saleable', nostalgia.[44] Writers, actors and theatre owners offered to the public an object of desire: an exotic representation of a foreign warrior; a historic, chivalric England writ large; an ancient Rome revisited. Their representations reinscribed a desire for the lost or unattainable artefact, a desire which reproduced *Tamburlaine* and Shakespeare's histories to meet demand. Are Shakespeare's history plays – English and Roman – history commodified? While I accept nostalgia's inimical possibilities, such a reading cannot consider that a history play, as a performance, is a singular experience, one not always and inevitably able to be repeated (as a simulacrum). These accounts imagine nostalgia's power to lie in its form as commodity, and that nostalgic desires have power only to produce that commodity.

Against this, I argue that Shakespeare stages nostalgia's power to act in history by dramatising the effects of nostalgic rhetoric. By then rendering such nostalgic rhetoric suspect through its multiplicity, Shakespeare's plays unsettle the idea that a fixed, idealised past can be located or possessed. His dramaturgy's use of that rhetoric resists the binary choice of past-or-future, a choice which characterises contemporary critical thinking about nostalgia. Rather, Shakespeare's drama identifies knowledge of the past, history itself, not as a refuge but as a necessary element in achieving future desires; the idealised past and its promised inheritance inspire the future, which – albeit briefly – becomes a place of hope rather than inevitable degeneration.

Nostalgia's capacity for hope and political action have figured in its ongoing, interdisciplinary critical rehabilitation.[45] Marx figures again in that process, as revisionists of modern nostalgia have used him to draw out nostalgia's revolutionary and utopic promise. In *The Eighteenth Brumaire*, he writes that 'The awakening of the dead in those revolutions [England's Civil War] served the purpose of glorifying new struggles, not of parodying the old; of magnifying the given tasks in imagination, not of taking flight from their solution in reality; of finding once more the spirit of revolution, not making its ghost walk again.'[46] Glorify, magnify, find: an active nostalgia possesses political potential, an ability to animate the revolution rather than speed its collapse. Frederic Jameson argues for nostalgia's political ambivalence, its ability to motivate present discontent into radical action; for Helmut Illbruck hope is essential to Ernst Bloch's interpretation of nostalgia as a good.[47] Similarly, in her bifurcation of modern nostalgia into two non-absolute 'tendencies' – 'restorative' and 'reflective' – the late Svetlana Boym has argued for a broader understanding of nostalgia. If restorative nostalgia is a treacherous 'anti-modern myth-making of history', then reflective nostalgia is a more salubrious co-habitation with loss, a 'modern' nostalgia that 'has a capacity to awaken multiple planes of consciousness' through its capacity for irony and humour.[48] Even Boym's nuanced arguments, however, effectively offer a good-and-bad nostalgia. Attractive solutions to this oversimplification, such as Jennifer Delisle's nostalgia spectrum, problematically posit individuals' experience of nostalgia at one end and cultural nostalgia at the other, shying away from nostalgia's ethical dimensions and ignoring the inevitable collapse of the experience-culture distinction.[49]

I am suspicious of tidy solutions for such an unwieldy, slippery concept as nostalgia.[50] As this book's early modern case studies illustrate, the boundaries of good/bad, individual/cultural or even restorative/reflective do not describe comprehensively the nostalgias at work in Shakespeare's drama and early English literature, nostalgias which push back, like early modern English culture itself, against clear delineations of time and space, past and present. In early modern England nostalgia is ambivalent: the longing for the past is welcome and it is anathema; it articulates anti-tyrannical rhetoric and legitimating absolutism; it is the source of hope and it inspires rebellion, which itself becomes a cause for despair.[51] Shakespeare's rhetorical use of nostalgia relies on this ambivalence, as his dramaturgy exposes how available nostalgia is, how no side of history possesses a truth claim to the past. It belongs to and can be voiced by monarchist and anarchist alike.

Rhetoric and Politics

A defining anxiety of early modern English culture was the recognition that acts of persuasion could be used for immoral ends. Anyone could use *ethos*, *pathos* and *logos*, as the early modern English stage made abundantly clear not only through Vice figures from Satan to Backbiter to Richard III, but through its own production: 'mere' actors possessed the (imagined) eloquence of kings and aristocrats. And as Elizabethan and Jacobean drama consistently depicted, status was not correspondent to virtue or virtuous speech. Argument *in utramque partem*, the ubiquitous rhetorical practice often exemplified by dialogues or conversation books, contributed to this anxiety: humanist scholars were trained to be able to 'argue both sides' of a given topic or commonplace.[52] Prevailing humanist attitudes towards rhetoric further emphasised its ambivalent nature, which resulted from the inherent duality in early modern ideas of rhetoric, as Victoria Kahn argues: 'On the one hand, rhetoric in this period was conceived of as an ethically and ideologically neutral technique of argument; on the other hand, rhetoric was seen as the embodiment of a faculty of practical reasoning, or prudential deliberation that is tied to ethical norms.'[53] Debates concerning the nature of rhetoric extended to who could, or should, possess the *ars rhetorica*, a question linked to beliefs about social status and the nature and virtue of the commons. For many humanists, rhetorical prowess was socially vital expertise which engendered good citizenship.[54] Because of the citizen's everyday social influence, humanists argued, it was in the state's interest to have him educated in the rhetorical arts. Others, however, were convinced that status should dictate who could possess such powers, ideally concentrated in an elite group of nobles and councillors and thus protecting the commonwealth from its greatest threat: 'the mighty weapon of eloquence in popular hands'.[55]

Richard Beacon's *Solon: his follie* (1594) offers a well-noted example of how the misuse of language is translated into misrule. In Markku Peltonen's account, Beacon's text argues that a balance of respect of powers – the commons for the nobles, and the nobles for their own power – prevents misgovernment and the fall of the *res publica*. Even while denouncing democracy or warning the common people against '"the aspiring minde" of ambition', late sixteenth-century authors could still recognise the need for a critique and mediation of absolute power.[56] This 'republican' discourse voices a tension between the humanist's ideal that rhetoric and the formation of a good citizen go hand in hand and the knowledge that the power of rhetoric, in the mouths of a wide range of citizens, may undermine the state.

These debates about access underscore further the extent to which early modern English culture granted language political power, and this question of who has access, or should have access, to the rhetorical arts assumes anyone *can* have access. Shakespeare notoriously explores this tension in *2 Henry VI* with the rise of Jack Cade, whose successful nostalgic rhetoric, I argue in Chapter 2, depends upon *what* he promises as much as *how* he promises.

Cade's use of nostalgic rhetoric to secure political support – and, in his fantasy, the crown – exemplifies just one of the ways Shakespeare's Elizabethan English and Roman histories engage with the political questions concerning right and legitimate rule that dominated the 1590s. At their core, the day's biggest political debates – under what conditions a subject could resist a tyrant, how subjects should be represented, the impact of queenship, the best form of government, who could take up political office – concern the nature of the public good and subjects' rights.[57] Shakespeare uses nostalgia as a central rhetorical strategy in exploring such questions, as he stages its ability to convince individuals and groups to acts that will 'make high majesty look like itself', as Northumberland declares in rejecting Richard's tyranny (2.1.295); or that will 'get what [they] have lost' in France, as Lord Clifford promises in *2 Henry VI*.[58] As these lines suggest, the 'good' that engenders action focuses on the political in the Aristotelian sense, the good of man and of the state.[59] However, against nostalgia's appeal to good in these plays, the rhetoric Shakespeare's dramatic political opponents use operates as a call to violence, be it as a threat (Bolingbroke's men 'march'ing outside Berkeley Castle at 3.3.51) or as a promise (Caesar's murder). In

2 Henry VI, Jack Cade's idea of social good elevates him to the height of power from which, he imagines, all laws issue; for Mark Antony in *Julius Caesar*, it is revenge for Caesar's death, a concentration of power and the exclusion of the conspirators from rule. Invoking the idealised past for political gain results in rebellion, conspiracy, riot and war. The diverse and contested political discourses extent in late Elizabethan England – republicanism, monarchism, monarchical republicanism, the mixed constitution – meant that how these actions were interpreted by spectators likewise inevitably varied with individuals, literate and illiterate men and women from differing religious, socio-economic and national backgrounds.[60] Irrespective of his diverse spectators' potential political sympathies, and conscious of his potential influence on them, Shakespeare dramatises nostalgia as a dangerously persuasive discourse, one that literally occupies centre stage in those events he frames as central to historical change.

Shakespeare's use of nostalgia is political in the sense that it is never exclusively individual. Its stakes are always collective, its concerns always communal, looking towards the *polis*. That community is both on and off stage, as character-auditors attend to nostalgia's plea for the reclamation of the past in the future, and off-stage spectators sit in judgement of that plea's use and power – even as that power is used on them. Notably, Shakespeare's dramaturgy stages nostalgic rhetoric at moments of communal crisis, suiting the language of rupture to moments of political rupture. The imagined futures that nostalgia articulates and desires reaffirm the commonplace recognition of the English popular theatre as dramatising political possibility even as it hedges the fruition of those possibilities. They are tied to past example and to the plays' own foreclosure of the promised future as desirable.

As I suggested earlier, *Henry V* exposes nostalgia as a rhetoric by staging a relationship between its uses and political gain, and Henry's St Crispin's Day speech, a rhetorical moment so celebrated it now seems enclosed unto itself, is no exception. Driven by his need to maintain his power and his kingdom, to affirm his own legitimacy, and to rally his troops against terrifying odds, Henry projects an idealised past to encourage his men to stay, promising:

He that outlives this day and comes safe home
Will stand a-tiptoe when this day is named[.]
[. . .]
He that shall see this day and live old age
Will yearly on the vigil feast his neighbours,
And say 'Tomorrow is Saint Crispian.'
Then will he strip his sleeve and show his scars,

> And say 'These wounds I had on Crispin's day.'
> Old men forget; yet all shall be forgot
> But he'll remember, with advantages,
> What feats he did that day. Then shall our names,
> Familiar in his mouth as household words,
> [. . .]
> Be in their flowing cups freshly remembered.
> This story shall the good man teach his son,
> And Crispin Crispian shall ne'er go by
> From this day to the ending of the world
> But we in it shall be remembered,
> We few, we happy few, we band of brothers. (4.3.41–60)

Tellingly, he imagines and employs nostalgia at a moment that must succeed rhetorically, and Shakespeare stages that 'anticipatory nostalgia' as a political response to a crisis.[61] His version of the romanticised Henry is a king who understands the cogent power of idealising the past and recognises how desire can rewrite history. In Canterbury's chronicle of his great-grandfather, Henry had been suspicious of embellishment. Now, acknowledging time's paradoxical power – in time old men's forgetfulness creates a memory burnished 'with advantages' – and fantasising the pride his (surviving) men will feel in the future, Henry idealises that future and its past, creating in the dramatic present a potent, persuasive desire to act. The Eastcheap gang's slow erasure from the play, and Henry's role in that erasure – traces of Eastcheap remain only in the king's bawdy humour of his wooing scene – suggest that the useful past, represented by Henry's questionable companions of his youth who enable his 'redemption', must be contained to that use. The tragic fates of Falstaff, Bardolph, Nym, the boy and Nell, and Pistol's own resolve to 'turn bawd' (5.1.86), together insist that the Elizabethans' idealised past, Henry V's medieval England, was just as violent and depraved as the present. In *Henry V* Shakespeare offers various models for thinking about the relationship between past, present and future, and the fact that he keeps displacing the ideal suggests that, despite all appearances, there isn't one. The play is not nostalgic; it stages nostalgia's power as a rhetoric.

Shakespeare's dramaturgy employs strategies of balance and expansion to articulate nostalgia's central role in the dramatic action. While key phrases might alert audience members to a nostalgic invocation ('it was never a merry England since . . .'), nostalgia works as a dramaturgical strategy through balance: political opponents are each shown to control the narrative of their respective idealised past. As I argue in Chapter 4, Cassius narrates the ideal of a lost, republican Rome to persuade Brutus to join the conspiracy; just one act later, Antony uses similar idealising techniques to elegise Caesar and to stir up the civic rage that will become 'the dogs of war'.[62] While *civitas* appears to lie at the heart of both men's respective values, by staging one nostalgic narrative after another Shakespeare casts doubt on these arguments, as the play encourages the audience to reflect on both the weight of nostalgic narratives and the on-stage auditor's susceptibility to such narratives. Moreover, Shakespeare expands dramaturgically the stakes of nostalgic rhetoric by staging first its claim on an individual and then on a crowd. Again in *Julius Caesar*, the audience watches the impact of nostalgia on Brutus (the individual) and later its effects on the Forum crowd: taken to its persuasive conclusion, nostalgic rhetoric results in one murder which then multiplies grossly as a result of Antony's own nostalgic arguments. In *Henry V*, Shakespeare stages nostalgia's effects at comparable dramatic moments. An early scene uses nostalgia to appeal to a singular individual (King Henry) upon whom the speakers' (the bishops) plans depend; late in the play we witness the expansion of nostalgia's power, as King Henry relies on it to ensure the support of his auditors (his army) and thus his victory.

By dramatising nostalgia's success with different audiences on stage, Shakespeare wants his off-stage audience to watch the power of nostalgia take hold, and he casts those spectators as recipients of nostalgia's effect. Tellingly, that off-stage audience takes the place of the large crowds imagined on stage, in Rome and in Agincourt. The dramaturgy furthermore suggests that nostalgia is catching; while we do not see the contagion of nostalgia working in its Enlightenment and Romantic modes (as a physical disease), Shakespeare does suggest that the desire embedded in nostalgia is contagious: it reproduces the desire it articulates in its on-stage auditor. This success is partially contingent on the fantasy of the future demanded of the nostalgic auditor. In a manner similar to the use of Shakespeare's staged silences, on-stage and off-stage auditors are left to fill in the blanks of the proposed perfect futures.[63] Shakespeare's dramaturgy simultaneously renders these spectators both participants in the theatre and critical witnesses to what unfolds, and thus to nostalgia's use as a political tool. Through the dramaturgy's shifting placement of the audience as objects and as observers of nostalgia's use, reflective space is created for questioning the claims of an idealised past.

Rupture and Continuity

Nostalgic discourse emerges from the possibility of comparing the past with the present, and inherent within that comparison is the conception of the past as past, as precedent. It is tantalising then to see nostalgia as a particularly Renaissance emotion and experience: it has become a critical commonplace that this sense of temporal discontinuity, of historical distance, was 'discovered' by Renaissance European humanists. From the fourteenth through the seventeenth centuries, scholars contend, a historical consciousness developed that rejected the perceived medieval practice of absorbing the past into the present, and that consciousness created a sense of anachronism and temporal rupture. Renaissance writers, scholars and artists, in comprehending that rupture which defined *now* and *then*, established the idea that the past could possess a proximity to the present without either subsuming the other; this idea enabled and encouraged the comparison of the present with the past in the Renaissance.[64] For Ricardo Quinones and Thomas Greene, it is the specific project of the Renaissance that articulates this discovery of time, which for Greene worked as a constant reminder to the humanists of what their era lacked, of its own belatedness. In his account, imitation provided a means for humanists to confront and cope with the pastness of the past, a panacea of sorts for the inescapable, irreparable sense of loss humanists experienced in their encounters with antiquity.[65]

Far from a dominant sense of estrangement, however, early modern texts suggest the Tudor humanists felt a 'strong sense of cultural unity' for their classical counterparts, exemplified in Thomas Wilson's 1570 translation of Demosthenes.[66] Providing an understanding of past and present characteristic of sixteenth-century England, he writes:

> And nowe most gentle Reader thinke that when I was occupied about this worke: to make Athens & the government thereof to be knowne to my Countrie men, my meaning was, that every good subject according to the levell of his witte, should compare the time past with the time present, and ever when he heareth Athens, or the Athenians, to remember England and Englishmen, and so all other things in like manner incident thereunto, that we maye learne by the doings of our elders how we may deale in our owne affayres, and so through wisedome by our neyghbours example avoyde all harme that else unwares might happen unto us.[67]

Wilson's explicit injunction to 'compare the time past with the time present' repeats the conventional early modern European belief in history's didactic use. In his readers' historical fantasies, Athens is writ as England; curiously, Wilson describes the Athenians who by example may teach his countrymen both as 'elders' and as 'neyghbours'. They are distinguished from the English by their ancient status and its implied attendant wisdom, while simultaneously Wilson imbues them with the Christian sense of a neighbour as a 'fellow human' and exploits the physical proximity inherent in 'neyghbour'.[68] In making this distinction, Wilson creates for his audience a simultaneous proximity to, and distance from, the past. It is the ability to sense contiguity through distance that makes the past – and the idea of the past – such a forceful means of instruction. Crucial to understanding nostalgia in early modernity, then, is this duality inherent in representations of the past. It is not only distant and therefore instructive; it is proximate and therefore relevant. The pervasiveness of the proximate-past duality distinguishes the Renaissance mindset from contemporary incarnations of nostalgia.

Contemporary nostalgia's conventional desire to relive and recreate a perfect past, particularly through its material reconstruction, was for some in the Renaissance not only suspect but, culturally and artistically, banal and devoid of genius. While a 'tragic pathos' confronted Renaissance humanists in the shape of their own imitations, Erasmus's *Ciceronianus* (1528) argues that the passage of time separating the humanists from antiquity was a source of debilitation and lifelessness in art only if artists and writers aimed solely at reconstructing that past.[69] Erasmus saw imitation in the Ciceronian's style as a 'dead copy', and thus the aim of imitation was 'self-expression', the assertion of one's own identity rather than its loss.[70] *Innovatio*'s essential role as an element of *imitatio*, which Erasmus's arguments suggest, further highlights the ambivalence attached to early modern English culture's engagement with the past. The *Adagia*, one of the period's best-selling and most important works, recognises the importance of *innovatio* even in the constant, seemingly atemporal form of proverbial discourse, which 'admit[s] metaphors of any degree of boldness, and unlimited innovation in the use of words'.[71] However, in late Tudor England innovation was viewed as a suspect practice, rejected by the period's rising Neostoicism.[72] Ambivalence pervades temporal comparison in the period: Michel de Montaigne praises the ancients *and* voices his scepticism of them.[73] George Puttenham's *The arte of English poesie* argues that the practice fundamental to the creation and expression of nostalgia – the comparison of times past to times present – is in fact the path to right action. Of memory, he writes that

> it maketh most to a sound judgement and perfect worldly wisedome, examining and comparing the times past with the present, and by them both considering the time to come, concludeth with a steadfast resolution, what is the best course to be taken in all his actions and advices in the world.[74]

For Puttenham, the future is formed by drawing on memory and comparing 'the times past with the present'. Nonetheless, in Ecclesiastes (one of Shakespeare's favourite biblical books), the preacher instructs: 'Say not thou, Why is it that the former dayes were better then [*sic*] these? For thou doest not enquire wisely of this thing' (7.12).[75] To prefer past to present is to question God's omniscience and providence. This verse enjoins against performing a discursive return to a preferable past and so implicitly reminds the reader that the past is not so different from the present, that 'there [is] no new thing under the sunne', as Ecclesiastes 1.9 states (and Shakespeare's Sonnet 59 echoes). As evidenced by its inclusion in the Anglican liturgy and its many printings and biblical commentaries, there was a significant cultural and literary interest in Ecclesiastes, and Shakespeare's audience would have been familiar with this text and its warning against temporal comparison.[76]

Desiring the past and seeking to recreate it was artistically an empty practice; simultaneously, newness – in art, religion and politics – was itself suspect. Such ambivalence extended to attitudes towards time and the early modern individual's relationship to the past. In the sixteenth century, the increasingly attractive idea of humanity's control over fortune – an idea consequent of the emblematic conflation of fortune and *occasio* in this period – was countered by the pan-European scepticism that developed in the same era.[77] Ernst Cassirer names that scepticism *chorismos* (separation), the idea that humankind is separated from absolute knowledge and consequently from stability in its world. Recognising that *chorismos* elicits *methixis*, a participation in the 'dark world of no past and no future', this awareness of alienation results in fact in 'a renewed participation in life'.[78] The behavioural and sentimental extremes which time elicits are mediated by the ambivalence that time itself produces. Ambivalence is the productive force, the 'mainspring' of humanist culture that represents the awareness of 'the paired intuitions of rupture and continuity'.[79] This ambivalence may encompass a range of attitudes voicing our relationship to, and use of, the past: rejection, anachronism, praise, longing. It is a consequence of early modern European culture's negotiation of, and meditation on, the role of the individual in time and the relationship between patterns of history and individual action. Shakespeare's own use of nostalgia as a politically successful and suspect rhetoric participated, then, in a culture that was seemingly always speaking from both sides of its mouth.

Of equal relevance for re-evaluating and expanding critical understanding of nostalgia in early modern England is its various and contradictory discourses of time. Alongside linear time that unfolds towards a providential telos, time could also be momentary and cyclical. With the development of the minute hand in 1577 and the steady proliferation of time-telling devices, the discourses of controlling time, particularly *occasio* (or *kairos*), circulated not only in drama but in early modern emblem books, tracts of Renaissance political thought (for example, Thomas Elyot's *The Book of the Governor*), and via printer's devices; Richard Taverner's device was used not only in the printing of Erasmus's works, but for *Romeo and Juliet*.[80] In *De inventione*, Cicero explains that

> An *occasion* is a period of time offering a convenient opportunity for doing or not doing something. And it is on the matter of opportunity that occasion differs from time [...] though *occasion* is of the same genus as *time*, it is something else, because it differs from it in some respect and, as we have said, belongs to a different species.[81]

As understood in antiquity, *tempus* encompasses *occasio* while each remains distinct from the other. Cicero partly identifies what that 'something else' is: an ephemeral quality. For example, Canterbury's appeal to Henry V that his time, his age, makes him 'Ripe for exploits and mighty enterprises', and that he is in the bloom ('May-morn') of his youth, not only presents the war in France as an opportunity that must be taken at the right time, but in using the imagery of the flower, which will inevitably fade, he insists on the fleetingness of the moment (and reproduces a motif common to Shakespeare's Sonnets) (1.2.121, 120). As the period's emblem literature shows, *occasio* has to be grasped by the forelock before she passes by and becomes unattainable, as she is unstable, ever-moving, and requires 'readiness'.[82] In early modernity, *occasio* adds real rhetorical weight to nostalgic discourses about the past's potential to return, since as a temporal discourse it gives to moments of action – Henry's St Crispin's Day speech or Northumberland's rousing of the rebels in *Richard II* – a sense of urgency and, equally, of possibility. By acting *now*, Northumberland will suggest, a peaceful past can return.

Likewise, the period's discourses of cyclical time and the idea of history's potential repetition invest laments for a lost, idealised past with a meaningful hope of that past's return. *Renovatio* offers one of early modernity's most powerful examples of this discourse, which represented not only a necessary element of the golden age *topos* but the 'return of the Golden Age' which could – for the Holy Roman Empire to which the term is consistently applied – signal a 'spiritual renovation' that would permit Christ's own return and consequent reign.[83] In her seminal *Astraea*, Frances Yates argues that the quattrocento humanists' hopes for renewal through successive Holy Roman Emperors continued in the person of Charles V, and this narrative of renewal laid the foundation for the cult of Astraea in early modern England. When the myth surrounding Charles dissipated with his abdication, it was reformed around Elizabeth I. In this argument, the monarch functions as the only possible vehicle for Astraea's return and the end of the Iron Age, and monarchy becomes then a unifying institution imbued with the powers to create a world of peace and prosperity.[84] But scholars have long taken issue with this idea of the 'cult of the monarch' that Yates associates with *renovatio* and Astraea, arguing rather for a constitutionalist understanding of monarchy.[85] Their critiques undermine the notion of a monarch as the singular source of justice in civil society and problematise the narrative of how a flawed present can be renewed and brought closer to perfection.

Shakespeare, ever attentive to the problems of (hereditary) monarchy, stages in *Henry V* a critique of the sovereign's central role in *renovatio*. In Act 4, Fluellen argues that King Henry is historically prefigured in Alexander the Great when he makes a serio-comic comparison of the king to the legendary emperor. 'If you mark Alexander's life well, Harry of Monmouth's life is come after it indifferent well, for there is figures in all things', he tells Gower (4.7.31–3). Noting as well geographic connections, Fluellen then insists that the king is a kind of improved 'Alexander the Pig', since 'As Alexander killed his friend Clytus, being in his ales and his cups, so also Harry Monmouth, being in his right wits and his good judgements, turned away the fat knight with the great belly doublet' (4.7.12–13, 44–7).[86] Shakespeare uses Fluellen's Welshness later in this scene to mock ideas of royalty's permanence – and his own drama. In a parodic echo of Richard II's 'Not all the water in the rough rude sea / Can wash the balm off from an anointed king' (3.2.54–5) – spoken in Wales – Fluellen insists to Henry that 'All the water in Wye cannot wash your majesty's Welsh plood out of your pody' (4.7.105–6). Recasting indissoluble kingship, a hubristic fault in *Richard II*, as indissoluble nationality, Shakespeare challenges his audience's impulse to locate the past's ability to return through an individual monarch. At the same time, he encourages such an impulse through the churchmen who laud Henry's perfection as a mortal 'paradise'.

Renovatio is however just one of the early modern modes of return Shakespeare explores in his dramaturgical staging of nostalgia. *Renovatio* originates in the Latin *renovatus*, from *renovare*; 'to make new anew'.[87] This sense implies a concrete, total loss that, in Yates's account, can only be restored by the monarch. In tension with this insistence on renewal and restoration is *reclamation*. Shakespeare's nostalgics articulate ideas of a pre-extant political inheritance, the security of which is contingent not upon monarchical influence but upon subjects' collective action to reclaim what is theirs. Reclamation derives from the classical Latin *reclamatio*, 'a shout of disapproval or protest', and in post-classical Latin a 'claim [or] counterclaim'; in early modern England, reclamation was defined as 'The action of protesting, objecting, or of expressing disapproval; opposition, disagreement; an instance of this, *esp*. a formal objection.' My use of reclamation also depends on its definition as 'The action of claiming something (formerly in one's legal possession) back or of reasserting a legal right; the legal right to make such an action; an instance of this' (traceable from 1626).[88] While the idea of restoration – renewing and granting again in the future what was taken away in the past – links renewal and reclamation, inherent in the latter is a sense of personal injustice that motivates action. What is crucial to remember about these modes of restoration is that they are not inevitably perceived or constructed as 'the anti-modern myth-making of history', as Boym characterises restorative nostalgia.[89] Shakespeare, I argue, crafts nostalgia as a suspicious practice, but he stages its speakers as ambitious men often seeking solutions to political crises or perceived injustice.

Shakespeare's Golden Ages

As staged by Shakespeare, nostalgia possesses five distinct qualities. These qualities are not prescriptive, but rather introduce some of the ways in which we can reconsider nostalgia in early modernity. First, in Shakespeare's use, an idealised space is articulated as coeval with an idealised time. Second, this idealised time and space offer the image of a rightful, extant political inheritance (a kingdom led by a just ruler, for example) which itself is presented as available for reclamation. Third, nostalgia is not exclusively focused on a longing for a limitless, unavailable past, but rather emerges from serious concerns for the future. Fourth, nostalgia is a rhetoric accessible to individuals across the early modern social hierarchy. Finally, Shakespeare exploits elements of early modern culture – temporal discourses such as momentary time (*occasio*), or the notion of *renovatio* – to nuance his depiction of nostalgia's power. Ambivalence about the idealised past is perhaps the most critical of those elements, and Shakespeare utilises it to dramatise a suspicion of nostalgia and to resist, as this book's title implies, the idea of anything like a historical 'golden age'. Shakespeare's own use of nostalgia exposes its openness to equivocation.

On Shakespeare's stage there is no singular idealised past, and he uses that plurality to render suspect the uses of nostalgia and its past-future orientations. This book attends to the dramaturgy and even the grammar of nostalgia to illustrate how that suspicion is created through Shakespeare's language and the staging of that language. His dramaturgy is invested in controlling stage action and shaping audience response; it is grounded in rhetoric. In the English histories particularly,

Shakespeare's dramaturgical choices create and invite scepticism – about the construction of history, about providence's role in daily life, about the power of the state – and they destabilise grand historical narratives.[90] His use of nostalgia is one such dramaturgical tool to achieve this disruption, as his stagecraft seeks to complicate the desire for an idealised past, and consequently it forms part of a larger, oft-noted dramaturgical project in his histories: the depiction of the past's instability and unknowability.

While this Introduction has focused on Shakespeare, Chapter 1 examines his contemporary dramatic influences to contextualise both the presence of nostalgic discourse in the emergent English public theatre and Shakespeare's own dramatic innovation in using that discourse. Shakespeare shares a 'dramatic vocabulary [...] with his collaborators and colleagues', and in this chapter I identify and examine those contemporaries' dramaturgical choices that Shakespeare develops and departs from.[91] This chapter first analyses two history plays adapted by Shakespeare – *The Famous Victories of Henry the Fifth* (1583/1588, pub. 1598), and *The True Tragedy of Richard the Third* (pub. 1594) – before turning to Marlowe's *Tamburlaine the Great* (1587), and the Queen's Men's *Selimus* (pub. 1594). I conclude the chapter with a brief analysis of the Queen's Men's *The Troublesome Reign of John, King of England* (1591) and Shakespeare's *King John* (1595–6) to demonstrate how Shakespeare incorporates a past-resistant dramaturgical model into his own work. Crucially, these plays use temporal consciousness – an explicit awareness of past, present and/or future – rhetorically, making that consciousness both ethical and political. Tamburlaine's refusal to look to the past, for example, marks him as dangerously future-oriented as he rejects past-dependent institutions like hereditary monarchy. These plays all stage a future-oriented temporal consciousness that highlights the limits of the past and consequently insists on focusing on the present-future. Having established the ways in which Shakespeare's dramatic influences staged temporal consciousness, the succeeding chapters offer case studies of how future-oriented nostalgic rhetoric drives political action in *2 Henry VI*, *Richard II* and *Julius Caesar*. Alongside these case studies, Shakespeare's dramatic and socio-historical contexts become a vital means of understanding how he stages nostalgia's power and his scepticism of it.

Chapter 2 examines a fantasy of the past central to the late Tudor idea of nostalgia: the *topos* of a 'merry world', or 'merry England'. I analyse the diverse articulations of the ubiquitous 'merry world/England' proverb that circulated in Tudor culture, in influential sixteenth-century plays and interludes (*Hick Scorner*, *Lusty Juventus*) and post-Reformation critiques of Catholicism. This context informs Shakespeare's own use of the *topos* in *The Second Part of Henry VI* (1590, rev. 1594–7), in which he employs a contested religious discourse to craft an ambivalent political rhetoric. The chapter demonstrates, for example, the cultural currency of the play's nostalgic proverbial discourse through an examination of Protestant writers who created and mocked their idea of a preferable Catholic past. *2 Henry VI* employs the culturally familiar language of proverbs to introduce political instability and radicalism into Shakespeare's play, as the crown's representatives and their opposition use nostalgic rhetoric to gain or to secure power. In the play, the 'merry world' discourse communicates a longing that will ultimately be revealed as fruitless in its desire for a place and time that never existed.

Chapter 3 identifies a nostalgic discourse of lost hospitality in *Richard II* (c. 1596). In the play, nostalgia functions as a political rhetoric engaged both with the socio-economic problems of the mid-1590s and with the changing landscape of English tradition instigated by the Reformation and the Dissolution of the Monasteries. Absent hospitality becomes a source of grief and a consequence of tyranny, and *Richard II* reveals an overwhelming sense of a lost golden age, as justice and equity have abandoned England. Again, the rhetoric of the idealised past articulates an interest in the future which reinforces the image of the present as post-lapsarian. Part of the play's historical context is how a potentially latent nostalgia was fomenting in the wake of failed harvests and diminishing and changing traditions of hospitality. I consider how Shakespeare, Stow and others represent the monastery ruins which symbolised the idea of lost hospitality. The chapter illustrates how the *topoi* of dissolution and desolation constitute a rhetoric of lost hospitality in *Richard II*. Moreover, I analyse the contemporary, anonymous play *Thomas of Woodstock* (c. 1590–4?) to illustrate how Shakespeare writes hospitality's absence in his own history. As in *2 Henry VI*, *Richard II* demonstrates how nostalgia provokes individuals to collective political action, as Northumberland and the rebels rally behind the idea of a reclaimable, idealised England.

Chapter 4 offers a final case study as it re-examines the relationship between *Julius Caesar* (1599) and Ben Jonson's *Sejanus* (1603/1605) to argue that Shakespeare's tragedy provides a model for dramatic nostalgic rhetoric that Jonson will develop further in his own Roman play. The playwrights' shared interest in and suspicion of nostalgia reinforces the conversation that critics have identified between these two dramas. Both Shakespeare and Jonson recreate Roman histories at a time when Tacitus's impact on history writing was steadily rising. While scholars have registered Tacitus's cultural and political importance in

Elizabethan England, the exact dramatic appeal of Tacitean history remains under-analysed, and *Julius Caesar* and *Sejanus* illustrate that appeal as they stage Tacitus's lament for a degenerate present and a longing for the republican past alongside his idea of the individual's role in shaping history. As elsewhere in Shakespeare's drama, in *Julius Caesar* the idealised past seems to be at hand; in this play, however, competing narratives of Rome and of its citizens together signal Rome's post-lapsarian state. By contrast, in *Sejanus* Jonson insists on the irretrievability of the past that seems so tantalisingly close in Shakespeare. In both plays, however, the language that articulates a perfect past becomes evidence of just how fallen the present is. That Shakespeare and Jonson make the act of interpretation within their plays crucial to their dramaturgy reinscribes how distant Rome and its cognate, early modern London, are from a perfect future. Ultimately, Shakespeare and Jonson employ nostalgia to different political ends, as *Sejanus* – in many ways a response to *Caesar* – formulates nostalgia as a strictly radical discourse which becomes sidelined and impotent in the play's politics.

I conclude this study by considering how Shakespeare takes his Elizabethan model of nostalgic rhetoric into his Jacobean histories. In *Antony and Cleopatra*, Shakespeare again demonstrates his suspicion of narratives of the perfect past as he uses his eponymous lovers to suggest both that ideals lie only in the future, and that those ideals can only ever be fantasy. The doubt Shakespeare sows around historical narratives in *Antony and Cleopatra* he repeats in *Henry VIII (All is True)*, where a similar focus on the future and an absence of nostalgic rhetoric intimate that, taking a cue from Jonson, nostalgic rhetoric cannot have a central place in a play that speaks so determinedly to its present.

Notes

1. William Shakespeare, *King Henry V*, ed. T. W. Craik, Arden Third Series (London: Routledge/The Arden Shakespeare, 1995), 1.1.27–30. All future references will be made in the text.
2. On nostalgic associations in *Henry V* cf. Katherine Eggert, 'Nostalgia and the Not Yet Late Queen: Refusing Female Rule in *Henry V*', *ELH*, 61:3 (1994), 523–50 and Linda Charnes, 'Anticipating Nostalgia: Finding Temporal Logic in a Textual Anomaly', *Textual Cultures*, 4:1 (2009), 72–83 and her 'Reading for the Wormholes: Micro-periods from the Future', in *Early Modern Culture: An Electronic Seminar*, 6 (2007), http://eserver.org/emc/1-6/charnes.html
3. Throughout, I refer to 'Shakespeare's dramatic nostalgia' and similar

phrases to avoid any confusion about making claims for 'Shakespeare's nostalgia' – that is, what I think he personally romanticises about the past.
4. Johannes Hofer defines nostalgia as a physical disease, see pp. 6–7; Susan Stewart, *On Longing: Narratives of the Miniature, the Gigantic, the Souvenir, the Collection* [1984] (Durham, NC and London: Duke University Press, 1993), p. ix; Achim Landwehr, 'Nostalgia and the Turbulence of Times', *History and Theory*, 57:2 (2018), 251–68, 253; Peter N. Carrol, *Keeping Time: Memory, Nostalgia, and the Art of History* (Athens: University of Georgia Press, 1990), p. 179.
5. On nostalgia and the pastoral, see Laurence Lerner, *The Uses of Nostalgia: Studies in Pastoral Poetry* (London: Chatto and Windus, 1972), pp. 40, 44 and *passim*; Harry Levin, *The Myth of the Golden Age in the Renaissance* (Bloomington and London: University of Indiana Press, 1969); Harry Berger, Jr., *Second World and Green World: Studies in Renaissance Fiction-Making*, selected and arranged, with an introduction, by John Patrick Lynch (Berkeley and London: University of California Press, 1988). On nostalgia and romance, see Richard Hillman, *Intertextuality and Romance in Renaissance Drama: The Staging of Nostalgia* (Basingstoke: Palgrave Macmillan, 1992); Donald Beecher, 'Nostalgia and the Renaissance Romance', *Philosophy and Literature*, 34:2 (2010), 281–301; J. K. Barrett, 'Shakespeare's Second Future: Anticipatory Nostalgia in Cymbeline', in *Untold Futures: Time and Literary Culture in Renaissance England* (Ithaca, NY: University of Cornell Press, 2016), pp. 147–76.
6. See most recently Yuichi Tsukada, *Shakespeare and the Politics of Nostalgia: Negotiating the Memory of Elizabeth I on the Jacobean Stage* (London: Bloomsbury, 2019); Curtis Perry, 'The Citizen Politics of Nostalgia: Queen Elizabeth in Jacobean London', *Journal of Medieval and Renaissance Studies*, 23 (1993), 89–111; Anne Barton, *Ben Jonson, Dramatist* (Cambridge: Cambridge University Press, 1984), pp. 300–20; James Knowles, '"In the purest times of peerless Queen Elizabeth": Nostalgia, Politics, and Jonson's use of the 1575 Kenilworth Entertainments', in *The Progresses, Pageants, and Entertainments of Queen Elizabeth I*, ed. J. E. Archer, Elizabeth Goldring and Sarah Knight (Oxford: Oxford University Press, 2007), pp. 247–67; Isabel Karremann, *The Drama of Memory in Shakespeare's History Plays* (Cambridge: Cambridge University Press, 2015), pp. 153–82; Hillman, *Intertextuality and Romance*; Lowell Gallagher, '"This seal'd-up Oracle": Ambivalent Nostalgia in The Winter's Tale', in *Exemplaria* (1995), 465–98; Susan Doran and Thomas S. Freeman, eds., *The Myth of Elizabeth* (Basingstoke: Palgrave Macmillan, 2003); Philip Schwyzer, *Literature, Nationalism, and Memory in Early Modern England and Wales* (Cambridge: Cambridge University Press, 2004); Lucy Munro, *Archaic Style: Archaic Style in English Literature, 1590–1674* (Cambridge: Cambridge University Press, 2014), Anita Gilman Sherman, *Skepticism and Memory in Shakespeare and Donne* (Basingstoke: Palgrave Macmillan, 2007), pp. 66–9, 121.
7. Karremann, *The Drama of Memory*, and 'Nostalgic Spectacle and the Politics of Memory in Henry VIII', *Shakespeare Survey*, 67 (2014), 180–90; Baldo, *Memory in Shakespeare's Histories: Stages of Forgetting in Early Modern England* (New York: Routledge, 2012); see also Schwyzer,

Literature, Nationalism, and Memory; and idem, 'Lees and Moonshine: Remembering Richard III, 1485–1635', *Renaissance Quarterly*, 63 (2010), 850–83.
8. *Shakespeare and Historical Formalism*, ed. Stephen Cohen (London: Routledge, 2007); Neema Parvini, *Shakespeare's History Plays: Rethinking Historicism* (Edinburgh: Edinburgh University Press, 2012).
9. For surveys of nostalgia criticism see Susannah Radstone, *The Sexual Politics of Time: Confession, Nostalgia, Memory* (London and New York: Routledge, 2007), pp. 112–32; Tobias Becker, 'The Meanings of Nostalgia: Genealogy and Critique', *History and Theory*, 57:2 (2018), 234–50, 235–41; Michael Hviid Jacobsen, 'Introduction', in *Nostalgia Now: Cross-Disciplinary Perspectives on the Past in the Present*, ed. Jacobsen (London: Routledge, 2020 [Vital Source Bookshelf], n.p.).
10. Those studies most relevant for this book include: Svetlana Boym, *The Future of Nostalgia* (New York: Basic Books, 2001); Nicholas Dames, *Amnesiac Selves: Nostalgia, Forgetting, and British Fiction, 1810–1870* (Oxford: Oxford University Press, 2001); Peter Fritzsche, 'Specters of History: On Nostalgia, Exile, and Modernity', *American Historical Review* (2001), 1587–1618; John J. Su, *Ethics and Nostalgia in the Contemporary Novel* (Cambridge: Cambridge University Press, 2005); Linda M. Austin, *Nostalgia in Transition, 1780–1917* (Charlottesville and London: University of Virginia Press, 2007); Renée R. Trilling, *The Aesthetics of Nostalgia: Historical Representation in Old English Verse* (Toronto: University of Toronto Press, 2009); Helmut Illbruck, *Nostalgia: Origins and Ends of an Unenlightened Disease* (Chicago: Northwestern University Press, 2012); Jennifer K. Ladino, *Reclaiming Nostalgia: Longing for Nature in American Literature* (Charlottesville and London: University of Virginia Press, 2012); Nadia Atia and Jeremy Davies, eds., *Memory Studies*, 3:3 (2010); Helen Dell, ed., *postmedieval: a journal of medieval cultural studies*, 2 (2011); Linda Hutcheon, 'Irony, Nostalgia, and the Postmodern', *Methods for the Study of Literature as Cultural Memory, Studies in Comparative Literature*, 30 (2000), 189–207; Kevis Goodman, 'Romantic Poetry and the Science of Nostalgia', in *The Cambridge Companion to British Romantic Poetry*, ed. James Chandler and Maureen N. McLane (Cambridge: Cambridge University Press, 2008), pp. 195–216 and '"Uncertain disease": Nostalgia, Pathologies of Motion, Practices of Reading', *Studies in Romanticism*, 49:2 (2010), 197–227; Becker, ed., 'Historical Forum' on Nostalgia in *History and Theory*, 57:2 (2018).
11. Jean Starobinski, 'The Idea of Nostalgia', trans. Will Kemp, *Diogenes*, 14 (1966), 81–103, 81.
12. Fritzsche, 'Specters of History', 1589; Nadia Atia and Jeremy Davies, 'Editorial: Nostalgia and the Shapes of History', *Memory Studies* 3:3 (2010), 181–6, 181; Boym, *The Future of Nostalgia*, p. 41; Nicholas Dames, 'Response: Nostalgia and Its Disciplines', *Memory Studies*, 3:3 (2010), 269–275, 271. On the valences of 'modern', see Margreta de Grazia, 'The Modern Divide: From Either Side', *Journal of Medieval and Early Modern Studies*, 37:3 (2007), 453–67, 453.
13. John Stow, *The Survey of London* (London, 1603), ff. 27, 29, 45.
14. Ibid., ff. 20–1, 18.

15. Cf. Chapter 3, pp. 106–7 below; Ian Archer, 'The Nostalgia of John Stow', in *The Theatrical City: Culture, Theatre and Politics in London, 1576–1649*, ed. David L. Smith, Richard Strier and David Bevington (Cambridge: Cambridge University Press, 1995); Benjamin Deneault on 'the overdetermined image of Stow as a nostalgic', in his '"The World Runs on Wheeles": John Stow's Indescribable London', *ELH*, 78:2 (2011), 337–58, 338; William Keith Hall, 'The Topography of Time: Historical Narration in John Stow's Survey of London', *Studies in Philology*, 88:1 (1991), 1–16.
16. Johannes Hofer, 'Medical Dissertation on Nostalgia by Johannes Holer, 1688', trans. Carolyn Kiser Anspach, *Bulletin of the Institute of the History of Medicine*, 2 (1934), 376–91, 380. Hofer, *Dissertatio Medica de Nostalgia, oder Heimwehe* (Basil, 1678 [1688]), A3^r. Hofer in fact writes 'Nosos', and Anspach repeats the error. The *OED*'s definition of the term uses Hofer's etymology but corrects the Greek: 'ancient Greek νόστος return home (see NOSTOS *n.*) + αλγία -ALGIA *comb. form*, after German *Heimweh*' (Oxford, draft revision September 2009).
17. Landwehr, 'Nostalgia', 256 and ibid., fn 21. *Heimweh* emerged from the Berne dialect and exists in contemporary German (*Heimweh*) and Dutch (*heimwee*).
18. Judith H. Anderson, 'Wonder and Nostalgia in *Hamlet*', *SEL*, 58:2 (2018), 353–72, 354.
19. Illbruck, *Nostalgia*, p. 5.
20. Anspach, 'Medical Dissertation', 381.
21. Ibid., 380.
22. Ibid., 384, 385; see 382ff. for case studies.
23. Landwehr, 'Nostalgia', 257.
24. Illbruck, *Nostalgia*, p. 41. Cf. William Cullen's *Synopsis Nosologiae Methodicae* (1792); Robert Pulteney's *A General View of the Writings of Linnæus* (1781), which includes a note on nostalgia (noted as 'Swiss Mallady'), p. 178; and the Rev. Dr John Trusler's *The Habitable World Described: Or the Present State of the People in All Parts of the Globe, from North to South* (1788). Evidence shows that nostalgia was still treated as a disease as late as 1946, and it was still defined as homesickness through the years following the Second World War; David Lowenthal, *The Past is a Foreign Country* (Cambridge: Cambridge University Press, 1985), p. 11, and Becker, 'The Meanings of Nostalgia', 239.
25. In in his 1770 ship journal for HMS *Endeavour*, Sir Joseph Banks refers to the dangerous effects of nostalgia on the crew – and demonstrates that the term was circulating in the English language less than a century after its initial coinage; see Dames, *Amnesiac Selves*, p. 24.
26. Burton, *Anatomy of Melancholy* (London, 1621), 2.3.4, f. 411.
27. William Shakespeare, *Richard II*, ed. Charles R. Forker, Arden Third Series (Walton-on-Thames: The Arden Shakespeare, 2002; repr. 2004), 1.3.275–6. All references will be made in the text.
28. Burton, *Anatomy of Melancholy*, d5^r.
29. Burton, *Anatomy of Melancholy*, C3^v.
30. Williams, *The Country and the City* (London: Chatto and Windus, 1973), p. 12. On Virgil see Lerner, *The Uses of Nostalgia*, pp. 40, 44, and David Lowenthal, who cites Virgil's epics and pastorals before moving through

centuries, *Foreign Country*, pp. 10, 4–13; on Ovid, see Illbruck, *Nostalgia*, pp. 9–10. A complex nostalgia infuses Ali Smith's Brexit-era Seasonal Quartet.
31. Cf. Renato Rosaldo, 'Imperialist Nostalgia', *Representations*, Special Issue: Memory and Counter-Memory, 26 (1989), 107–22, 109; Malcolm Chase and Christopher Shaw, 'The Dimensions of Nostalgia', in *The Imagined Past: History and Nostalgia*, ed. Chase and Shaw (Manchester and New York: Manchester University Press, 1989), pp. 3–6, p. 3.
32. Linda Charnes, 'Anticipating Nostalgia', 81; Phyllis Rackin, *Stages of History* (London: Routledge, 1990), p. 99; and see Susan E. Harlan, *Memories of War in Early Modern England: Armor and Militant Nostalgia in Marlowe, Sidney, and Shakespeare* (Basingstoke: Palgrave Macmillan, 2016); on Shakespeare's possible suspicion, see Christopher Warley, 'Shakespeare's Fickle-Fee Simple: A Lover's Complaint, Nostalgia, and the Transition from Feudalism to Capitalism', in *Shakespeare and the Middle Ages*, ed. Curtis Perry and John Watkins (Oxford: Oxford University Press, 2009), pp. 21–44, p. 31; Natasha Korda, '"The Sign of the Last": Gender, Material Culture, and Artisanal Nostalgia in The Shoemaker's Holiday', *Journal of Medieval and Early Modern Studies*, 43:3 (2013), 573–97; Harriet Phillips, *Nostalgia in Print and Performance, 1510–1613: Merry Worlds* (Cambridge: Cambridge University Press, 2019); Anderson, 'Wonder and Nostalgia in *Hamlet*'.
33. Eggert, 'Nostalgia and the Not Yet Late Queen', 523ff. Cf. Frances A. Yates, *Astraea: The Imperial Theme in the Sixteenth Century* (London and Boston, MA: Routledge and Kegan Paul, 1975) and Yates, 'Queen Elizabeth as Astraea', *Journal of the Warburg and Courtauld Institutes*, 10 (1947), 27–82.
34. Stephen Cohen, 'Introduction', in *Shakespeare and Historical Formalism*, pp. 1–30, p. 16.
35. Alex Davis, 'Coming Home Again: Johannes Hofer, Edmund Spenser, and Premodern Nostalgia', in Approaches to Early Modern Nostalgia special issue, ed. Kristine Johanson, *Parergon*, 33:2 (2016), 17–38, 17.
36. Karl Marx, *The Eighteenth Brumaire of Louis Bonaparte*, in *The Marx-Engels Reader*, ed. Robert C. Tucker, 2nd edn (New York: Norton, 1978), pp. 594–617, p. 597. Fred Davis, *Yearning for Yesterday: A Sociology of Nostalgia* (New York and London: The Free Press and Collier Macmillan Publishers, 1979), p. 109.
37. Marcos Piason Natali, 'History and the Politics of Nostalgia', *Iowa Journal of Cultural Studies*, 5 (2004), 10–25, 13.
38. Davis, *Yearning for Yesterday*, p. 109.
39. Stewart, *On Longing*, p. x.
40. Ibid., p. 23.
41. Munro, *Archaic Style*, p. 21; see Trilling, *The Aesthetics of Nostalgia*, p. 5.
42. Munro, *Archaic Style*, pp. 21–2.
43. Korda, '"The Sign of the Last"'.
44. Phillips, *Nostalgia in Print and Performance*, p. 30 and cf. 1–30.
45. Cf. Su, *Ethics and Nostalgia*, p. 5; Constantine Sedikides et al., 'Nostalgia Motivates Pursuit of Important Goals by Increasing Meaning in Life:

Nostalgia, Meaning, Motivation', *European Journal of Social Psychology*, 48:2 (2018), 209–16; Anderson, 'Wonder and Nostalgia in *Hamlet*', 355; Landwehr, 'Nostalgia', 253; Becker, 'The Meanings of Nostalgia', 236.
46. Marx, *The Eighteenth Brumaire of Louis Bonaparte*, p. 596.
47. Frederic Jameson, *Marxism and Form* (Princeton, NJ: Princeton University Press, 1971), p. 82 and idem, *Postmodernism: Or, The Cultural Logic of Late Capitalism* (Durham, NC: Duke University Press, 1991), p. 171; Illbruck, *Nostalgia*, pp. 22, 249, 233 and 213–51; see also Kiernan Ryan, 'Measure for Measure: Marxism before Marx', in *Marxist Shakespeares*, ed. Jean E. Howard and Scott Cutler Shershow (New York: Routledge, 2001), pp. 228, 229.
48. Boym, *The Future of Nostalgia*, pp. 41, 49–50.
49. Jennifer Delisle, 'For King and Country', cited in Jennifer K. Ladino, *Reclaiming Nostalgia*, p. 12.
50. On complicating nostalgia see Helen Dell, 'Nostalgia and Medievalism: Conversations, Constructions, Impasses', *postmedieval: a journal of medieval cultural studies*, 2 (2011), 115–26, esp. 116–20.
51. Few critics have pursued this ambivalence in earnest, with the notable exception of Phillips, *Nostalgia in Print and Performance* (who attaches it to the production of mirth); Warley, Korda, Karremann and Hillman all suggest nostalgia's ambivalence; Lowell Gallagher's serious engagement with its possibility relies on a psychoanalytic lens in '"This seal'd-up Oracle"'.
52. Joel Altman, *The Tudor Play of Mind* (Berkeley and London: University of California Press, 1978), pp. 3, 31ff; Victoria Kahn, *Rhetoric, Prudence, and Skepticism in the Renaissance* (Ithaca, NY and London: Cornell University Press, 1985), p. 22; G. K. Hunter, 'Rhetoric and Renaissance Drama', in *Renaissance Rhetoric*, ed. Peter Mack (Basingstoke: Palgrave Macmillan, 1994), pp. 103–18, p. 111ff.
53. Victoria Kahn, *Machiavellian Rhetoric: From the Counter-Reformation to Milton* (Princeton, NJ: Princeton University Press, 1994), pp. 9, 10, and Kahn, *Rhetoric, Prudence, and Skepticism*, esp. pp. 27–9, 47.
54. Markku Peltonen, 'Rhetoric and Citizenship in the Monarchical Republic of Queen Elizabeth', in *The Monarchical Republic of Early Modern England: Essays in Response to Patrick Collinson*, ed. John F. McDiarmid (Aldershot: Ashgate, 2007), pp. 109–27, pp. 110, 111.
55. Peltonen, 'Rhetoric and Citizenship', p. 111.
56. Markku Peltonen, *Classical Humanism and Republicanism in English Political Thought 1570–1640*, Ideas in Context Series, gen. ed. Quentin Skinner (Cambridge: Cambridge University Press, 1995), pp. 79, 72, but see pp. 72–102, and cf. Andrew Hadfield, *Shakespeare and Republicanism* (Cambridge: Cambridge University Press, 2005), pp. 28–31.
57. Hadfield, *Shakespeare and Republicanism*, p. 12.
58. Shakespeare, Marlowe, and others, *2 Henry VI*, ed. Rory Loughnane in *The New Oxford Shakespeare*, gen. ed. Gary Taylor et al. (Oxford: Oxford University Press, 2017), 4.8.45. All further citations will be made in the text.
59. Cf. Aristotle, *The Nicomachean Ethics*, trans. H. Rackham. Loeb Classical Library 73 (Cambridge, MA: Harvard University Press, 1926), I.ii.8.

60. Cf. Hadfield, *Shakespeare and Republicanism* and Hadfield, *Shakespeare and Renaissance Politics* (London: Thomson Learning, 2004); A. N. McLaren, *Political Culture in the Reign of Elizabeth I: Queen and Commonwealth 1558–1585* (Cambridge: Cambridge University Press, 1999); Chris Fitter, 'Introduction: Rethinking Shakespeare in the Social Depth of Politics', *Shakespeare & the Politics of Commoners: Digesting the New Social History*, ed. Chris Fitter (Oxford: Oxford University Press, 2017), pp. 1–39.
61. Discussing *Cymbeline*, J. K. Barret has termed the imagined longing for the past in the future 'anticipatory nostalgia' in *Untold Futures*, pp. 21–2.
62. Shakespeare, *Julius Caesar*, ed. Sarah Neville, in *The New Oxford Shakespeare: Modern Critical Edition*, 3.1.277.
63. Jean Howard, *Shakespeare's Art of Orchestration* (Urbana: University of Illinois Press, 1984), pp. 79–100, esp. p. 86.
64. Thomas M. Greene, *The Light in Troy* (New Haven, CT and London: Yale University Press, 1982); Ricardo J. Quinones, *The Renaissance Discovery of Time*, Harvard Studies in Comparative Literature, vol. 31 (Cambridge, MA: Harvard University Press, 1972); cf. also Erwin Panofsky, *Renaissance and Renascences in Western Art* (New York: Harper and Row, 1972); Peter Burke, *The Renaissance Sense of the Past* (London: Edward Arnold, 1969); Jacques LeGoff, *Time, Work, & Culture in the Middle Ages*, trans. Arthur Goldhammer (Chicago: University of Chicago Press, 1980) esp. pp. 29–42.
65. Greene, *The Light in Troy*, p. 3.
66. Quentin Skinner, *Reason and Rhetoric in the Philosophy of Hobbes* (Cambridge: Cambridge University Press, 1996), p. 40.
67. Thomas Wilson, 'The Bounding of Greecelande According to Ptolomeus', in Demosthenes, *The Three Orations of Demosthenes*, trans. Wilson (London, 1570), Bi^v.
68. *OED*, 'neighbour', n. sense A.1.b, 2nd edn (Oxford: Oxford University Press, 1989).
69. Greene, *The Light in Troy*, pp. 8–10; Terence Cave, *The Cornucopian Text* (Oxford: Oxford University Press, 1979), pp. 40ff.
70. Cave, *Cornucopian Text*, pp. 42ff, 46; Betty I. Knott, 'Introduction', in Desiderus Erasmus, *The Ciceronian: A Dialogue on the Ideal Latin Style*, in *Collected Works*, ed. A. H. T. Levi, intro. and trans. Betty I. Knott (Toronto and London: University of Toronto Press, 1986), vol. 28, p. 328.
71. William Barker, ed., *A Selection from Erasmus's Adages* (Toronto and London: University of Toronto Press, 2001), p. 26.
72. Lisa Ferraro Parmelee, 'Neostoicism and Absolutism in Late Elizabethan England', in *Politics, Ideology and the Law in Early Modern Europe*, ed. Adrianna E. Bakos (Rochester, NY: University of Rochester Press, 1994), pp. 3–19, 6ff. On Neostoicism and its relationship to nostalgia, see Chapter 4.
73. Cf. Michel de Montaigne, 'On Ancient Customs', in *The Complete Essays*, trans. and ed. M. A. Screech (Harmondsworth: Penguin, 2003), p. 334.
74. George Puttenham, *The arte of English poesie* (London, 1589), F[v^r].
75. *The Bible* (London, 1583). Shakespeare most frequently used the Geneva translation of the Bible, cf. Hannibal Hamlin, *The Bible in Shakespeare* (Oxford: Oxford University Press, 2013), pp. 9–11, 16.

76. On Shakespeare and Ecclesiastes, see Kristine Johanson, '"Our brains beguiled": Ecclesiastes and Sonnet 59's Poetics of Temporal Instability', in *The Sonnets: State of Play*, ed. Hannah Crawforth, Elizabeth Scott-Baumann, and Clare Whitehead (London: Bloomsbury, 2017), pp. 55–76, esp. pp. 58–9.
77. Frederick Kiefer, 'The Conflation of Fortuna and Occasio in Renaissance Thought and Iconography', *Journal of Medieval and Renaissance Studies*, 9 (1979), 1–27; Quinones, *Discovery*, p. 179.
78. Quinones, *Discovery*, pp. 183, 184, 497.
79. Greene, *The Light in Troy*, p. 193.
80. See Kristine Johanson, 'Regulating Time and the Self in Shakespearean Drama', in *Staged Normality in Shakespeare's* England, ed. Rory Loughnane and Edel Semple (Basingstoke: Palgrave Macmillan, 2019), pp. 89–108; cf. Tiffany Stern, 'Time for Shakespeare: Hourglasses, Sundials, Clocks, and Early Modern Theatre', *Journal of the British Academy*, 3 (2015), 1–33; David Houston Wood, *Time, Narrative, and Emotion in Early Modern England* (Farnham, UK: Ashgate, 2009); Simona Cohen, *Transformations of Time and Temporality in Medieval and Renaissance Art* (Brill: Leiden, 2014); Joanne Paul, 'The Use of *Kairos* in Renaissance Political Philosophy', *Renaissance Quarterly*, 67:1 (2014), 43–78; Jonathan Gil Harris, *Untimely Matter in the Time of Shakespeare* (Philadelphia: University of Pennsylvania Press, 2009); Phillip Sipiora and James S. Baumlin, eds., *Rhetoric and Kairos: Essays in History, Theory, and Praxis* (Albany: State University of New York Press, 2002); Gerhard Dohrn-van Rossum, *History of the Hour: Clocks and Modern Temporal Orders*, trans. Thomas Dunlap (Chicago and London: University of Chicago Press, 1996).
81. 'Occasio autem est pars temporis habens in se alicuius rei idoneam faciendi aut non faciendi opportunitatem. Quare cum tempore hoc differt: nam genere quidem utrumque idem esse intellegitur, verum in tempore spatium quodam modo declaratur quod in annis aut in anno aut in aliqua anni parte spectatur, in occasione ad spatium temporis faciendi quaedam opportunitas intellegitur adiuncta. Quare cum genere idem sit, fit aliud quod parte quadam et specie, ut diximus, differat'. Cicero, *De inventione*, trans. H. M. Hubbell (London: William Heinemann Ltd; Cambridge, MA: Harvard University Press, 1949), 40.XXVII, pp. 78, 79.
82. See Erasmus, *Proverbes or adagies with newe addicions gathered out of the Chiliades of Erasmus*, trans. Richard Taverner (London, 1539), sig. [C8ᵛ], fol. Xxiiii.
83. Yates, 'Queen Elizabeth as Astraea', and Yates, *Astraea*, p. 4.
84. Yates, *Astraea*, pp. 1–28, esp. 11–16, 15, 38.
85. Cf. Alan Cromartie, *The Constitutionalist Revolution: An Essay on the History of England, 1450–1642* (Cambridge: Cambridge University Press, 2006); David Norbrook, *Poetry and Politics in the English Renaissance* (London: Routledge & Kegan Paul, 1984); Peltonen, *Classical Humanism and Republicanism*, esp. pp. 54ff; Cathy Shrank, *Writing the Nation in Reformation England, 1530–1580* (Oxford: Oxford University Press, 2004), p. 5; Paul Strohm, *Politique: Languages of Statecraft between Chaucer and Shakespeare* (Notre Dame, IN: University of Notre Dame Press, 2005); Blair Worden, *The Sound of Virtue: Philip Sidney's Arcadia*

and Elizabethan Politics (New Haven, CT and London: Yale University Press, 1996).
86. See also Hadfield, *Shakespeare and Renaissance Politics*, pp. 57–9, and Judith Mossmann, '*Henry V* and Plutarch's *Alexander*', *Shakespeare Quarterly*, 45:1 (1994), 57–73.
87. *OED*, 'Renovate', v.; see also the prefix 're-', sense iii (Oxford: Oxford University Press, 2009). OED Online, November 2009, Oxford University Press. https://www-oed-com.proxy.uba.uva.nl/view/Entry/162502?rskey=HDeSqE&result=2&isAdvanced=false (accessed 1 November 2009).
88. *OED*, 'reclamation', n., 2.b; 'reclamation', n., 3.a. *Reclamatio* derives from the Latin *reclamare*, 'to call out in response, (of places) to shout back, to cry out in protest, object loudly, to appeal'.
88. Boym, *The Future of Nostalgia*, p. 41.
90. Janette Dillon, *Shakespeare and the Staging of English History* (Oxford: Oxford University Press, 2012); see also Howard, *Shakespeare's Art of Orchestration*.
91. Karremann, *The Drama of Memory*, p. 32, and see Dillon, *Shakespeare and the Staging of English History*, *passim*.

Chapter 1

Against Nostalgia: Looking Forward to the Future in the Queen's Men's Plays and Marlowe's *Tamburlaine*

[I]f the old king my father were dead, we would be all kings.[1]
Prince Henry, *The Famous Victories of Henry the Fifth*

To understand Shakespeare's development and staging of nostalgic discourse as a political rhetoric, we cannot begin with Shakespeare. By examining his contemporary dramatic influences and contextualising the presence of nostalgic discourse in the emergent English public theatre, we witness both Shakespeare's dramatic innovation in his use of nostalgia and the changing uses of the past in early modern drama. This chapter attends predominantly to plays by the Queen's Men and by Christopher Marlowe, as the success of these plays not only made the success of Shakespeare's own histories possible, but these dramas significantly influenced Shakespeare's craft as sources for his plays and for action, character and language.[2] *The Famous Victories of Henry the Fifth*, *The True Tragedy of Richard the Third*, *Selimus* and *Tamburlaine* all stage a future-oriented temporal consciousness that highlights the limits of the past, concentrating attention on events in the (dramatic) present. Simply stated, this chapter asks: why is there no past to the past in these plays?

Since the revolutionary work of *The Queen's Men and Their Plays*, and, more recently, the *Locating the Queen's Men* collection, literary scholars have not only been increasingly interested in the relationship between Shakespeare's plays and this troupe's repertory but also in the Queen's Men themselves as offering a foundation for public theatre's ascendancy as an art form at the end of the sixteenth century. The Queen's Men's repertory – the limited representation of it that we have – offers one of the most significant bodies of work for examining how Shakespeare crafted his own history plays and the historical consciousness they present. While a long tradition of the historical play predates the Queen's Men, the troupe invented it as a successful genre for the public theatre.³ Scholars may agree on the Queen's Men's importance, but debate remains both regarding the troupe's presence and influence through the 1590s, and concerning their overarching 'style', certainty of which is curtailed by the limited body of work available. Nevertheless, repeated dramatic practices signify dramaturgical interest, a recognition of the success of a set of ideas and practices. The Queen's Men's plays demonstrate just such an interest in their representation of past and future. Recent scholarship, revising the 'duopoly' theory that the Queen's Men's final obsolescence was brought about by the rise of the Admiral's Men and the Chamberlain's Men, shows that the troupe '[i]n spirit and overall dramatic structure [. . . was] still not out of fashion by the end of the century'.⁴ Given the persistent influence of the Queen's Men through the 1590s, these plays and their future-oriented, past-less histories provide therefore both a foundation and a potential foil to the ways in which Shakespeare constructs an idealised past in his own works.

I am interested in those plays that provide a dramaturgical model for explicitly thinking about the complex relation between past, present and future which is at work in Shakespeare's use of nostalgia, and the plays under analysis in this chapter approach that complexity. While the histories I analyse are not exhaustive of the future-oriented plays from this period, their clear influence on Shakespeare's dramaturgy as a whole and his historical concerns in particular justify their inclusion here. In these plays, temporal consciousness – that is, an explicit awareness of past, present and/or future – is ethical and political. Tamburlaine's refusal to look back, for example, marks him as subversively future-oriented, as he rejects past-based institutions like hereditary monarchy. This chapter discusses three pairs of plays: two adapted by Shakespeare, *The Famous Victories of Henry the Fifth* (1583/1588, pub. 1598) and *The True Tragedy of Richard the Third* (pub. 1594); Marlowe's *Tamburlaine the Great* (1587) and the Queen's Men's response, *Selimus* (pub. 1594); and finally George Peele and Shakespeare's respective King John dramas, *The Troublesome Reign of King John* (1591) and *King John* (1595–6). Peele's play concerns itself even less with its past than other plays I analyse, but my brief discussion illustrates how Shakespeare draws on and turns away from the future-focused model of the Queen's Men. I have excluded *The True Chronicle History of King Leir* because it – not unlike Shakespeare's dramatisations of the Lear story – offers no sense of history beyond the play. *Leir*'s story emerges immediately in the present from an unknown and undiscussed past and looks with hesitation and anxiety on the future; there is no sense either of what the past was or why it should be yearned for.⁵

In the analyses that follow, I locate and examine these plays' temporal investments: the extent to which they linger on and actively consider past, present and future. As plays set in the past for an Elizabethan audience, the simple fact of their production itself presumes and asserts a relationship between past and present. Simultaneously, that relationship can be understood as a relationship between the play's past and its future, the Elizabethan present.

Early forms of the history play appear resistant to idealising the past and to offering any kind of rhetoric that might be labelled 'nostalgic' in the sense outlined in the Introduction. Modern spectators and readers, conditioned by Shakespeare's histories and their chronicling speeches, might assume that these earlier plays demonstrate an interest in their own past and establish for an audience what has preceded the stage action. This is consistently not the case. Dramaturgically, the Queen's Men's plays and *Tamburlaine* do not create conditions that provide a nostalgic glance into the past. These plays are not invested explicitly in the kind of historical chronicle that grounds the claims for a political inheritance and that forms the object of nostalgic longing in Shakespeare's works. Rather, they are driven by the anticipation of an unknown future, and the plays' obsessions with this future provided Shakespeare with a dramaturgical model of historical future orientation.

The Queen's Men's model, I argue, stages a temporal consciousness that participates in their national political project. Scholars disagree on the success and earnestness of the Queen's Men's purpose 'to spread Protestant and Royalist propaganda through a divided realm' and offer 'a coherent English nationalism'; and some have identified works like *The Famous Victories* and *The Troublesome Reign* as subverting the ideology ascribed to them.[6] What remains undebated is that the Queen's Men produce political messages. To fully understand the troupe's political dramaturgy, we would do well to consider how they render the temporal political. Attending to the Queen's Men's future orientations also calls into question the process by which the troupe could create 'historical consciousness'. In his important work on the company, Brian Walsh argues that it the embodied actor himself who temporally disrupts the presumed nostalgic longings of the Queen's Men's audiences. The player's body both forces 'audiences into awareness that the actual past is always irrecoverable' and shows how the desire to commune with the past is 'a desire that is doomed from the start to remain unfulfilled'.[7] Walsh's account assumes a nostalgic longing latently produced by the play itself. I argue that the Queen's Men's plays themselves refuse such longing in their dramaturgy. The plays' ever-forward focus tempers such a desire for the past, ironically seeming even to deny its existence.

For while these plays insist on history's construction, they also demonstrate a significant disinterest in the past beyond that of the play world. This idea implies the impossible: that history plays are disinterested in history. And this is precisely my point: the disinterest and the exclusion of any past lurking beyond the confines of the play is necessary for their Elizabethan project.

Perhaps it is not so surprising that the Queen's Men's drama is future-oriented. It is the natural temporality of a play, which traditionally does not go backwards, but rather unfolds in time, creating within its world its own time scheme of past, present and future. But to ascribe such a focus to the function of genre alone offers a myopic view of what the Queen's Men's temporal consciousness does. Their future-focused dramaturgy cannot be disjoined from what we know of the troupe's political ideology, and analysing their history plays and those plays' temporal consciousness reveals the political valences attached to articulations of the past, present and future as they were being used by the troupe. Attitudes towards time – again, primarily a focus on the future – are used to reveal character and chart character change; to create anxiety (will Henry kill his father?); to concentrate attention on the (Elizabethan) present. In short, these attitudes play a vital role in the subtle and not-so-subtle ideology that these histories present, as the dramas consistently link temporal consciousness to political choice and gain.

If desiring the past drives its reproduction in the cultural sphere, why is it that that past is offered up as undesirable? For the Queen's Men, the answer to this question lies in their larger political project. However nuanced that project is, it would be undermined by any depiction of the past that seemed to suggest history was in decline and to perpetuate any audience longing to inhabit that past.

Future Longings in *The Famous Victories of Henry the Fifth*

'Reading that chaotic anonymous production *The Famous Victories* is like going through the *Henry IV–Henry V* sequence in a bad dream', Arthur Humphreys harrumphed in his 1960 edition of *1 Henry IV*.[8] Whatever Humphreys's reading experience, *The Famous Victories* (1583/88) possessed a varied and lengthy lifespan on the Elizabethan stage, one that guaranteed its influence across dramatic genres in the 1590s.[9] The play's popularity is clear not only from the legendary status of its protagonist, nor from the evident impact it had on Shakespeare's rewriting of it, but on earlier evidence from Thomas Nashe's *Pierce Penilesse* (1592), which uses the play to reject anti-theatricalist claims of the theatre's immorality and to insist on the necessity of historical drama. In an oft-cited passage, he declares that plays, 'borrow[ing] out of our English Chronicles', 'reviv[e]' 'our forefathers['] valiant acts'; and with those forefathers 'raised from the Grave of Oblivion, and brought to plead their aged Honours in open presence', Nashe asks: 'what can be a sharper reproofe to these degenerate effeminate dayes of ours?'[10] By casting the present as 'degenerate' and equally 'effeminate', Nashe implies that the passage of time and history's decline has made humanity increasingly, problematically, feminine. His comments locate the genre's potential for topicality and critical commentary: in reviving the acts of English forebears, players provide a historical exemplar with which to reprove the imperfect days of the early 1590s. In what now looks like an act of self-promotion, Nashe then uses *Harey the VI* (presumed to be the Shakespearean collaboration *1 Henry VI*) and a recollection of the *Famous Victories* to support these claims, declaring: 'a glorious thing it is to have Henrie the fifth represented on the Stage, leading the French King prisoner, and forcing both him and the Dolphon to sweare fealty'.[11] Nashe captures here the success of the Queen's Men's historical project in their chauvinistic, exclusively masculine pageant of English conquest.

While it is nothing new to observe history plays' ability to speak to the present, I argue that the troupe's histories employ specific temporal strategies to do so. Ironically, in the *Famous Victories* the Queen's Men create a future-focused history play to ensure their audience's attention to their own present – the play's time-to-come. Spectators are not asked to imagine a better or different or endless sense of history. There is no sense of countless 'sad stories of the deaths of kings' here.[12] Rather, the play orients its spectators (and readers) consistently towards the future through two primary means. First, the play's episodic dramatic structure keeps the audience anticipating Henry's accession, reign and victory; there are no constructed moments for reflection on the past beyond the events that have occurred in the play itself. This structure and attendant absence lead to the second strategy: while characters fantasise about the reign of Henry V, as this chapter's epigraph shows, they also demonstrate either no or very limited knowledge of the past. Their sense of the future is grounded in their present. This idea is one that Shakespeare will largely reject, as his nostalgic rhetoric constructs an intimate, dependent relationship between past and future – even as he uses that connection to attend to the Elizabethan present. As I argue in the next chapter, Shakespeare lampoons the idea of a 'merry England' by using it as a source of dissatisfaction with the present which encourages change in the future. Contrarily, it could be argued that simply by presenting a future-oriented medieval past, *Famous Victories* binds the past and the future. But if that staged past itself depicts no awareness of its precedent, then any future it imagines is always and only grounded in the present it depicts.

The dramatic influences and generic conventions which shape *Famous Victories* may provide a partial explanation for this forward-looking past. The first professional history play and the earliest drama from the English professional theatre, it innovatively combines the traditions of saint plays, morality plays, ritual-historical drama, and comedy.[13] In their constructions of temporality, medieval dramatic traditions are particularly significant for early modern drama. These plays often offer an image of time which, while cyclical in its anticipation of a union with Christ through his return, nonetheless focuses on that future event. The crucial acts which imbue the dramas with purpose – the saint's martyrdom, Mankind's (here, Henry's) redemption – are always anticipated in the unfolding of their plays. Of course, such anticipation is an essential part of any play; genre provides knowing audiences clues to how the drama will progress. Additionally, the play's seeming disinterest in its own past could be a consequence of its status as memorial reconstruction. The players who put together the final manuscript for the printing house perhaps attenuated or absented any chronicle history which was present in staged versions.[14] Regardless, the play's dramaturgy relies on the refusal of historical knowledge, which is crucial both to the prince's character and to the Queen's Men's political strategy.

In enacting the past, this play almost categorically resists considering the age from which its story emerges. *Famous Victories* focuses its first nine scenes on what will become of the unruly prince, signifying for the audience that the past outside of the play matters little compared with the present's juggernaut towards Henry's accession. Significantly, *Famous Victories* uses laments of the present – a common signal of nostalgic discourse, as I have discussed – to orient its audience not towards an idealised past, but towards a problematic-but-promising future. Prince Henry himself relies on a treasonous rhetoric that twice imagines the death of the king. In the first scene, he insists on his equality with his friends, rejecting their deferential 'We are ready to waite upon on your grace' with: 'Gogs wounds waite, we will go altogither, / We are all fellowes, I tell you sirs, and the King / My father were dead, we would be all Kings' (A3^v, ll. 111, 112–14). Henry identifies here at least two faults with the present rule: his father is still alive; and, consequently, they are not all equals, 'all Kings'. The play's early audacity, howsoever fitting with the prince's character, appears to undermine any pro-monarchical agenda that could be ascribed to the Queen's Men and could likely have delighted, shocked and horrified spectators. The prince's anticipation of his rule and his father's death is not, however, an exceptional moment in the play. In fact, *Famous Victories* imagines it twice more. Following the prince's assault on the Lord Chief Justice and his brief foray into prison life, Henry laments:

> heres such ado now adayes, heres prisoning, heres hanging, whipping, and the divel and all: but I tel you sirs, when I am king, we will have no such things, but my lads, if the old king my father were dead, we would be all kings. (C^r, ll. 511–15)

While the repetition of the dead father fantasy suggests the play's status as memorial reconstruction, in this scene it creates a decidedly different effect.[15] John Oldcastle's immediate rejoinder – 'Hee is a goode olde man, God take him to his mercy the sooner' – repeats the prince's insistence on his father's age, and, more importantly, emphasises the comic intention of the lines, where the audience is invited to laugh and gasp at these dark desires (C^r, ll. 516–17). Unlike the play's previous use of this fantasy, here comic intent trumps the line's secondary purpose to insist on and demonstrate the fellowship between Henry and his mates. Nevertheless, Henry's focus on the present, his lament for the punishing times in which he and his ruffian crew live ('such ado now adayes'), promises that when he succeeds his father, a 'merry world' of disorder will be created: thieves will be kings and Lord Chief Justices, and hierarchy and status will be abolished. The social structure of England will be eradicated and rewritten, and the past as represented in these institutions will cease to exist.

An audience may have been tired of such fantasies, or thrilled by them. But however this particular fiction may have tapped into individual desires, the drama itself works to make the past undesirable in these fantasies.[16] Scholars have noted the irony of these lines and their subversive desires, but they have largely ignored the repetitive nature of this fantasy and the temporal consciousness that the lines express.[17] The prince's future-oriented politics have no basis in the past. Henry's vision of rule is its absence, and such a vision is unprecedented – royalty's legitimacy depends on its apparent perpetuity through succession and inheritance. He pushes the fantasy further, inviting the audience deeper into his ideal future England as he creates a world-upside-down that perhaps inspired Shakespeare's Jack Cade. The prince transforms his regret of England's rule of law into a land full of 'couragious[]' highwaymen whom he promises to reward with 'an annual pension out of my Exchequer, to maintain him all the days of his life' (C^v, ll. 529, 532–3). Such men, we are led to believe, will propagate due to the replacement of prisons with fencing schools (C^r, ll. 524–5).

To maintain this riotous future fantasy, the Queen's Men invert the expectations of the *sensus communis* through Sir John Oldcastle's proverbial assent: 'we shall never have a mery world til the old king be dead' (C^v, ll. 535–6). On the surface, his line represents the perfect collapse of past into future; the return of the 'mery world' is predicated on what is to come. He rewrites well-known proverbial discourse to focus on the future ('never a merry world *til*') instead of the past ('never a merry world *since*', discussed in the next chapter). However, as this remark illustrates, the prince's rule does not depend on the example or idea of the past, on what that 'mery world' actually is. Rather, it ridicules the present by imagining it *as past*, and envisions a future defined by its disconnection from that past. The play's only explicit nostalgic rhetoric is associated with a carnivalesque and treasonous wish for the king's death, and as such is disassociated from any positive use or successful act of persuasion. The laughter surely elicited by Henry's and Oldcastle's exchanges emerges from the taboo of such a statement and such a reaction. This compassing of the king's death is critical for the play's dramaturgy, as it directs the audience to anticipate the inevitable, the king's demise and Henry's redemption. It also creates dramatic anxiety about right rule and such a prince's fitness to govern. If, as has been claimed, Henry does come to appreciate the past, then it remains curious that a play so invested in creating historical consciousness and in constructing the past refuses to reflect backwards from its present.[18]

With *Famous Victories*, the Queen's Men argue that there is no past to wax nostalgic for. Through these statements and audacious jokes, the troupe insists upon the past as problematic and undesirable. In the play's staged past, the heir to the throne promises power to his rascal companions and builds his own claim to power on the pretence of reconciliation. His cloak of needles, 'all of [his] owne devising', signals 'that [he] stand[s] upon thorns, til the Crowne be on [his] head' (C^v, ll. 545–6, 549–50). Once more, that 'til' creates the anticipation of the future. Indeed, everyone from the clowns to the king laments the play's present: following the prince's attack in the law courts, Dericke and John Cobler bemoan the exceptional quality of the present moment.

> *Der.* Sownds maisters, heres adoo,
> When Princes must go to prison:
> Why John, didst ever see the like?
> *John.* O Dericke, trust me, I never saw the like.   (B[4]^r, ll. 431–4)

Had the play offered any image of a past to long for, Dericke and John's exchange would be the proper dramatic moment for its invocation. That past is only weakly implied, however, as the clowns insist not on a longing for the past, but rather the singularity of the present. Similarly, Henry IV despairs of what the shameful present indicates for the future, telling the prince: 'I had thought once whiles I had lived, to have seene this noble Realme of England flourish by thee my sonne, but now I see it goes to ruin and decaie' (sig. C2ʳ, ll. 584–6). In an inversion of the fantasies of the king's death, here the future is oriented on Henry IV's witnessing his son's triumph – or rather, his failure to witness that success 'once whiles I had lived', again underlining the fallibility of the present-past. Significantly, that decline was not inevitable in the king's vision of linear history: he had imagined 'flourishing' where now its opposite occurs.

The absence of chronicle history in the play makes the focus of *The Famous Victories* both on the present and its fallibility all the more striking. With one notable exception, nothing is specified about how the England depicted in the play came to be. King Henry's vague allusion to his usurpation of Richard II's throne exemplifies the disinterest in the play's past:

> Hen.4.   God blesse thee and make thee his servant,
>   And send thee a prosperous raigne.
>   For God knowes my sonne, how hardly I came by it,
>   And how hardly I have maintained it.
> Hen.5.   Howsoever you came by it, I know not,
>   But now I have it from you, and from you I wil keepe it[.]
>
> (C[4]ᵛ, ll. 762–7)

This moment presents a fascinating rejection of historical consciousness within a work that emerges out of a distinctly historical culture. On the one hand, Henry's 'God knows' and his son's explicit ignorance represent history as privileged knowledge: only God has access to the truth of how Henry came to the throne. On the other, reading this exchange rhetorically renders Henry's deathbed 'God knows' as a dark foreboding, and the prince's innocuous 'I know not' difficult to believe from one so versed in the murkier sides of English culture (as the play has shown). Where in *Henry V* Shakespeare makes history a disturbing, ineluctable fact of the king's precarious power, here the throne is secure because that history is not known and, moreover, not pursued.[19] The play's characterisations of the two men to this point make it difficult to accept scholars' redemptive readings of the prince's lines. It has been interpreted as 'a temporary loss of memory' 'inspire[d]' by the play's 'holiday atmosphere', one which renders Henry oblivious to his claim to the throne. Henry has been characterised as 'free of the guilt of usurpation against King Richard II that so haunts his father, innocent' of how he arrived in his position – as if *ex nihilo*.[20] *The Famous Victories* does not support such forgiving interpretations: the prince's lack of historical knowledge would, for the informed playgoer, require a significant suspension of disbelief.

The prince's wilful ignorance of his past is part of the Queen's Men's dramaturgical strategy. Staging the prince's refusal of knowledge cuts off any recourse to the past, foreclosing a discussion of history that could trouble Henry's legitimacy as king. Indeed, such ignorance serves Henry at the moment of his succession. When Ned demands that he 'put away these dumpes' and declares, 'What man, do you not remember the old sayings, / You know I must be Lord chiefe Justice of England?', a strange thing happens. Ned suggests that Henry's promises have somehow entered into the proverbial lore of the play's own immediate past. The prince's assurances for the future have become 'the old sayings'. But just as the audience will be familiar with Henry IV's past, they will remember, from their own witnessing, Henry's promise. They also witness how the past represented in 'the old sayings' fails to persuade, or even interest, the new king, who instructs Ned and his companions to 'mend thy manners' (D^v, ll. 830, 832–3, 838).

The exceptional moments where history takes on significance for Henry V depend upon questions of empire and future power. *The Famous Victories* gives the Archbishop of Canterbury three lines in which to outline the king's right in France, in response to Henry's question concerning his 'Embassage'. 'Your right to the French Crowne of France, / Came by your great grandmother Izabel, / Wife to King Edward the third, / And sister to Charles the French king', the Archbishop informs him (D2^r, ll. 857, 858–61). Here, history as dynastic narrative persuades Henry to action, as does Oxford's proverbial wisdom, which contradicts the Archbishop's advice to fight Scotland first. Oxford advises, 'He that wil Scotland win, must first with France begin: / According to the old saying' (D2^v, ll. 879–80). From one perspective, these brief but persuasive moments represent part of the king's redemption, his progress towards wisdom as he recognises the importance of the past to his present and future. To this point, Henry has resisted that past, and notably these invocations come not from him, but from his counsellors. From a counter perspective, in *The Famous Victories* the past as historical narrative is important only insofar as it can be used for personal gain, a motivation also staged in *Richard II* and *Julius Caesar*. Unlike those plays, in this historical drama the past in and of itself does not hold an exclusive, authoritative claim on the unfolding action.

The Famous Victories reveals its attenuated interest in a past beyond that which it stages, focusing rather on the future as part of its dramatic and political strategy. Arguably, what I interpret as dramaturgical strategy could be the result of an assumed familiarity with the story on the part of the play's author(s), who relied on the chronicles to speak for themselves, as certain incidents (the box on the ear, the taking of the crown) would be recognisable from known sources like Hall or Holinshed. It could also be argued that our familiarity with Shakespeare creates particular expectations for how to stage a history, and that this leads to an expectation of a Russian-doll-like past, history nestled within history, a past without concrete end. Shakespeare's English and Roman histories create a sense of the past that itself possesses a past, and his plays are littered with references to never-seen historical characters like Edward III, the Black Prince, Tarquin, Junius Brutus. By contrast, while *The Famous Victories* offers ample moments to go further back in its past, it actively resists them, even explicitly desires not to know them. In the Queen's Men's staging, history is oriented on the future, on what will be of England, and as their other plays will do, *The Famous Victories* refuses nostalgic longing for its past.

The True Tragedy of Richard the Third

Like *The Famous Victories*, this history too concerns itself not with a prior past that has created the present of the play, but rather with an anticipation for the future that is its audience's present.[21] In crafting a longing for the future, and in its service to Tudor hagiography, *The True Tragedy* cautions against any kind of nostalgia for the past, as it depicts that past as wholly undesirable: tyrannous, inhospitable, unusually cruel. *The True Tragedy*'s concluding warning about what will follow Elizabeth I places the present unambiguously at the apex of a hierarchy of time, insisting in that placement that history is both progress – from past to present – and decline – from present to future.

To construct an unfavourable past, *The True Tragedy* places in dialogue two epistemologies of history. In marked contrast to *The Famous Victories*, at certain moments *The True Tragedy* dramatises explicit concerns about the record of history – through references to the chronicles, for example, or what will be recorded and what has been recorded of men's lives. Rejecting Richard's accusation of treason, Rivers argues that history is on his side: 'The Chronicles I record, talk of my fidelitie, & of my progeny, / Wher, as in a glas yû maist behold, thy ancestors & their trechery'.[22] Primarily, *The True Tragedy* uses history to undermine the idea of a desirable past. The drama first insists on Fortune's role in determining the present; it then places the present on a historical spectrum where events themselves, rather than the abstract power of Fortune, influence personal outcomes. *The True Tragedy* thus proposes competing accounts of how to understand the past's relationship to the present. In the Fortune model, the past is an object of longing, as Fortune's wheel inevitably turns, and the present represents either decline or its anticipation. In contrast, the historical model views the ancient past – and only the ancient past – as a standard to be re-established in the present/future through the person of Richmond. What is striking about both models is that they share an apparent circularity and linearity. In the *de casibus* tradition, Fortune possesses an ironic linearity – her wheel lifts you, it hurls you down, but rarely does it lift you up again. The events on the historical spectrum, while oriented towards the future, in fact rely on idealised models from the past, thus suggesting cyclicality in an otherwise linear narrative. Dramaturgically, these models together focus the play's politics on the future by rejecting a return to the past via Fortune, and by placing political hope and success in the future as embodied by Richmond.

A ubiquitous actor on the early modern English stage, Fortune finds herself busy enough in *The True Tragedy*. From King Richard to lowly Jane Shore she is invoked, and the circular imagery attached to her highlights the world's inherent instability and emphasises the providential power so often featured in the Queen's Men's dramaturgy. Fortune seems unknowable, as Richard asks, 'Doth Fortune so much favour my happinesse, / That I no sooner devise, but she sets abroach? / Or doth she but to trie me, that raising me aloft, / My fall maybe be the greater?' (ll. 393–4). These questions not only articulate the anxieties of 'great' men (like Tamburlaine), but they stress an uncertainty about the future that is linked only to the present, through Richard's fortune-blessed actions *now*. To maintain that uncertainty and focus on the future, the Queen's Men make effective dramatic use of Richard's page. Closing the scene by directly addressing the audience, the page interprets what he and the audience have just witnessed. 'I see my Lord is fully resolved to climbe', he states: 'but how hee climbes ile leave that to your judgements, but what his fall will be that's hard to say' (ll. 475–6). As with *The Famous Victories*, knowledgeable spectators will know exactly what awaits Richard, and *The True Tragedy* thus makes a curious move in eliciting the audience's critical engagement. They must 'judge' Richard's path to power, and they must wait and watch his inevitable fall (which 'will be'). In an exceptional turn, the Page rewrites the circular image of Fortune's wheel offered by Richard into a linear historical certainty. While he 'can't say' what will happen, the point is that the fall *will* happen – it is a dramatic and historic certainty.

Fortune's fickleness provides a means to critique the play's present, imply a preferable past, and question the future. The Jane Shore subplot provides a multivalent lament for the fallen present, which under time's power brings only decay and the preferment of vice. Lodowick complains:

> A time how thou suffrest fortune to alter estates, & changest the mindes of the good for the worst. How many headlesse Peeres sleepe in their graves, whose places are furnish with their inferiours? Such as are neither nobly borne, nor vertuously min-ded. (ll. 1037–41)

Articulating Elizabethan anxieties about social-climbing subordinates, Lodowick urges the imperfection of the play's present: a villain not 'vertuously minded' has declared himself king, and Lodowick's image of time passing is an image only of decay – the minds of the good change for the worse. Mistress Shore herself relates the cruelty of the present: 'where neede was, there was I / bountifull, and mindfull I was still upon the poore to releeve / them, and *now* none will know me nor succour me' (ll. 1088–90, my emphasis). The subplot of Shore's Wife insists on the medieval past's inferiority, so crucial to the larger dramaturgy at work in *The True Tragedy* that focuses spectators on the anticipation of a historical future. Need may be constant in the past, but in the play's present, the king – 'next under the degree of God' (l. 356) – denies not only charity to the needy, but even the possibility of charity to the needy (here, Jane Shore). The drama renders the past utterly inhospitable. Those who would provide hospitality, such as the Host ('Oste'), are made criminal accomplices, as when Richard schemes to have Earl Rivers murdered in Rivers's favourite inn.[23] The Host communicates his difficult position in asides, asking the audience:

> Alassa what shall I do? Who were I best to offend? Shall I betraie that good olde Earle that hath laine at my house this fortie yeares? Why and I doe hee [Richard] will hang me: nay then on the other side, if I should not do as my Lord Protector commands, he will chop off my head, but is there no remedie? (ll. 569–73)

'[T]here is no remedie', the Page advises, and the Host remains on stage alone to confess he'll see the plan carried out. In this past, hospitality is made the servant to revenge.

This dark image of the past aligns with Truth's initial monologue, which establishes the play's historical background and relays what 'the Chronicles make manifest' (l. 23). Outrage abounds, virtue is murdered; one wonders how precisely the pageant of an unstable state led by a tyrant, 'A Tragedie in England done but late' will, as Truth promises, 'revive the hearts of drooping mindes' (ll. 17–18).[24] Truth narrates how 'Outragious' Richard Duke of York warred against 'vertuous' Henry VI, 'by outrage suppressed' (ll. 34, 31) and by Richard of Gloucester 'cruelly murthered' (l. 44). In catechistic fashion, Truth reveals the York brothers' misdeeds. Edward is a 'shame to parents stocke' (l. 51) for having his brother Clarence imprisoned, while Richard's crimes continue apace following Henry VI's murder. We learn of his guilt in drowning Clarence, and when pressed by Poetry to tell 'What maner of man' he was, Truth concludes that he was a man 'Valiantly minded, but tyrannous in authoritie' (ll. 58–60). To 'revive' spirits, the Queen's Men must rely then on the attenuated history of Richmond's triumph and the Tudor dynasty's origin.

Late in *The True Tragedy*, concrete parallels between the present-future and the idealised ancient world replace the vagaries of a pre-Ricardian past which were articulated in the Shore subplot, as this ancient world becomes associated with Richmond. In Scene 16, the would-be-king's vision of England depends on eradicating a cankerous present:

> I will so deale in governing the state,
> Which now lies like a savage shultred grove,
> Where brambles, briars, and thornes, over-grow those sprigs,
> Which if they might but spring to their effect,
> And not be crost so by their contraries,
> Making them subject to these outrages,
> Would prove such members of the Common-weale,
> That England should in them be honoured,
> As much as ever was the Romane state,
> When it was governd by the Councels rule,
> And I will draw my sword brave country-men,
> And never leave to follow my resolve,
> Till I have mowed those brambles, briars, and thornes
> That hinder those that long to do us good.   (ll. 1684–1700)

Tellingly, Richmond's speech depends on the future mood ('will so deale', 'will draw my sword', 'Till I have'). Relying on the 'garden of England' commonplace, he promises to prune a 'savage' grove whose wild state is repeatedly described as dominated by 'brambles, briars, and thornes' that paralyse virtue in the 'Common-weale'.[25] This claim relies on the idea of a better England waiting in the future, as the present is stunted, rendered barbarous and uncivil by Richard and his supporters. In his analogy of England as the Consul-governed Roman Empire, Richmond performs that quintessentially Renaissance act of collapsing time and acknowledging its passing. Again, his grammatical mood is crucial to his argument. England 'should [. . .] be' like Rome, if only those 'sprigs' impeded by the tyrant Richard could be made to grow. Fundamentally, England *is* like Rome; it just needs a good gardener to 'root abuses [. . .] which *now* flowes faster' than the Nile through the land (ll. 2099–2100, my emphasis). Richmond's invocation of Consul-led Rome asserts that the country's future goodness is contingent upon its leader as much as its citizens, who 'would prove such members of the Common-weale, / That England should in them be honoured'. Lord Oxford attaches the idealised ancients explicitly to Richmond, wishing him 'as / many honours [. . .] as *Cæsar* had in conquering / the world' and prophesying that he will be honoured 'as *Hector* was among / the Lords of *Troy*, or [Tully] mongst the Romane Senators' (ll. 2058, 61–2). Oxford shares Richmond's confidence that the glorious, ancient past will return – or at least, that the new present will be like that exemplary past, a connection made possible through the figure of Richmond and as such suggestive of Yates's notion of *renovatio*.[26] Notably, Oxford's praise imagines Richmond as the conqueror, as a singular Caesar. Richmond however is not the sole image of the ancient world. The Page elegiacally describes Richard 'mounted on / horsback, with as high resolve as fierce *Achillis* mongst the stur-/die Greekes [. . .] to encounter worthie Richmond' (ll. 2019–21). Here, the uses of the ancient past conflict: in the *Iliad*, Achilles destroys Hector. The Queen's Men seem to rewrite classical history in the English past, in which the historical victor is now conquered, and which links Tudor power to England's own mythology of Brute.[27]

Having staged a bleak medieval past brightened only by Richmond's alignment with revised classical mythology, *The True Tragedy* concludes with dramatic chronicle, a teleological genre apt for expressing the Queen's Men's final argument. The play's last scene transforms characters into chroniclers whose speeches briefly narrate the history of the Tudor dynasty, providing a literal past as prologue to celebrating 'Worthie Elizabeth, a mirrour in her age' (l. 2193). This structure demonstrates starkly the temporal consciousness that the Queen's Men align with political ideology, as the speeches offer historical judgements of the recent royal past: Henry VII's reign 'was vertuous every way', Henry VIII was a 'worthie, valient, and victorious Prince', Edward VI was 'wise'; Mary receives no epithets, and much is said in the consequent silence (ll. 2168, 2173–4, 2185). Elizabeth naturally outshines her Tudor forebears as 'that lampe that keeps faire Englands light, / And through her faith her country lives in peace', and this theme of peace continues throughout the speech, which praises Elizabeth's 'wise life and civill government' and chronicles the many ways that she is the centre of international politics and a general source of concord (ll. 2203–4, 2194).

Because of Elizabeth, England is 'happie' and 'blessed' and lives 'in such prosperitie' (ll. 2199, 2214, 2202). Whatever the merits of Tudors past, the Queen's Men suggest, the ideal time is now. Through this panegyric of Elizabeth, the troupe refuses and rejects any longing for the past, for the classical past was reborn in Richmond, and the Golden Age is come in his granddaughter. But history's progress, asserted in the chronicle of Henry VII to Elizabeth, is ephemeral. Elizabeth's rule itself represents a temporal zenith, and the speech warns of the future, intimating that the queen's successor will be found wanting. Using an amusingly cautious 'if', the play concludes: 'For if her Graces dayes be brought to end, / Your hope is gone, on whom did peace depend' (ll. 2223–4). When Elizabeth dies, despair and war will return. Throughout *The True Tragedy*, the Queen's Men orient their audience towards the future, towards their own present, only to insist that that future-present itself is circumscribed, its goodness contingent on the life of Elizabeth.

Tamburlaine's Future Imperative and *Selimus*, the Queen's Men's Response

As in the Queen's Men's plays, *Tamburlaine* eschews any direct idealising of the past, rejecting history as an object of desire in the present. While outside the genre of English chronicle history as scholars have come to define it, *Tamburlaine* regardless provided an example to Marlowe's fellow playwrights of the triumph of blank verse and rhetorical set speeches in a historical play.[28] Moreover, Marlowe's manipulation of audience expectations is a manipulation of temporal expectation when Tamburlaine's awaited reversal of fortune never arrives. As critics across generations have noted, he appears to stand fast upon Fortune's wheel.[29] Marlowe's foreign worlds staged concerns familiar to the Elizabethans – what is the individual's relationship to their community? What are the limits of an individual's power?[30] In his protagonist, Marlowe constructs a character for whom the past is a cipher. Tamburlaine takes no part in lauding or idealising figures of the past, refusing to allow the past's legitimising narrative to affect his own course of action. The play stages the rise of the quintessential anti-hero, the man seemingly without remorse or memory – and therefore without nostalgia. Indeed, *Tamburlaine* stages the fall of those who would wax nostalgic or attempt to cling to power because of their personal history or pedigree rather than their political and military aptitude. The eponymous character's near-total disdain for history and memory, and his projection of himself ceaselessly into the future, represent constitutive elements of his limitless power. Unbounded disdain – so essential to the 'Marlovian form of theatrical wonder' – lies at the heart of Tamburlaine's willingness to abjure historical example, and his triumph despite such abjuration creates awe in character and audience.[31] Like the Queen's Men, Marlowe represents personal achievement as bound to temporal perspective, and unlike them he offers foils to Tamburlaine's way of thinking – Bajazeth's failure, for example, simply reasserts the power of future-focus. Both Fortune and time assume political significance in his play, as they appear to be under Tamburlaine's control. Neither can function as persuasive discourses to interrogate or check his acts of conquest.

Temporal consciousness dictates success in the play, as Marlowe stages in the successive falls of the Persian usurper Cosroe and the Turkish emperor Bajazeth; lackeys of the past are doomed to fail. In the sole instance of nostalgic discourse in *Tamburlaine*, Cosroe laments the state of his brother's realm, which he seeks to rule:

> [T]his it is that doth excruciate
> The very substance of my vexèd soul:
> To see our neighbours that were wont to quake
> And tremble at the Persian monarch's name
> Now sits and laughs our regiment to scorn.[32]

Loss – of reputation, of riches – underlies Cosroe's wish here to reclaim the Persians' legacy, to make Persia great again, and the humiliation 'excruciate[s his] soul'. This speech frames Cosroe's usurpation as a political act committed in the interest of returning Persia, a 'maimed empery', to the status Mycetes squandered by his incompetent reign (1.1.126). Cosroe's language presents the possibility of a return to past glories, and that possibility instigates his investiture as king. Nostalgic narrative becomes prelude to political action, a sequence that Shakespeare will repeat. The nobleman Ceneus substantiates the loss Cosroe alludes to, depicting a Persepolis 'heretofore [...] filled' with 'Afric captains' whose ransoms dressed the 'warlike soldiers' and 'gentlemen' in 'coats of gold', 'costly jewels' and 'shining stones' (1.1.141, 142, 140, 143–5). These men, 'Now living idle',

> Begin in troops to threaten civil war
> And openly exclaim against the King.
> Therefore, to stay all sudden mutinies,
> We will invest Your Highness emperor. (1.1.147–51)

The notion of a rupture between past and present turns on Ceneus's use of 'now': 'Now' that the victorious soldiers lack employment and pay, 'now' that they are dangerously idle, Cosroe is the instrument to create 'martial discipline' and to restore Persia to its former glory. Explicitly recognising the discrepancy between present lack and past excess, the soldiers' threats voice their desire and discontent. In *Tamburlaine*, the installation of Mycetes creates the binary of the idealised past and the failed present, and it is precisely that pre- and post-lapsarian rhetorical structure upon which nostalgic *topoi* turn, as the following chapters show.

Marlowe, however, quickly extinguishes the suggested power of the past and of nostalgic desire that he initially stages. Tamburlaine's ambitions are realised through his rhetoric of possibility, a rhetoric embedded in the future. Although allied with Tamburlaine against Mycetes, Cosroe learns the cost of memorialising the past and wishing for its reconstruction: he is deposed by Tamburlaine's own desire and his future-centric, violent policy of conquest. Tamburlaine looks only forward to what he will vanquish and rule. Recognising the power of his future-oriented rhetoric, he fashions himself as a prophet of sorts: 'Nor are Apollo's oracles more true / Than thou shalt find my vaunts substantial', he declares to Mycetes's captain Theridamas, persuading him to abandon his attack and join his army (1.2.212–13). Tamburlaine's language, reflective of his action, is concerned exclusively with future imperatives, and he himself identifies the effectiveness of such speech. When Theridamas remarks that Tamburlaine 'shall rouse [the Turkish emperor Bajazeth] out of Europe', he replies:

> Well said, Theridamas! Speak in that mood,
> For 'will' and 'shall' best fitteth Tamburlaine,
> Whose smiling stars give him assured hope
> Of martial triumph ere he meet his foes.   (3.3.38, 40–3)

That 'mood' refers explicitly to the grammar by which the future ('will' and 'shall') is constructed. Tamburlaine, loyal only to himself or to the fulfilment of his word (his 'vaunts substantial'), is loyal to the unconditional tense, which is the imperative mood. Because that mood is imperative, he must remain committed to the imperative as the form of the future that negates uncertainty. In fact, his mood determines the structure of his language. He claims that he is suited only for futurity, as he announces in the same scene when he commands his lieutenants to 'Fight all courageously, and *be* you kings! / I speak it, and my words are oracles'; of Damascus he asserts, 'Those walled garrisons will I subdue, / And write myself great lord of Africa' (3.3.101–2; 3.3.244–5; my emphasis). Taken together with his 'hope', these lines suggest that Tamburlaine exists in a self-contradicting position. He will 'write' his own future, leaving nothing to depend on chroniclers and suggesting himself as the exemplar of the anti-history hero; but that future depends on the assurance his 'smiling stars give'.

In accordance with the play's sense of 'anti-history' heroism, Tamburlaine rejects any recourse to past action for present example, refusing the fashionable idea of history's didacticism. His is an anti-Polybian – truly, anti-Renaissance – perspective on Fortune: rather than looking to Fortune's wheel as a sign that his success will inevitably end, he simply does not look at all.[33] Tamburlaine detaches himself from any hope and asserts his independence of virtually any tie – historical, memorial – save to himself. When his beloved Zenocrate pleads to remember her countrymen and father Bajazeth and to spare Damascus, to 'have some pity for my sake, / Because it is my country's, and my father's', Tamburlaine rejects her with brutal self-interest: 'Not for the world, Zenocrate, if I have sworn' (4.2.123–5). His pledge represents an action to be made in the future, and consequently one that Tamburlaine is devoted to and cannot repeal. His commitment to the linguistic constructs of the future functions equally as an exercise of self-devotion.

Nevertheless, Tamburlaine's future cannot exist without the idea of the past. Even while scorning history and historically derived power, Tamburlaine declares throughout the play that it is in history that he shall live and be immortal: 'The ages that shall talk of Tamburlaine, / Even from this day to Plato's wondrous year, / Shall talk how I have handled Bajazeth' (4.2.95–7). Tamburlaine provides a model for Brutus's and Cassius's own self-projection in *Julius Caesar*, and yet unlike the conspirators, to guarantee him the eternity he craves Tamburlaine depends paradoxically upon the very practice of memorialisation that he consistently derides. By keeping Tamburlaine's concern with legacy visible, Marlowe maintains expectations about the rhythm of 'rise-and-decline and pride-goes-before-a-fall' in order to shock his audience when he interrupts, indeed refuses to satisfy, those expectations.[34] In a play that had fundamental ramifications for English drama, a longing for the past and a reliance on its institutions are enthusiastically denounced, as Marlowe stages nostalgia as a weak motivation for political rule. His future-oriented Tamburlaine provides a rhetorical model for the persuasiveness of the future mood, a mood that occupies a central place in Shakespeare's dramatic nostalgia.

Marlowe rightly anticipated that his own age would talk of how Tamburlaine handled Bajazeth: the Queen's Men produced *Selimus*, the tale of Bajazeth's power-thirsty son, in response to the play. Likely first performed in 1588 and first printed in 1594, questions persist regarding *Selimus*'s provenance. It may have been written by Robert Greene, who as a Queen's Men playwright would probably have had a hand in it; nothing is known of the play's success.[35] The play's title character is a Tamburlaine off the rails, whose unabashed ambition and shocking cruelty certainly recall his Scythian predecessor. Remarkably, the Queen's Men create a subtle future-focused dramaturgy by turning to an idealised vision of the past to suggest the danger of such a vision. In Selimus's Golden Age speech, they again attach an ethics to dramatic temporal consciousness.

Selimus's use of the golden age *topos* relies on an image that would have been recognisable to the varied audience of a Queen's Men play. Closely following Arthur Golding's translation of Ovid's *Metamorphoses*, the play's author lightly reworks a source familiar to the many grammar school-educated spectators; together with Virgil's *Fourth Eclogue*, knowledge of the *Metamorphoses* was 'an essential pre-requisite for understanding the discourse of the Elizabethan elite'.[36] This is not to suggest that the myth itself and its political implications were unintelligible to the masses. It had circulated publicly and politically since Elizabeth I's 1559 coronation procession at least, from which time Elizabeth was publicly associated with Astraea, the virgin goddess of Justice, and the attendant idea that she represented the hope of a new and peaceful gilded age (just as *The True Tragedy*'s closing speeches intimate). In classical mythology, Astraea was the last of the immortals to abandon the 'blood-soaked earth' with the coming of the Iron Age.[37] Elizabeth's entry procession through London, *Veritas Temporis Filia* (Truth is the Daughter of Time), imagined her as a pure force of peace after the turbulence and conflict of the preceding decades since Henry VIII's break from Rome, the Dissolution of the Monasteries, and the religious violence that marked the reigns of Edward and Mary.[38] The procession included staged pageants at fountains and conduits which underscored metaphorically Elizabeth's role as 'cause alone' of England's peace.[39] In his contemporary account of her progress through London, the influential schoolmaster and scholar Richard Mulcaster describes how the new Queen 'implanted a wonderful hope in [her subjects] touching her worthy government in the rest of her reign'.[40] In these public acts, hope signals a recognition of the past's potential to return.

Thirty years later that hope may have eroded, but the association between Elizabeth, Astraea and the Golden Age remained topical to the playwrights of the burgeoning public theatres. In addition to the invocations of peace, hope and happiness in *The True Tragedy*, Robert Greene included Astraea briefly in his *A Maidens Dreame upon the Death of the Right Honorable Sir Christopher Hatton* (1591), in which the goddess comforts the narrator over the death of the Lord Chancellor.[41] In the same year, Queen's Men playwright George Peele made the connection between the Queen and Astraea more explicit in his *Descensus astraeae*, in which 'Astraea [. . .] tendes her flocke / With watchfull eyes, and keep this fount in peace'. She does not permit 'blind superstitious ignorance, / [to] Corrupt so pure a spring', and Peele rejoices, 'O happie times / That do beget such calme and quiet daies', concluding: 'Long may she live, long may she governe us / In peace triumphant [. . .] / Our faire Astraea, our Pandora faire, / Our faire Eliza'.[42] Employing the imagery of the fount and 'pure spring' that has been associated with the idea of Elizabeth as a 'cause alone' for peace, his celebratory rhetoric lauds the present in these 'happie times'. The Astraea he describes has returned (hence his title's 'descensus'), signalling the arrival of a new age governed by her justice.

As with Greene's and Peele's respective verses, *Selimus* exemplifies the political and literary interest in maintaining the associations between Elizabeth and the Golden Age which appeared on stage in the early 1590s. The titular tyrant describes the history of the golden world:

When first this circled round, this building faire,
Some God tooke out of the confused masse,
(What God I do not know, nor greatly care)
Then every man of his owne dition was,
And every one his life in peace did passe.
Warre was not then, and riches were not knowne,
And no man said, this, or this, is mine owne.
The plough-man with a furrow did not marke
How farre his great possessions did reach:
The earth knew not the share, nor seas the barke.
The souldiers entred not the battred breach,
Nor Trumpets the tantara loud did teach.
There needed them no judge, nor yet no law,
Nor any King of whom to stand in awe.
But after *Ninus*, warlike *Belus* sonne,
The earth with unknowne armour did warray,
Then first the sacred name of King begunne:
And things that were as common as the day,
Did then to set possessours first obey.[43]

Selimus identifies widely known characteristics of the Golden Age and exemplifies its common romanticisation in his description of an Edenic pre-history when wealth, property and violence were unknown. The speech demonstrates how the construction of a nostalgic narrative – of longing for an idealised time and space – depends upon both content and form, as Selimus uses topographia – when a poet 'fayne[s] places untrue' – to give shape to a fantasised past.[44] He enforces the present's distance from this space and time by identifying rupture as he introduces the post-lapsarian world 'after *Ninus*', which includes institutions such as hereditary monarchy and private property that would be recognisable to his early modern audience. His monologue offers something unknown to this point in the Queen's Men's dramaturgy: an explicit, detailed invocation of an idealised past designed to create a sense of longing in their auditors.

Nevertheless, the context of this speech complicates a seemingly straightforward reprise of Ovid. Selimus is a bloodthirsty, atheist despot who murders his family. The ambition and lust for power that he exhibits therefore make his longing for a time when 'Warre was not' an unexpected rhetorical and ethical turn, as is his observation that kings were unnecessary and superfluous. In fact, this entire speech seems grossly out of character, until it turns abruptly to reflect his true villainy, disrupting his idyll and reminding the audience of his true nature. He recounts how 'some sage man' 'did first devise / The names of Gods, religion, heaven, and hell', calling them 'meere fictions' (ii.26, 28–9, 33). While the speech illuminates Selimus's villainous atheism (and the play's Marlovian influence), it simultaneously undermines the virtuous longing present in his initial discourse of the Golden Age. First citing God's role in creating 'this circled round, this building faire', Selimus now states that God is fictitious, and heaven and hell – the former tied to the idea of an attainable utopia – 'meere fiction'. To be persuaded by Selimus's tempting image of the Golden Age suddenly becomes, in light of his blasphemy, a heretical and morally compromising position.

The Queen's Men's political remit offers one way to understand both the reason for this shift and the speech's dramaturgical role. As I discussed above, the troupe's plays could offer a range of readings, from the explicit support of the queen offered in *The True Tragedy* to the more ambivalent politics found in *The Famous Victories*. This monologue's multiple positions might very well have accommodated the political message the group needed to convey. To honour the Golden Age is to honour Astraea, which in turn is to honour Queen Elizabeth. On a superficial and rhetorical level, Selimus's speech does commit to that honour. However, to stress the infallibility of a fantasised Golden Age – and its freedom from private property and hierarchy – is to criticise the common law support of private property, the practice of enclosure and the existence of hierarchy that defined the structure of early modern English society. Selimus's speech therefore represents a sophisticated political balancing act, as what it suggests initially, the past's greatness, is then rejected by Selimus's contradicting rhetoric and character. Issuing from the mouth of a blasphemous tyrant, his vitriol against the present state in fact encourages an appreciation for those institutions (religion, monarchy, family, property) that he denigrates. In this speech the Queen's Men propose that expressing nostalgia, or being persuaded by it, is potentially damning. Even as Selimus suggests the lure of the Golden Age idyll, the temptation to idealise the past leads one to neglect society's moral values and priorities, which are grounded in the duty to one's God, one's monarch, one's country and one's family.[45] *Selimus* depicts the negative connotations of nostalgia evident in the period's anti-papist rhetoric, which George Peele's *The Troublesome Reign of King John* (1591) explicitly embraces in its dramaturgy.[46]

King John

Provided its close (and debated) relationship with Shakespeare's *King John*, attending to how *Troublesome Reign* stages time reveals that *King John* reworks the insistent future-focus of its source play.[47] *Troublesome Reign*'s past is in fact part of what makes John's reign so troublesome, as the question of his usurpation haunts him. Even his mother has no wish to linger in praise of her elder son: she laments Richard I's death in two lines and immediately turns the barons' attention to the 'second hope' of 'this womb'.[48] In the play, the future becomes the site of hope and salvation, as the past – even the play's most recent past – is unknown and unknowable, its present rife with internecine and international violence, and England enfeoffed to the Catholic Church. It is only the distant future beyond the play's temporal confines that could appear as an object of longing, for the drama's staging of futurity through the predictions of Peter the Prophet and the questions about Arthur's death destabilise its world. Characters' attempts to control the future of the play's present consistently create conflict. The immediate and future peace between France and England and the diffusion of the competing kingship claims, promised with the marriage of Blanche and Lewis, implodes with Cardinal Pandulph's demand that France go to war with England, and reveals the tenuous, political nature of any hope for the immediate future (1:1.4.168–72, 1:5.63–4). The appearance of the prophet Peter late in the play's first part (1:11) concentrates in particular dramatic attention on the future – the play's and England's. While the audience witnesses a realised dramatic future when the prophecy that 'King John shall not be king as heretofore' comes true, the ideal state of England, its best version, lies in the time to come. Peter's vision of the moons, in which 'Albion, / [. . .] 'gins to scorn the See and state of Rome, / And seeks to shun the edicts of the Pope', anticipates England's future Protestant course, and that anticipation forms a crucial part of the play's conclusion (2:2.28, 1:13.171–3). Only the Tudor future offers the space where the problems of sovereignty, right rule and tyranny might be resolved, as John acknowledges to himself:

> Thy sins are far too great to be the man
> T'abolish Pope and popery from thy realm,
> But in thy seat, if I may guess at all,
> A king shall reign that shall suppress them all.   (2:2.170–3)

The audience knows well which king that is. By positioning John as a forerunner to Henry VIII, the play follows a narrative already established in Foxe's *Actes and monuments* and John Bale's *King Johan*. John's deathbed speech, granted all the more authority because these lines are his last, reaches back into the biblical past to authorise his prophecy of a Solomon (a Henry) to come:

> As did the kingly prophet David cry,
> [. . .]
> I am not he shall build the Lord a house,
> [. . .]
> From out of these loins shall spring a kingly branch
> Whose arms shall reach unto the gates of Rome,
> And with his feet tread down the strumpet's pride
> That sits upon the chair of Babylon.   (2:8.100, 102, 105–8)

The *Troublesome Reign*'s prophecies do not end with John. 'Thus England's peace begins in Henry's reign', declares Philip the Bastard, and his proclamation creates a sense of doubled time as it invokes both Henry III in the play's present and the Elizabethans' recent past in their image of Henry VIII (2:9.43). Superficially, 'Henry's reign' refers to John's son and successor Henry III. But in light of the play's insistent repudiation of Catholicism, and its linking of war and strife with England's subservience to the pope and the Catholic Church, the rejection of Rome by Henry VIII represents in this sense the beginning, the origin, of 'England's peace'. At the end of Part 1, John himself admits how England's allegiance to the Church has stained the past, and again orients the longing for a paradisal England towards the future: 'I grieve to think how kings in ages past, / Simply devoted to the See of Rome, / Have run into a thousand acts of shame' (1:13.24–6). *Troublesome Reign* consistently rejects the idea of the past as a repository of ideals to be recreated in the present or future. England's peace and security depends, rather, on the time to come.

Like *The True Tragedy*, *Troublesome Reign*'s use of the classical past as exemplary orients its audience towards the present-future, and its analogies employ dark, violent episodes of that past that trouble its status as ideal. Philip, who most frequently makes these comparisons, alternatively compares himself to Hector and 'the Prince of Troy' as well as to Phaeton and even Nero, threatening Lady Margaret that 'As cursèd Nero with his mother did, / So I with you' if she does not reveal who his true father is (1:3.14, 2:6.34, 1:1.342, 1:1.374–5). In her revelation, Margaret suggests that she is a failed Lucrece and had learned better from that 'Roman dame / That shed her blood to wash away her shame' (1:1.406–7). The play's two heroes are tainted in this moment. The comparison directly implies Richard I's likeness to Tarquin – an analogy no critic seems to have acknowledged – and consequently corrupts the idealised image of the former king with which the play begins ('Victorious Richard, scourge of infidels', 1:1.3). Additionally, Philip's status as reincarnation of the 'ideal' Coeur de Lion seems cast into some doubt here, first with his twice-made threat to murder his mother (following the invocation of Nero, he declares 'Let son's entreaty sway the mother now, / Or else she dies', 1:1.378–9), and second, *pace* Forker, with the invited rhetorical wish that his mother would have killed herself. Given this repeated matricidal rhetoric I find it difficult to accept the Bastard as an 'invo[cation of] a more idealistic past'.[49]

In *Troublesome Reign* neither the classical nor the immediate past can offer ideals to be emulated in the present, and the play rejects and even lampoons concepts of time that are not structured towards the future. Arthur's faith in temporal cycles, for example, provides him with what the play reveals to be an empty, misplaced hope when he tries to reassure his mother that 'Seasons will change, and so our present grief / May change with them, and all to our relief', his couplet sounding a misleading certainty (1:4.194–5). Friar Lawrence invokes commonplace classical and biblical ideas of time in his rhymes, 'O *tempus edax rerum*. / Give children books, they tear them. / O *vanitas vanitatis*, / In this waning *aetatis*' (1:11.107–10), which make Time and children equal devourers of the material world before rendering the sacred profane with his superficial citation of Ecclesiastes 1.2. These rhymes suggest little hope in the future: knowledge passed to children ('books') will only be neglected and destroyed, perhaps an additional sign of 'this waning *aetatis*'. While these lines have been characterised as part of the scene's 'absurd' linguistic 'gobbledygook', in fact they slot nicely into the play's anti-Catholic rhetoric and rejection of historical longing.[50] As the next chapter shows, ventriloquising a Catholic nostalgia is not uncommon to sixteenth-century drama, and this ridiculing of representatives of the Catholic Church is particularly suited to the Queen's Men's larger ideological commitments – notably, this scene is Peele's invention – as *Troublesome Reign*'s future-focus insists on the fallibility of a Catholic past and therefore anticipates the preferable Tudor, Protestant present.

Howsoever that Shakespeare's *King John* turns away from antipopery and the anticipation of the Tudors to place a crisis of legitimacy at the play's core, like *Troublesome Reign*, the drama provides no concept of an idealised past that Shakespeare's audience might long for. Rather, such a crisis illustrates the real proximity of past and present, of the Angevin to the Elizabethan through the spectre of Elizabeth's own legitimacy crisis, the threat of 'powers from home and discontents at home', in the Bastard's words.[51] Such topicality suggests a temporal collapse that insists on looking to a future both bleak and hopeful, as *King John* emphasises the fallenness of the play's present. At Hubert's insistence that he will burn out Arthur's eyes with hot irons, the prince cries, '[N]one but in this iron age would do it!' (4.1.60). Reflecting on Arthur's supposed death, Pembroke declares, 'Bad world the while' (4.2.100), and in 'the while' he stresses that world's immediacy, its happening-now. With the prince's actual demise, Shakespeare suggests a pinnacle of evil has been reached, as Pembroke makes Arthur's a paragon of deaths, declaring that

> All murders past do stand excused in this,
> And this so sole, and so unmatcheable
> Shall give a holiness, a purity,
> To the yet unbegotten sin of times[.] (4.3.51–4)

Christ-like, Arthur's death purifies future evil, and this association highlights simultaneously the singular quality of Arthur himself, the depravity of the present, and the possibility of the future's superiority (as its 'unbegotten sin' will yet be sanctified). But the Bastard curtails that possibility in his own response to Arthur's death: anxious that he will 'lose my way / Among the thorns and dangers of this world' (4.3.140–1), he laments present and future:

> From forth this morsel of dead royalty,
> The life, the right and truth of all this realm
> Is fled to heaven, and England now is left
> To tug and scamble, and to part by th' teeth
> The unowed interest of proud-swelling state.
> Now for the bare-picked bone of majesty
> Doth dogged war bristle his angry crest
> And snarleth in the gentle eyes of peace.
> Now powers from home and discontents at home
> Meet in one line, and vast confusion waits,
> As doth a raven on a sick-fallen beast,
> The imminent decay of wrested pomp.
> Now happy he, whose cloak and ceinture can
> Hold out this tempest. (4.3.143–56)

Surely a model for Gaunt's anaphoric use of 'Now' in *Richard II*, this speech insistently constructs the present by repeating 'now' four times, but its topic is in fact the temporal entrapment of the play's present. Unlike *Troublesome Reign*'s possibility of a liberating Protestant future, the Bastard's certainty that 'the life, right and truth of all the realm' have Astraea-like fled to heaven suggests that the moment of Arthur's death creates yet another Iron Age, an age – the Elizabethan present? – 'To tug and scamble'. 'Now' exists only in relation to a doubtful future, as 'war' and 'peace' confront each other 'for the bare-picked bone of majesty'. While 'The imminent decay of wrested pomp' declares that usurpation will meet its just end, the fact that 'vast confusion waits' stresses inevitable decline and, like so many of the play's prophetic moments, *King John* looks queasily ahead. The Bastard's temporal discomfort persists to the play's end, when his grammar itself signifies the uncertainty of the time to come:

> This England never did, nor never shall,
> Lie at the proud foot of a conqueror,
> But when it first did help to wound itself.
> Now these her princes are come home again.
> Come the three corners of the world in arms,
> And we shall shock them. Nought shall make us rue,
> If England to itself do rest but true.   (5.7.112–18)

His prophetic certainties about the future ('England [. . .] never shall', 'we shall', 'Nought shall'), rooted partially in the past ('but when it first did help to wound itself'), are all conditional. Successful resistance to foreign conquest depends both upon domestic harmony and that ideal so evasive throughout *King John*: truth. Recent criticism has posited this contingency as hopeful, as it concludes Shakespeare's dramatic construction of 'a historical origin-point for that conception of secure island nationhood' which, in its 'Anglo-French "bastard" nature [. . .] endows it with unique possibilities for future adaptation and renewal'.[52] Intimated in that identification of origin points – the origin which is itself dependent on the look backwards from a future perspective – is a sense of nostalgia for that moment of creation. However, Shakespeare rejects such a sense in this play, which even as it reproduces the future-focus of *Troublesome Reign*, does not allow that focus to transform into providential fantasy or narrative ideal. By refusing to stage John as a Reformation ancestor to the Tudors, Shakespeare refuses to locate any kind of origin for the Elizabethans here. He eliminates a crucial way of imagining the future in his play and rather reveals, as he will do elsewhere in his drama, how the hopes of the future become mired in the self-serving actions of the present.

That future orientation, this chapter has argued, Shakespeare develops from the Queen's Men's and Marlowe's respective dramaturgies, which ignore or, as in *Selimus*, mock nostalgic rhetoric. The Queen's Men's plays demonstrate how temporal consciousness can be political, for however invested the troupe was in representing English history, that interest in the past itself had clear limits in their plays. These limits, and Marlowe's own future-focus in *Tamburlaine*, exemplify that these early dramatists, so important for Shakespeare, consistently stage how the past keeps returning to the present. While *King John*, like *Troublesome Reign*, makes no earnest use of nostalgic rhetoric, its construction of past, present and future illustrates one dramaturgical strategy Shakespeare uses to resist nostalgia's idealising processes, as he refuses to construct any past in the play that could feed such idealisation.

Shakespeare's strategic use of nostalgic rhetoric elsewhere in his drama represents his own negotiation of the values attached to staging and narrating the past within early modern English culture. The succeeding chapters establish how crucial the promise of reclamation becomes to Shakespeare's rhetorical nostalgia, how essential the transformation of the past into the future is for his rhetoric of the idealised past. Shakespeare's inclusion of nostalgic discourse into a genre that he himself was shaping represents an important divergence not only from the Queen's Men's plays but from Marlowe's proved success as well.

Notes

1. *The Famous Victories of Henry the Fifth*, ed. Chiaki Hanabusa, The Malone Society Reprints, 171 (Manchester: Manchester University Press, 2007), ll. 499–500. Further citations will be made in the text.
2. Scott McMillin and Sally-Beth MacLean, *The Queen's Men and Their Plays* (Cambridge and New York: Cambridge University Press, 1998), pp. 165–6; Bernard M. Ward, '*The Famous Victories of Henry V*: Its Place in Elizabethan Dramatic Literature', *The Review of English Studies*, 4 (1928), 270–94; Brian Walsh, *Shakespeare, the Queen's Men, and the Elizabethan Performance of History* (Cambridge: Cambridge University Press, 2009); William Glasgow Bowling, 'The Wild Prince Hal in Legend and Literature', Washington University Studies vol. XII, Humanistic Series, No. 2 (1926), 305–34; Karen Oberer, 'Appropriations of the Popular Tradition in *The Famous Victories of Henry V* and *The Troublesome Raigne of King John*', in *Locating the Queen's Men, 1583–1603: Material Practices and Conditions of Playing*, ed. Helen Ostovich, Holger Schott Syme and Andrew Griffin (Farnham, UK: Ashgate, 2009), pp. 171–82; Charles R. Forker, 'Marlowe's *Edward II* and its Shakespearean Relatives: The Emergence of a Genre',

in *Shakespeare's English Histories: A Quest for Form and Genre*, ed. John W. Velz (Tempe, AZ: Medieval & Renaissance Texts and Studies, 1997), pp. 60–89; J. Dover Wilson, 'Shakespeare's Richard III and The True Tragedy of Richard the Third, 1594', *Shakespeare Quarterly*, 3:4 (1952), 299–306; T. W. Craik, 'Introduction', in *King Henry V*, ed. T. W. Craik (London: Routledge/The Arden Shakespeare, 1995), pp. 7–10; Lorna Hutson, *The Invention of Suspicion* (Oxford: Oxford University Press, 2007), p. 219; Geoffrey Bullough, ed., *The Narrative and Dramatic Sources of Shakespeare*, 8 vols (London and New York: Routledge and Kegan Paul, 1957–75), IV (1962), p. 348; see also Peter Corbin and Douglas Sedge, eds., *The Oldcastle Controversy: Sir John Oldcastle Part 1 and The Famous Victories of Henry V* (Manchester: Manchester University Press 1991), p. 28.
3. McMillin and MacLean, *The Queen's Men*, p. 167, and see Benjamin Griffin, *Playing the Past: Approaches to English Historical Drama, 1385–1600* (London: DS Brewer, 2001), esp. Prologomena through Chapter 2.
4. Ostovich et al., 'Introduction', in *Locating the Queen's Men, 1583–1603: Material Practices and Conditions of Playing* (London and New York: Routledge, 2016), p. 10; on the duopoly see Andrew Gurr, *Playgoing in Shakespeare's London* (Cambridge: Cambridge University Press, 1987), and McMillin and MacLean, *The Queen's Men*, p. 50.
5. We learn one fact about the past in the play's opening lament for the recent death of the queen (given its publication date, this could be a nod to Elizabeth). By the play's end the future looks brighter with Gaul, Cordella, Leir and Perillus all alive and content to let Leir rule again. There are no gods to suggest the play's pre-Christianity, and there is nothing about this play that signals its ancientness other than the names and their connection to chronicle history; see *The True Chronicle History of King Leir, and his three daughters, Gonorill, Ragan, and Cordella* (London, 1605).
6. McMillin and MacLean, *The Queen's Men*, p. 166; Ostovich et al., 'Introduction', in *Locating the Queen's Men*, p. 15; Jennifer Roberts-Smith argues that a staged shared past becomes a dramatic method of shoring up political unity, '"What makes thou upon a stage?": Child Actors, Royalist Publicity, and the Space of the Nation in the Queen's Men's *True Tragedy of Richard the Third*', *Issue in Review: Making Theatrical Publics on the Early Modern Stage*, ed. Paul Yachnin, *Early Theatre*, 15:2 (2012), 192–205, esp. 194; Larry S. Champion, '"What Prerogatives Meanes": Perspective and Political Ideology in "The Famous Victories of Henry V"', *South Atlantic Review*, 53:4 (1988), 1–19; Karen Oberer, 'Appropriations', esp. p. 172.
7. Walsh, *Shakespeare*, pp. 26, 1.
8. Humphreys, ed., 'Introduction', in *King Henry IV, Part 1*, Arden Two Series (London: Routledge, 1960), p. xxxii. Cited in Dutton, '*The Famous Victories* and the 1600 Quarto of *Henry V*', in Ostovich et al., *Locating the Queen's Men*, pp. 140–1.
9. Precise dating of the play remains a subject of discussion, but the play's connection to the Queen's Men's actor Richard Tarlton's *Jests* (London, 1611/1613, cf. C2^v–C3^r) places a first performance sometime between 1583 and 1588. It was not registered with the Stationers' Company until

14 May 1594 and not published until 1598. Henslowe records a 'ne' 'harey the v' performed on 28 November 1595, and critics believe this to be *The Famous Victories*, perhaps in a newly revised form. See E. K. Chambers, *The Elizabethan Stage*, 4 vols (Oxford: Oxford University Press, 1923, reiss. 2009), II, pp. 145–6; R. A. Foakes, ed., *Henslowe's Diary*, 2nd edn (Cambridge and New York: Cambridge University Press, 2002), p. 33. That *Famous Victories* is memorially reconstructed remains an uncomfortable critical conclusion, particularly since the demise of 'bad quarto' theory; cf. Hanabusa, ed., *The Famous Victories*, p. xx.
10. Nashe, *Pierce Penilesse, his Supplication to the Devil*, in *The Works of Thomas Nashe*, ed. R. B. McKerrow, corr. F. P. Wilson, 5 vols (Oxford: Oxford University Press, 1958), I (1958), p. 212.
11. Nashe, *Pierce Penilesse*, p. 213, and cf. Anon., *Famous Victories*, G2^r. Sarah Neville notes that Nashe likely penned most of Act 1; *1 Henry VI*, ed. Sarah Neville in *The New Oxford Shakespeare: The Complete Works, Critical Reference Edition*, vol. 2, gen. eds Gary Taylor, John Jowett, Terri Bourus and Gabriel Egan (Oxford: Oxford University Press, 2017), p. 2387 and cf. p. 2389.
12. William Shakespeare, *Richard II*, ed. Charles R. Forker, Arden Third Series (London: The Arden Shakespeare, 2002), 3.2.156–7.
13. McMillin and MacLean, *The Queen's Men*, p. 167; Griffin, *Playing the Past*; Edgar T. Schell, 'Prince Hal's Second "Reformation"', *Shakespeare Quarterly*, 21:1 (1970), 11–16.
14. Cf. the brief genealogy offered to Henry in Scene 9, ll. 841–4, discussed below.
15. If we allow that the 'till the king is dead' line is a memorial reconstruction of a forgotten line, then that line could have offered another dig at the king and thus its consistent inclusion in this play fits with the content – whoever was transferring or reading out the play believed this to be dramaturgically appropriate.
16. The feast day traditions of the Lord of Misrule and other inversions of hierarchy would have made these desires familiar, even if an audience recognised that their realisation was pure fancy. As Peter Laslett argues, in early modern England, 'Social revolution, meaning an irreversible changing of the pattern of social relationships [. . .] was almost impossible to contemplate. Almost, but not quite'; Peter Laslett, *The World We Have Lost*, 2nd edn (London: Methuen, 1970), p. 4.
17. Cf. Griffin, *Playing the Past*, p. 62 and Corbin and Sedge, *The Oldcastle Controversy*, p. 22.
18. Brian Walsh, 'Theatrical Temporality and Historical Consciousness in *The Famous Victories of Henry V*', *Theatre Journal*, 59:1 (2007), 57–73, 64.
19. 'Not today, O Lord, / O not today, think not upon the fault / My father made in compassing the crown.' *Henry V*, 4.1.289–91, but cf. ll. 94–302 and 1.2.
20. Griffin, *Playing the Past*, p. 61, and Walsh, 'Theatrical Temporality', 63.
21. First entered into the Stationers' Register in 1594 and published in the same year, *The True Tragedy* was probably in performance by the end of 1588 or 1589, and possibly performed for the queen; the absence of a clown role in the play suggests the tragedy was written following Tarlton's death. Cf.

Walsh, *Shakespeare*, pp. 76, 104 n 8, citing Lewis Mott, 'Foreign Politics in an Old Play', *Modern Philology*, 19 (1921), 65–71.
22. John Johnson, ed., *The True Tragedy of Richard the Third*, the Malone Society Reprints, gen. ed. W. W. Greg (London: the Malone Society, 1929), ll. 621–2. All future citations will be made in the text.
23. For Shakespeare's own construction of absent hospitality and its relationship to a rejection of nostalgia, see Chapter 3.
24. See Philip Schwyzer on the problem of 'late', '"Late" Losses and the Temporality of Early Modern Nostalgia', in Approaches to Early Modern Nostalgia special issue, ed. Kristine Johanson, *Parergon*, 33:2 (2016), 97–114.
25. Shakespeare will place a similar critique in the mouths of gardeners in *Richard II*, and in *Henry V* the image is used to castigate the two kings who have turned 'this best garden of the world, / Our fertile France' into a battlefield (5.3.59–60). On the *topos* of the garden in early modern literature, see Amy L. Tigner, *Literature and the Renaissance Garden from Elizabeth I to Charles II: England's Paradise* (Farnham, UK: Ashgate, 2012).
26. Cf. Introduction, pp. 21–2.
27. At the close of Robert Greene's *Friar Bacon and Friar Bungay*, Bacon imagines Elizabeth as the descendant of Brute's 'Troynovant'; idem, *Friar Bacon and Friar Bungay*, ed. Daniel Seltzer (London: Edward Arnold, 1963), xvi.44–8. My thanks to Bronnie Johnston for bringing this passage to my attention. As George Chapman's English translation of the *Iliad* was not published until 1598, the play's author(s) likely relied on common knowledge and/or on the Latin or Greek versions of the poem.
28. David Scott Kastan, 'The Shape of Time: Form and Value in the Shakespearean History Play', *Comparative Drama*, 7 (1973), 259–77, 263ff.
29. E. M. W. Tillyard, *Shakespeare's History Plays* (London: Chatto and Windus, 1944), p. 8, and Stephen Greenblatt, *Renaissance Self-Fashioning* (Chicago and London: University of Chicago Press, 1980), p. 202.
30. See John S. Mebane, *Renaissance Magic and the Return of the Golden Age: The Occult Tradition and Marlowe, Jonson, and Shakespeare* (Lincoln and London: University of Nebraska Press, 1989), pp. 5–6; Mark Hutchings, 'The "Turk Phenomenon" and the Repertory of the Late Elizabethan Playhouse', *Early Modern Literary Studies*, Special Issue 16 (2007), 10.1–39 (http://purl.oclc.org/emls/si-16/hutcturk.htm, point 8); Greenblatt, *Renaissance Self-Fashioning*, p. 194.
31. Anthony Dawson, 'Introduction', in Marlowe, *Tamburlaine the Great: Parts One and Two*, ed. Anthony Dawson (London: A & C Black, 2005), p. xiii.
32. Marlowe, *Tamburlaine the Great: Parts One and Two*, ed. Anthony B. Dawson, 1.1.113–17. Further citations will be made in the text.
33. Cf. Polybius, *The Histories*, trans. and ed. W. R. Paton (London and Cambridge, MA: Harvard University Press, 1954), I.35.1–3. On history's power to stir readers to virtue, see Thomas Blundeville, *The true order and Methode of wryting and reading hystories* (London, 1574), Hii^v–Hiii^r, and cf. Hii^r.
34. Greenblatt, *Renaissance Self-Fashioning*, p. 202.

35. Scholars cannot agree on authorship. McMillin and MacLean do not ascribe a definite author to the play, cf. *The Queen's Men*, pp. 155–67; Jean Jacquot follows J. C. Collins's conclusion that 'there is little ground' for Greene's authorship; Jacquot, 'Ralegh's "Hellish Verses" and the "Tragicall Raigne of Selimus"', *The Modern Language Review*, 48:1 (1953), 1–9, 5; Hutchings follows Daniel Vitkus to argue that 'Greene is the most likely candidate', 'The "Turk Phenomenon"', n 13; Walsh attributes the play unequivocally to Greene in *Shakespeare*, p. 55.
36. Peter Mack, *Elizabethan Rhetoric: Theory and Practice* (Cambridge: Cambridge University Press, 2002), p. 12; on Virgil's influence, see also Levin, *Golden Age*, pp. 15–17. Arthur Golding, trans. *The. Xv. Bookes of P. Ovidius Naso, entytuled Metamorphosis, translated oute of Latine into English meter, by Arthur Golding Gentleman, A worke very pleasaunt and delectable. London: William Seres, 1567*, The English Experience no. 881 (Amsterdam and Norwood, NJ: Johnson, 1977).
37. Ovid, *Metamorphoses*, Books I–XIII. Trans. Frank Justus Miller, rev. G. P. Goold, 2nd edn (Cambridge, MA and London: Harvard University Press, 1984), I.150, but cf. 89–150. See Frances Yates, 'Queen Elizabeth as Astraea', *Journal of the Warburg and Courtauld Institutes*, 10 (1947), 27–8 and her *Astraea*; Levin, *Golden Age*, p. 22.
38. Eamon Duffy, *The Stripping of the Altars: Traditional Religion in England 1400–1580*, 2nd edn (New Haven, CT and London: Yale University Press, 2005), p. 564.
39. Hester Lees-Jeffries, 'Location as Metaphor in Queen Elizabeth's Coronation Entry (1559): *Veritas Temporis Filia*', in Archer et al, eds., *Progresses*, pp. 65–85, p. 79; see also her *England's Helicon: Fountains in Early Modern Literature and Culture* (Oxford: Oxford University Press, 2007); see Paulina Kewes, 'History and Its Uses', in *The Uses of History in Early Modern England*, ed. Paulina Kewes (San Marino, CA: The Huntington Library, 2006), p. 14.
40. Richard Mulcaster, 'The Receiving of the Queen's Majesty', in *The Queen's Majesty's Passage and Related Documents*, ed. Germaine Warkentin (Toronto: University of Toronto Press, 2004), p. 76.
41. Robert Greene, *A Maidens Dreame* (London, 1591), C3^r–C3^v.
42. George Peele, *Descensus astraeae* (London, 1591), A2^r–A2^v.
43. Anon, *The Tragical Reign of Selimus: 1594*, prep. W. Bang (London: the Malone Society, 1909), ii.305–23. Further citations will be made in the text.
44. George Puttenham, *The arte of English poesie* (London, 1589), Ddiii^v; see also 'topothesia' in Henry Peacham, *The Garden of Eloquence* (London, 1577), Pi^v.
45. 'An Homilee agaynst disobedience and wylfull rebellion' in John Jewel, *The second tome of Homilees* (London, 1571), Llviii^v–Qqiii^v, and Sir Thomas Smith, *De Republica Anglorum [1583]*, ed. Mary Dewar (Cambridge: Cambridge University Press, 1982).
46. Peele's authorship has been asserted at least since Malone, who argued that it was his or Robert Greene's work, Ivor B. John, 'Introduction', in Shakespeare, *The Life and Death of King John*, ed. John (London: Methuen & Co., 1907), p. xi; Charles R. Forker maintains this claim in his edition,

relying on Brian Vickers, 'The Troublesome Reign, George Peele, and the Date of King John', in Words that Count: Essays on Early Modern Authorship in Honor of MacDonald P. Jackson, ed. Brian Boyd (Newark: University of Delaware Press, 2004), pp. 78–116; Forker, 'Introduction', in George Peele, The Troublesome Reign of John, King of England, ed. Charles Forker, The Revels Plays series (Manchester: Manchester University Press, 2011/2016), pp. 6–30.

47. On the plays' relationship see Peter Lake, How Shakespeare Put Politics on Stage (New Haven, CT: Yale University Press, 2016), pp. 195–235; Forker, 'Introduction', pp. 79–87; Beatrice Groves, 'Memory, Composition, and the Relationship of King John to The Troublesome Raigne of King John', Comparative Drama, 38:2, 3 (2004), 277–90.

48. Peele, The Troublesome Reign of John, King of England, ed. Forker, 1:1.6. Further references will be made in the text.

49. Forker, 'Introduction', p. 5.

50. Forker, 'Introduction', p. 26; Lake, How Shakespeare Put Politics on Stage, p. 205.

51. William Shakespeare, King John, ed. Jesse M. Lander and J. J. M. Tobin (London: Bloomsbury, 2018), 4.3.152. All further citations will be made in the text. Cf. Michael Gadaleto, 'Shakespeare's Bastard Nation: Skepticism and the English Isle in King John', Shakespeare Quarterly, 69:1 (2018), 3–34, 26.

52. Gadaleto, 'Shakespeare's Bastard Nation', first quote at 34, second at 7–8.

Chapter 2

What Merry World in England? Nostalgic *Paroemia* and *The Second Part of Henry VI*

[I]f more over we can sette a parte al affections, as fretting cares & thoughtes, dolefull or sorowfull imaginations, vaine feares, folysh loves, gnawing hates, and geve oure selves to lyve quietly, frendlie, & merily one with an other, as men were wont to do in the old world, when this countrie was called merye Englande, and every man to medle in his own matters, thinking theim sufficient, as thei do in Italye, and avoyde malyce and dissencion, the destruction of commune wealthes, and private houses: I doubte not but we shall preserve oure selves, bothe from this sweatinge syckenesse, and other diseases also not here purposed to be spoken of.[1]

In his book on the sweating sickness, the Tudor physician, scholar and religious conservative John Caius relies on the nostalgic *topos* of 'merye Englande' to advise his readers on how to 'preserve' themselves against the disease and other afflictions.[2] The past, exemplary for Caius, is also proximate, and his 'merye Englande' invocation orients his readers towards the future. By signalling Italy's present possession of 'old world' values, and through his confident hope ('I doubte not but we shall'), Caius tempers his lament for an idealised, neighbourly England by suggesting that recovering those values is possible and even necessary as a social and physical panacea. The ubiquitous 'merry world' trope is expansive and complex. Its use signals temporal rupture and a general dissatisfaction with the present, one in sixteenth-century England associated with the Reformation and the change in the 'ritual season' of England. As this chapter demonstrates and as Harriet Phillips has recently shown, the Protestant polemic imagination attached its use to recusancy and sedition, and the 'merry world/England' circulated as a more shadowed cultural phenomenon than its carnival or festive associations have allowed.[3]

In *The Second Part of Henry VI* (1590, rev. 1594–7),[4] in the rebel Nick's complaint that 'it was never merry world in England since gentlemen came up', Shakespeare offers his audience a familiar lament, one they could have heard in a sermon, play, or ballad.[5] How various religious and dramatic Tudor texts employ the 'never a merry world' *topos* is this chapter's first concern. By mocking projected Catholic fantasies, these texts establish and reiterate a suspicion of nostalgia, insisting on its futile longing even as they implicitly acknowledge the power of idealising the past. The values these texts attach to the merry world provide an important context for *2 Henry VI*. Shakespeare crafts a clear object of desire in the play: a sense of a common inheritance that existed in the past and is available to be reclaimed for the future. That inheritance is always competing with other constructions of the past, and therefore other possible inheritances, as the play's persistent concerns with historical narrative and conflicting truth claims demonstrate. These competing claims on the past destabilise any available or triumphant claim to an 'English inheritance' in the play. Significantly, Shakespeare dramatises that inheritance's role in the play's various nostalgias and consequently nostalgia's ability to persuade, its power to influence, even as he does not stage the attainment of that inheritance and thereby suggests the futility of desiring it.

The 'merry world' maxim participates in the play's sustained attention both to historical uncertainty and the interpretive process required by its contending historical narratives. The drama's investment in such narratives is evident not simply from its status as history play, but in its first title, *The First Part of the Contention Betwixt the Two Famous Houses of York and Lancaster*; those families' rival claims provide a crucial background to the play's unfolding events. From the early debate about the significance of losing Anjou and Maine, to the conflict between the apprentice Peter and Thomas Horner his master, to Gloucester's trial of 'blind' Simpcox and his wife's claims, to Jack Cade's and Lord Stafford's arguments over the alternative facts of Cade's birth, *2 Henry VI* unfailingly asks its spectators to weigh versions of the past, and these competing histories stage and expose nostalgic rhetoric's role in such narratives. The Duke of Gloucester's first speech, when he 'unload[s. . .] the common grief of all the land' at the news of Anjou and Maine's loss, exemplifies the idea of a communal loss bound with a history of inheritance that the 'merry world' proverb will capture later in the play (1.1.72–3).[6] While pasts contend in *2 Henry VI*, the 'merry world' proverb's use commences a series of explicit alternative futures: that projected by the rebels, the Cockaignian idyll lauded by Cade, and finally the harmonious England which Lord Clifford locates, ironically, as a consequence of war. Shakespeare binds each of those futures to an idealised past, and, staging these fantasies' suasive ability, introduces nostalgia as successful political rhetoric.

Paroemia and the Rhetoric of Reformation

2 Henry VI uses *paroemia*, the rhetorical use of a proverb, as a *topos* of nostalgia. Employing the totalising narrative of the 'merry world' adage appeals to the *sensus communis* of an early modern English audience, who would have been familiar with a wide body of proverbs and with variants of 'It was never a merry world since . . .' more generally. Proverbs share with nostalgia an impulse and an ability to express collective understanding, as they too can articulate an appeal to collective memory. *Paroemia* relies on both contemporary use and historical commendation, as it must be both 'a sentence in every mans mouth' as well as 'pretty [. . .] witty, that is to say: that it may be decearned, by some note and marke from common speeche, and also commended by antiquity, and learning'.[7] Erasmus's *Adagia* played a central role in shaping proverbs' cultural significance in early modernity, and his 1508 *Adagiorum chiliades* expanded upon his previous editions of the *Collectanea*, this time including Latin translations of his Greek text.[8] An English translation appeared with Richard Taverner's 1539 *Proverbes or adagies*, and that text's reprintings in 1545, 1552 and 1569 indicate its relative success. Perhaps the appeal of aphorisms lay in their collective, anonymous nature, their implied malleability. By some counts Shakespeare used over 4,600 proverbs in his plays; the 'merry world' is just one of seventy-two identified in *2 Henry VI*.[9] As Obelkevich argues, '[p]roverbs put the collective before the individual, the recurrent and stereotyped before the unique, external rules before self-determination, common sense before the individual vision', a sequencing that the frequent use of introductory phrases such as 'We say . . .' and 'As we say' suggests.[10] Such phrasing makes explicit what the proverb itself possesses implicitly: an appeal to a common idea, a common belief; they provide a cultural education, a window into a specific society and time.[11] By invoking a source of shared ideas and a rhetoric which distils larger problems and themes into a forthright saying, proverbs like the 'merry world' both participate in creating a nostalgic tone and represent what nostalgia actively appeals to – a shared ideal.

Alongside the rhetoric of a 'merry world', the idea of a 'world never being so . . .' summarised in the totalising expression that the 'world was never', flourished in the sixteenth century in diverse writings ranging from literary texts to religious pamphlets to reported speech. In his 1567 translation of John Calvin, Arthur Golding anglicises Calvin's argument with the phrase: 'the worlde was never shaken with more cruell tempestes of warre, nor never drowned in so manifold & déepe a sinke of evils'.[12] The English (as the Latin) enables a nostalgic comparison between contemporary Europe and the imagined tranquillity of Christ's birth, when 'there was peace and singular quietnesse everywhere'.[13] This image presents both the Reformation project that Calvin promoted and the goals of Protestantism in England: to return to the days of the early church. Where Calvin sees a rupture resulting from a rejection of the Gospels, 'citezein of London' John Carr observes only decay since the days of Eden:

> More whoredom, filthy fornication, was never used, since the first originall, more dissimulation, never was hard of nor seene[.] What more should I say, sithe the state of all thynges doth decay: and the world was never more full of impietee.[14]

In addition to internal rhyme (m*ore* wh*ore*dom) and alliteration (filthy fornication), Carr – like Golding – uses *paroemia* to create general extremes in his focus on the disgraceful present, as his 'never' expresses absolutes; society has reached its apex of sinfulness. The Iron Age unfolds still, as 'the state of *all* thynges doth decay' establishes the present's singular wickedness and the future's inevitable evil. This rhetoric of extremes comes to constitute a crucial element of nostalgic dramatic discourse.

Indeed, drama from the early sixteenth century makes potent use of that rhetoric, as the interlude *Hick Scorner* (c. 1514) illustrates.[15] As 'merry England' and the 'never' world circulated and transformed during the Tudor era, performance and the burgeoning English public theatre became powerful means for their dissemination. In *Hick Scorner* the 'world was never' trope offers social critique as it focuses attention on the degenerate present to stress the importance of a future in heaven. The play predates the Reformation and was printed only in Henry and Mary's respective reigns (1515, 1530, 1550), but the archive, the Stationers' Register, and the period's drama itself all reveal late Elizabethan attention to the play. As with so many texts, *Hick Scorner*'s explicitly Catholic material was revised and redeployed for Protestant England, and by the end of the sixteenth century the term 'hick scorner' could signal disgruntled Catholics.[16] In the play, Perseverance, Contemplation and Pity articulate moral teachings, while Freewill, Imagination and the vice Hick Scorner celebrate libertine ways until the former two are converted at the play's end; Imagination becomes Good Remembrance, and both pledge to serve Perseverance. The play's eponym, however, proves to be a less conventional morality character. Upon his arrival in England, ship's master Hick Scorner offers a vision that, in its imaginative destruction of all that is good, not only reproduces a traditional complaint theme but echoes Ovid's description of the beginning of the Iron Age, when Astraea, goddess of justice and last of the gods on earth, abandoned the mortal world. The vice informs Freewill and Imagination that on his crossing to England he met ships full of those leaving for Ireland, 'who will nevermore come to England'.[17] Those emigrating were 'Great':

> All true religious, and holy women:
> There was Troth and his kinsmen,
> With Patience, Meekness, and Humility,
> And all true maidens with their virginity,
> Rial [Royal] preachers, Sadness and Charity,
> Right Conscience and Faith with devotion,
> And all true monks that kept their religion,
> True buyers and sellers and alms-deed doers,
> Piteous people that be of sin destroyers,
> With Just Abstinence and good counsellors,
> Mourners for sin with Lamentation,
> And good rich men that helpeth folk out of prison.
> True Wedlock was there also,
> With young men that ever in prayer did go. (ll. 338, 339–52)

Glancing at the possibility of justice and goodness escaping the world's corruption, the play describes how all that is virtuous – 'patience', 'charity', 'right conscience', 'faith' – has fled the island, never to return since 'God shoop a remedy' for this 'unhappy company': all perished in a shipwreck (ll. 354, 353, 356). In their absence, the vicious sail for England, including 'Hatred' who vows his presence there 'forever' (ll. 379, 380). Hick Scorner's reports establish and implicitly laud a proximate virtuous past and, significantly, negate the possibility of its return, insisting on the inevitability of a vicious future.

The *Hick Scorner* dramatist notably uses both vice and virtue to assert temporal degeneracy in the play. Put in the stocks and then abandoned by Freewill, Imagination and the eponymous vice, Pity relies on the *paroemia* of the 'world was never' idea to lament:

> We all may say 'wellaway!'
> For sin that is now-a-day.
> Lo, virtue is vanished forever and aye.
> Worse was it never![18]
> We have plenty of great oaths,
> And cloth enough in our clothes,
> But charity many men loathes,
> Worse was it never! (ll. 550–7)

The refrain 'worse was it never!' appears three more times, concluding a lengthy speech depicting an England inhabited only by the vicious, violent and proud, and punished by God with disease. Pity presents an image of an utterly corrupted society: sophistry has led to a redefinition of values, so that 'lechery [is] called love', 'murder manhood named' and 'Exhortation is called law'; vanity, in the form of 'goodly gilt knaves' and 'apparelled wives', goes forth, while 'Devotion' and 'charity' are absent (ll. 558, 559, 560, 574, 575, 583, 556). Even when Pity suspends the 'worse was it never' refrain (ll. 553, 557, 561, 597, 601), the text still insists on present weakness through a second refrain, 'Now-a-day(s)' (ll. 551, 565, 573, 599). Using *paroemia* and numerous examples of extant vice, Pity performs a degenerative reading of history that offers an implicit nostalgia. For even while it refuses to explicitly invoke the past, the speech calls upon its audience to imagine the proximate past of the play just described by Hick Scorner, when virtue thrived in England and then collectively abandoned it. Apart from this important example, however, the play pays no attention to the past. Rather, *Hick Scorner* denounces the imperfect mortal present to attend to the soteriological and focus on a divine future with Christ. The play's concluding lines, 'Of all our mirths here we make an end, / Unto the bliss of heaven Jesus your souls bring' (ll. 1027–8), underscore how *Hick Scorner*'s message depends upon the creation of a wicked present to stress the importance of personal amendment to reach heavenly respite. Again, as I argued in Chapter 1, early modern drama weds temporal consciousness to ethical and political values. *Hick Scorner* uses nostalgia as a chastising discourse, as it holds up the abstract past as an exemplar for early modern English society. Significantly, however, that past remains unobtainable – its virtues literally drowned – and the play insists that past goodness can only be claimed outside the material world, through salvation.

Paroemia circulated nostalgic discourse across dramatic, religious and political texts, but one constant shared across the 'merry world' proverb and its variants is temporal rupture: it was never a merry world or England *since*. As noted above, this 'since' is capacious. However, in Protestant polemicists' use, 'merry world' *paroemia* is the touchstone for their imagined, uniform Catholic longing for a plentiful and illiterate past.[19] In *A plaine subversyon* (1555) by 'Gracious Menewe' (a possible pseudonym for Thomas Becon, chaplain to Archbishop Cranmer), an apprentice and a priest debate the fallacy of confession. The priest, bemoaning that a 'prentyse' should attempt to understand the Gospel as a religious man does, complains: 'It was never mery with us, sythens such ionge boyes presumed to reade the scriptures.'[20] This proverbial rhetoric is deployed in Protestant mythology in John Foxe's *Actes and monuments*: 'The Notable Historie of William Hunter Martyr' parallels events in Menewe's 'dialogue' almost exactly.[21] William, a young

London apprentice in the first year of Queen Mary's reign, is discovered reading the Bible by one Father Atwell. The latter, outraged by William's response to his interrogations, declares, 'it was never mery since the Bible came abroad in English'.[22] Both Menewe and Foxe imagine Catholic longing for the past as a longing for ignorance, for a pre-Reformation era of Biblical illiteracy and inaccessibility. It is precisely this rupture that the Protestant authors exploit: their narratives mock nostalgic discourse and in so doing attempt to shape the temporal consciousness of their readers by arguing that the present, the time when the Bible *has* come abroad in English and young boys *can* read scriptures, must be superior to the past.

In ventriloquising an imagined papist in his baldly anti-Catholic *A caveat for Parsons Howlet* (1581) – Catholics are a 'darke broode' in an 'uncleane cage' – John Fielde uses nostalgic *paroemia* to attach ethical implications to longing for the past and, critically, the future.[23] Describing at length 'Catholic' actions and character, he writes:

> They will whisper from place to place, and from one to another upon their ale-bench, what dayes are these, what wickednesse is in the world [. . .] O the golden world is gone, when we had 24 egges for a peny, when we mighte goe to this religious house and that, and have good chere and our bellies ful [. . .] They say the Masse is naught, but I can not tell, then we had a mery world, and all things plenty [. . .] and as for mens servants [. . .] *Nowe* they are so bookishe, become so wise and learned, that they wil meddle with the scriptures. It was never mery world since there was so muche talke of the scripture, since every cobler and Tinker durst meddle with it, and a byble must stande in every window.[24]

As with Becon's and Foxe's texts, *paroemia* is used here to make the *topos* of nostalgia a place of scorn: Fielde's sarcastic and derogatory tone associates a longing for an idealised past with the illicit, the ignorant, the evil – with the papists. His rhetoric derides the impulse to imagine an ideal world, one not unlike that proposed by Jack Cade (where seven half-penny loaves will be sold for a penny). Of equal significance, and unlike the previous accounts, Fielde's 'speech' opposes nostalgic discourse to the state by promising a Catholic future. Having lamented 'these days', invoked the image of the 'golden world' and crowned this with the 'merry world' vision, Fielde's 'papist' declares, 'the Queene cannot live alwaies, and when our day commeth, we will be even with them'.[25] The treasonous speaker suggests that the Queen's death will enable the golden world's return, a riposte to the Elizabeth-Astraea narrative. The discourse of the ideal past becomes the source of a preferable future, as Fielde's imaginary papist suggests that a return to the 'merry world' depends upon one inevitable future event.

Into the late Elizabethan period, popular preachers such as Henry Smith and William Burton maintained that a longing for the past represented undesirable belief, as their writings continued to circulate the idea that the desire for the 'merry world' is foolish and baseless. In his sermon on Paul's first letter to the Thessalonians, the 'Silver-Tongued Smith' explicitly associates 'merry world' nostalgia with heresy and hypocrisy:

> If Paule woulde have us abstaine from everie appearance of evill, sure he would have us abstaine frome heresie and hypocrisie. [A]nd not to surfet with the blessings of peace, and then saye it was never merry world since this newe Religion came up.[26]

Notably, Smith urges the irenic Protestant present as a foil to the perceived rupture of 'newe Religion'. In his 1594 sermon 'The Anatomie of Belial', Burton uses the 'merry world' to collapse biblical past with the present, railing against vanity and the profane nature of those 'persons as preferre earth before heaven, the world before the word':

> Such were they that said in *Jer.* 43.[27] *It was well with us when we made cakes for the Queene of heaven*: as many say now adaies: It was never merry world since we had so much preaching: it was a good world when we could go to the Abbeys and other religious houses, and have our bellies full of good cheare for nothing. *Jeremie* is a babler (said they) and preaching is babling, say these.[28]

Notably, Burton opposes a vicious preference for material succour to evangelism. His repetition of 'as many say' and 'say these' reiterates the communality inherit in *paroemia* as he constructs a simplifying fantasy of a Catholic community united both in its discontents and in its desires, a fantasy that must have been doubtful to his more reflective readers.[29]

Deploying the 'merry world' proverb enabled these polemicists to avoid the ventriloquist's 'dilemma' that requires the repetition of ideas he must refute, as they argue that the proverb represents a heretical and unethical longing.[30] But beneath these ventriloquists' mocks lies an anxiety about the desirability of the merry world fantasy and the need to highlight the virtues of the present. As these authors and religious pamphlets suggest, the burden of proof lay with the Protestants. The question of the Protestant present's superiority over the Catholic past again comes to the fore in the pamphlets between the Bishop of Salisbury John Jewel and the Catholic doctor of divinity Thomas Harding. In *A confutation of a booke intituled An apologie of the Church of England* (1565), Harding writes: 'That the people be now otherwise instructed, then they were in times past, we confesse. But whether better now, then

[sic] in our forefathers dayes, they that can consider the lives of them now, and of them that were then, may easely judge.'[31] Harding's is an ecumenical appeal that, apart from 'forefathers dayes', offers nothing of the concrete material lament about which Protestant polemicists gleefully fantasise (although his reference to 'these most perilouse times' states his position clear enough).[32] In *A defence*, Jewel rejected the charge that Protestantism signalled regression, demanding:

> Certainely you must néedes confesse, there are fewer blasphemies, fewer Othes, fewer breaches of Matrimonie, fewer Stewes, fewer Concubines, fewer Fraies, fewer Murthers emongst us this daie, then commonly were at any time emonge our Fathers.[33]

For Jewel, Protestantism purifies society: life is more peaceful and people more secure, marriage and sex more sanctified, speech godlier and more refined. He needs temporal comparison to make this point, and the vision of history he offers is, significantly, one of social progress that counters the ubiquitous idea of an ever-declining state of man outlined in the Golden Age myth and implied in the 'merry world' proverb. He makes his attitude towards nostalgia definitive in his paraphrase of Ecclesiastes: 'Never demaunde wherefore the times past were better than the times presente. For indeed it is a foolishe question.'[34]

Where 'merry England' appears in historical narratives of Henrician England, its use intimates that it is this England at stake in Henry's reforms. John Lassells (or Lascelles) anticipates the accounts of Becon and Foxe in his report that following Henry VIII's split from Rome and the Dissolution of the Monasteries, an outraged Duke of Norfolk 'was not ashamed to say that he had never read the Scriptures nor ever would, and it was merry in England before this New Learning came up'.[35] While the explicit context is religious, its use is in fact political: Lassells's report is perhaps the first instance of the use of the 'merry England' proverb as a means of documenting and employing the text against its supposed speaker. A century later, Sir William Thomas in 1641 and Sir Richard Baker in 1643 reported in their respective works the Duke of Suffolk's rage at ecclesiastical opposition to Henry VIII's divorce and remarriage. Learning that Wolsey and Campeius refused to judge the lawfulness of the king's marriage, 'the Duke of Suffolke said, and that truly, It was never merry in England since Cardinall Bishops came amongst us'.[36] Baker's account in his *A chronicle of the Kings of England* repeats the anecdote, an uncommon instance of a report of Protestant use of the adage.[37] Published at the inception of the Civil War, these Caroline histories reinforce the political quality of the 'merry world' proverb which the Elizabethan religious tracts initially suggest.

As I've been arguing, Protestant fantasies of Catholic discontent encapsulated in accounts of nostalgic *paroemia* articulated a temporal consciousness that rejects historical decline, emphasising the futility and impotence of such desires and insisting on the superiority both of the present and, implicitly, the future. This model, which ventriloquises supposed Catholic displeasure, is also put to work in drama of the mid-sixteenth century. While *Hick Scorner* attacks the present to convey its moral of future salvation, R. Wever's Reformation interlude *Lusty Juventus* (comp. 1550x1553; pub. 1561x1575) reworks religious ideas and dramatic trends as it co-opts and inverts a sub-genre of the Catholic morality play and adopts previously reported Catholic dialogue for Protestant didactic purposes.[38] From the play's outset, Good Counsel and Knowledge distinguish their teachings from what Juventus has learned from his elders and parents, a metaphorical separation of Protestantism and Catholicism that aligns the old with the sinful and the new with what is godly. In the course of the play Good Counsel persuades Juventus to give up his pleasure-seeking ways, but the Devil, through his intermediary Hypocrisie, tempts him again before he is converted a final time, and the play ends with a speech by God's Promises and a prayer for King Edward (Queen Elizabeth in later editions). *Lusty Juventus* exemplifies how the genre of early Reformation interlude reversed and reworked the typical pattern in the era's 'Prodigal Son' plays, which were originally interested in training up youth in a humanist tradition.[39] As Pamela King argues, 'When [...] the Reformation rendered the values of elders synonymous with those of the corrupt old faith, the youthful protagonist [of an interlude] might be encouraged by characters representing the voice of Reformation to cast aside the values of his elders in order to conform to a new orthodoxy.'[40] We can see this project at work in one of Hypocrisie's monologues, which Wever uses to voice an ironic nostalgia:

> I may say to you secretly
> The worlde was never mery,
> Since children where so bolde.
> Now every boy wyl be a teacher
> The father a foole, and the chyld a preacher
> Thys is preaty geare
> The foule presumption of youth
> Wyl turne shortly to great ruth
> I fere, I feare, I feare.[41]

Hypocrisie articulates every stereotype of Catholic speech so far examined in this discussion of *paroemia* and nostalgia. That he must speak in secret recalls Fielde's report of Catholic whispering; the idea that 'every boy wil be a teacher / The father a foole, and the chyld a preacher' repeats the supposed Catholic anxiety concerning access to the scriptures. The 'fathers' of the old Catholic Church are thus pushed aside for the young Church of England and its children to become 'preachers'. In the play, it is precisely the inversion of hierarchy, the young now ranking above the old, that Wever uses as the metaphor for the superiority of the Reformation and, in the play's larger context, to suggest the importance of a monarch's careful selection of those 'old' teachers to whom she or he submits.[42]

Ironic nostalgia appears in fact as a dramatic trend that critiques any earnest longing for the past. In the contemporaneous play *Respublica* (1553), Avarice laments that

> Suche gredie covetous folke as nowe of daies been
> I trowe before these present daies wer never seen.
> An honest man can goe in no place of the strete
> But he shall I thinke with an hundred beggers mete.
> 'Geve for goddes sake, geve for Saincte Charitee,
> Geve for oure Ladies sake, geve for the Trenitee,
> Geve in the waye of your good spede, geve, geve, geve, geve'.[43]

As with Hypocrisie in *Lusty Juventus*, here a devious voice communicates nostalgic longing for a superior past: 'before these present daies wer never seen', 'Suche gredie covetous folke as nowe of daies'. Much in the same way that Protestant writers ventriloquise to alert their readers to the dangers of a seemingly innocuous 'merry world' lament, these Tudor dramatists use vice characters to alert their audience to the temptations of bewailing the present, an act aligned with sin. Nevertheless, in presenting wittily ironic vices, both plays present guarded social satire. Avarice's ventriloquising of the beggars provides the audience with a real indictment of the present, even though its phrasing comes from a disreputable source. These interludes articulate a complex, ambivalent nostalgia that primarily highlights its heretical, vicious associations while also revealing nostalgia's capacity to express recognisable social realities (poverty, the neglect of the needy, and greed).

Lusty Juventus's ideals and arguments continued to entertain the Elizabethans: it was republished in 1565 and it appears in the multi-authored *The Book of Sir Thomas More* (1591–93x1595). In that play, the Lord Cardinal's players visit More as he entertains the Lord Mayor of London, and the lead player proposes a drama. More enquires about the troupe's repertory, which includes 'the Cradle of Securitie, / hit nayle o'th head, impacient povertie, / the play of foure Pees, dives and Lazarus, / Lustie Juventus, and the mariage of witt and wisedome'.[44] Of these plays, only one is definitively contemporaneous with More;

the remainder are undated or anachronistic in the context, illustrating that the scene's author draws on interludes that he knew – like *Lusty Juventus*. When More declares he'll 'none but' *The Marriage of Wit and Wisdom* (l. 924), the play that follows is a hodge-podge of various interludes that relies heavily on *Lusty Juventus*, in particular Witt's Song.[45] Fifty years after its first appearance, this interlude, with its ironic nostalgia and suspicion of the idealised past, still functioned as a cultural referent in Elizabethan England and provided a dramatic model for a complex rhetorical nostalgia.

Throughout the Tudor period, in religious and literary texts as well as public performance, the 'merry world' and 'merry England' proverbs and their 'world was never' analogue work beyond a proverb's most basic function as a pithy communal saying to complicate significantly what appears as straightforward *paroemia*. With the exception of Pity's monologue in *Hick Scorner*, the texts analysed above imagine nostalgia to be a Catholic discourse, aligning it with heresy, ignorance and sin. Nostalgia's proponents, these texts suggest, are heretic fools. Through such consistent literary presentation of the 'merry world', early modern English culture makes nostalgia and its related attitudes to the past and present emphatically moral problems. Notably, the paroemiac discourse of the 'merry world' is attenuated: it looks from present to past; the future plays no part in the laments of temporal discrepancy. Of equal importance, this emphasis on moral crisis suggests both nostalgia's impotence and its potential consequence. Against this trend, in Shakespeare's early dramatic use of nostalgia – partially constituted by *paroemia* – the past becomes a model for the future and a powerful impetus to dramatic political action.

Nostalgia's Ambivalence in *The Second Part of Henry VI*

As I have been arguing, Protestant writers rendered 'merry world' nostalgia a morally and politically dubious speech act, and when this proverb is used on stage in *2 Henry VI*, there is accordingly a set of values and judgements already attached to its use. Shakespeare was surely aware of how this proverb was being used in late Elizabethan culture when he deployed it as a key part of the nostalgic rhetoric he crafts in the play, and his dramaturgy reproduces Protestant suspicion of nostalgia circulating at the time. Additionally, Shakespeare dramatically exploits the explicit and implicit understanding of nostalgia as always available, made evident through the various ventriloquists of nostalgia I've discussed. Vice or Catholic or (rarely) Protestant, earnestly or ironically, a variety of characters could speak nostalgia and thereby unsettle any truth claims that might attach to constructions of the idealised past.

Shakespeare innovates in his dramatic use of *paroemia* by dissociating it from explicitly religious terms, and in fact makes nostalgic rhetoric free of 'party politics': it is available to, and used by, the play's various factions. The earlier Tudor dramas I've discussed rely on a lost ideal and the assumed persuasiveness of nostalgic discourse; Protestant writers repeat 'Catholic' nostalgia to insist on such discourse's futility and impotence. Shakespeare's innovation is to reject that futility by staging how nostalgia's persuasiveness operates. 2 *Henry VI* illustrates first how individuals across the social hierarchy – labourers, pseudo-claimants to the throne, and lords – can all use the language of the idealised past, and second how its use persuades others to dramatic action. Shakespeare avoids any explicitly pro-Protestant, anti-nostalgia positions, rather staging the moral implications of nostalgia by revealing that it is without morality: it floats, superficially, on the possibilities of rhetoric. The polemicists' paroemiac use of the 'merry world/England' trope decried the longing for a past ideal and, through that critical use, insisted on the present's superiority, orienting readers and auditors towards an equally benevolent future. Rejecting the separation of future from past, Shakespeare employs 'merry world' *paroemia* to linger in and on the past and equally to look towards the future, as his dramaturgy insists that how the relationship between past and future is constructed can shape individual and communal dramatic action.

The 'merry world' proverb encapsulates the sense of temporal discontinuity, dissatisfaction and displacement which nostalgia articulates, and in 2 *Henry VI* a commoner's use of *paroemia* establishes a rhetoric that figures prominently in the play's succeeding rebel scenes.[46] When the rebel Nick laments, 'it was never merry world in England since gentlemen came up', his dissatisfaction with the present articulates nostalgia's narrow, selective narrative of the past, and parsing this proverb shows how nostalgia operates in this scene at large.[47] Nick's line may be understood in separate, equally meaningful phrases. The 'It was never' idea behind 'never a merry world' exemplifies the totalising and extreme rhetoric which comprises one necessary element of a nostalgic narrative, a narrative which not only the rebels but their leader Jack Cade and the king's representative Lord Clifford make successful use of. In religious and dramatic texts, characters or speakers who use such language are Catholics and vices – wayward fools. For spectators familiar with the uses of 'never a merry world', Nick's complaint would immediately align him with viciousness and emphasise the idea that the mob is ignorant and 'incapable of political thought'.[48] While scholarly opinion of these rebels remains mixed, there is consensus that they act without motive, as a gang of ignorant brutes, 'buffoons' who need only 'A few rousing speeches from the aristocrats, with the invocation of the name of Henry V and the threat of a French invasion' to abandon Cade; as 'an irrational mob unilaterally focused on butchery' that offers 'a chaotic and contradictory' image of their purpose.[49] In these readings, the rebels' actions not only find no justification, but are coherently incoherent.

I posit that the rebellion scenes offer clear grounds for their action, grounds established in the first appearance of the rebels and their nostalgic rhetoric, and which are carried through to their final abandonment of their would-be king Jack Cade. The rebels evaluate their present through the lens of the past and the promised future, and their loyalties follow potential political realities, calling into question the commonplace characterisation as a mob acting without rationale. From the beginning they are unconvinced by Cade: during the Cockaigne speech they both assent and consistently dissent from him in a series of hilarious asides. As Cade declares his claim to England's throne in a speech outlining his ancestry and his qualities as a leader, his auditors continuously interrupt and discredit him with stinging commentary (4.2.26–60).[50] In opposition to the man Cade constructs – a Mortimer of 'honourable', 'valiant' breeding – Cade is a Cade 'for stealing of a cade of herring'; his father was a bricklayer and his mother 'a pedlar's daughter'; he was 'born under a hedge; for his father had never a house but the cage'; he is a known criminal; and his laws, which Cade famously declares shall come from his mouth, will be 'stinking law, for his breath / stinks with eating toasted cheese' (4.2.41, 45, 27, 32, 37, 43–4, 4.7.8–9).[51] These asides construct their own history of Cade as they reject his account and link him from his arrival to an epistemological process that renders any knowledge about the past uncertain. Grounding his promise of a better future in his legitimacy, Cade exploits the certainty of his own falsehoods. Nevertheless, Shakespeare stages clearly that Cade's power is circumscribed by the crowd's self-interest. Their comments 'continually subvert' Cade's world, as they see through his performance of gentility, and consequently they possess no reason to follow Cade beyond what he will deliver to them.[52] More than establishing a carnivalesque act of inclusion, the asides create the possibility of Cade's future rejection, which these rebels perform at the end of the play. The rebels' abandonment of Cade suggests that they choose a new utopian vision; between competing theoretical futures, they choose one that promises honour and material gain in reprising the wars of their fathers. Nick's 'it was never' establishes from the beginning of the rebel scenes the dissatisfaction with the present that demands action and inspires longing for an ideal future.

While 'it was never' implies a foolishness that the rebels both confirm and call into question, the second half of the proverb establishes a temporal rupture essential to Shakespeare's construction of a persuasive nostalgic rhetoric. To speak of a 'merry world *since*' explicitly invokes a circulating cultural image of the nation, one which Protestant writings mocked as a Catholic yearning for the past, and one which Nick's dissatisfaction with the coming into fashion of gentlemen reveals as representative of anxieties about social status rather than exclusively about religious beliefs and practices. Nick does not ventriloquise: the rise of gentlemen has changed the cultural topography of the 'merry world in England', and the subsequent discontent – so the play suggests – persuades him to join Cade. In complaining about the upstart gentry, Nick reprises the idea that religious change engenders a sense of loss, identifying that loss rather as a consequence of an expanding social hierarchy. This notion circulated throughout the Elizabethan period, and it possessed political significance particularly in the 1590s, when it was used in a 1596 Oxfordshire rising. As Buchanan Sharp notes, 'The miller Richard Bradshawe was reported to have declared "that he hoped that before yt were long to see some of the ditches throwne downe, and that yt wold never be merye till some of the gentlemen were knocked down"', an expression that assumes these gentlemen have 'come up'. A continental example of 'living merrily' offered some inspiration to the Oxford men, as '"the commons, long sithens in Spaine did rise and kill all the gentlemen in Spaine and sithens that time have lyved merrily there"'.[53] The phrase's use in the Oxfordshire rising illustrates its potential function as a commonplace 'rallying cry', and in using it Shakespeare 'bring[s] the successive histories of past risings and rebellions [. . .] into direct contact with latter-day representations of class conflict, thereby giving added currency to an apparently old complaint'.[54] In the space of this single line, through the nostalgia of the 'merry world', Shakespeare employs *paroemia* as a critical socio-economic discourse that draws its audience into some sympathy with the rebels before alienating them with those same rebels' actions.

The historical sources of *2 Henry VI* illustrate the established relationship between proverbial rhetoric, nostalgic *topoi* and expressions of class conflict. As this book argues, Shakespeare's nostalgic rhetoric was not created in a vacuum. In addition to popular Tudor interludes and religious discourses mocking Catholics, historical texts communicating nostalgic ideas were also available to him, and he drew on accounts of the 1381 Great Revolt that was led by Wat Tyler and John Ball.

According to Richard Grafton's *A Chronicle at Large* (1569), the rebels were motivated by a sense of a utopic past free from hierarchy and servitude: 'sayd they [the rebels], in the beginning of the worlde, there were no bond men: neyther oughte there be any nowe'.⁵⁵ Ball preached this egalitarianism as the explicit future aim that would cure England's ills. '[M]atters go not wel to passe in England in these dayes, nor shall not do *untill* every thing be common, and that there be no Villeynes nor gentlemen, but that we be all as one', Grafton reports him saying (my emphasis).⁵⁶ Ball's vision of the future is dependent both on a longing for a known, Edenic past whose emphasis on 'common' status recalls an essential element of the Golden Age, and present discontent, which requires immediate action to eradicate the social hierarchy. Raphael Holinshed's account of the Great Revolt in *The Third Volume of Chronicles* (1586) reports that Wat Tyler demanded not an absence of hierarchy to make all in common, but rather that 'all warrens, waters, parks and woods should be common' for the purposes of hunting and fishing access for the poor.⁵⁷ In Jack Cade, Shakespeare conflates the characters of Ball and Tyler that we encounter in Grafton's and Holinshed's respective accounts, and this dramatic expediency erases any explicit connection between the church and its role as a source of rebellion in the Revolt (a source to which Ball, according to Holinshed, was unconnected).⁵⁸ While Shakespeare's dramaturgy maintains the suspicion of nostalgia articulated by those religious and dramatic texts mocking Catholicism, he sets aside explicit religious critique to emphasise economic and political gains, a future prosperity, as the source of nostalgia's success with the rebels.

Shakespeare had recourse to historical precedent for nostalgic rhetoric through another maxim, one that became associated with Ball in various chronicles and which was dramatised around the same time as *2 Henry VI*'s first production (as *The First Part of the Contention*). As Holinshed and John Stow both record, Ball used the aphorism, 'When Adam delv'd, and Eve span, / Who was then a gentleman?' to interrogate England's hierarchical society and rally rebels to his cause. Stow describes how Ball's *paroemia* 'infect[ed]' the people, suggesting the proverb's dangerously contagious power in a manner decidedly opposite to the salutary effects imagined by Caius in this chapter's epigraph.⁵⁹ In *2 Henry VI*, to Stafford's accusation that Cade's father was 'a plasterer, / And thou thyself a shearman', Cade replies, 'And Adam was a gardener' (4.2.109–110, 111).⁶⁰ His curt response calls up these associations, repeating the status conflict with which the scene began. *The life and death of Jack Straw* (1591–2), an anonymous history play dramatising the eponymous Great Revolt leader, recreates a historical scene from Blackheath where

Ball is reported to have spoken the Adam/Eve adage.[61] In that play, which possesses verbal and structural parallels with *2 Henry VI*, Parson Ball initiates the drama's exploration of socio-economic inequity:

> England is grone to such a passe of late,
> That rich men triumph to see the poore beg at their gate.
> But I am able by good scripture before you to prove,
> That God doth not this dealing allow nor love.
> But when Adam delved, and Eve span,
> Who was then a Gentleman.
> [. . .]
> But merrily with the world it went,
> When men eat berries of the hauthorne tree,
> And thou helpe me, Ile helpe thee.[62]

Drawing first on the now familiar trope of England's decline, Ball then explicitly links the world's former merriment with the interrogation of a hierarchical society and the implied creation of status difference. Significantly, that explicit connection is suggested in another contemporary source of the Adam and Eve proverb, writer and Queen's Men's playwright Robert Greene's *A quip for an upstart courtier* (1592). Through the voice of 'cloth breeches', Greene interrogates the socio-economic strata that determine an individual's worth, demanding:

> Mounsier Malapart are you therefore my superiour, because you are taken up with Gentlemen, and I with the yeomanry? Doth true vertue consist in riches, or humanity in welth? Is auncient honour tied to o[u]tward bravery? Or not rather true Nobility, a mind excellently qualified with rare vertues? I will teach thee a lesson worth the hearing, proud princocks, how Gentility first sprung upe, I will not forget the olde wives logick, when Adam delvd and Eve span, who was then a Gentleman?[63]

Greene's claims against inequality based on status rely on *paroemia* as the summary and potent climax of his argument. His dialogue indicates the currency of the complaint – of this discontented language and the relationship between a perfect past embodied in a 'merry world'/Eden and the intolerable present peppered with 'upstart' gentry.

In historical, dramatic and prose sources contemporary with Shakespeare, a nostalgic rhetoric of temporal displacement and present dissatisfaction circulated in print and performance. This circulation reveals not simply the topicality of Nick's line, that it responds to concerns present in the early 1590s; in its larger dramatic context, this line is part of the drama's reflection on how nostalgic rhetoric works and why it is persuasive. Simultaneously, the rebel's complaint collapses past and present: in its nature as proverb, as 'old wives logick', the line is both contemporaneous and past, in a sense old and tired – and therefore available to be mocked, as Protestant writers mocked Catholic contemporaries. Howsoever he repeats a 'rallying cry', Nick produces a nostalgic statement that Shakespeare uses first to establish a motive for rebellion but which he also employs to create distance between his spectators and the nostalgic project that the rebels, and then the crown, construct.

The status conflict established by Nick's *paroemia* continues with the rebels' ruminations on the state of the commonwealth, and their language affirms nostalgia's association with that conflict. Amplifying the lament of the rising gentry, his fellow rebel George declares, 'O miserable age! Virtue is not regarded in handicraftsmen'; Nick adds that 'The nobility think scorn to go in leather aprons' (4.2.8–9).[64] His rhetoric calls attention to the visual markers of rank, and in coupling that observation with his invocation of a 'miserable age', George suggests – like Nick, and like Parson Ball in *Jack Straw* – that elitist behaviour and the rise of the gentry are developments characteristic of *this* time, Elizabethan England, even though it's dressed up dramatically to look like the medieval past. Creating a causal relationship between the present's inferiority and the gentry's ascension, Nick and George's discourse imagines a temporal rupture that has distanced them from a golden age when socio-economic hierarchies did not exist.

2 Henry VI translates chronicle record into both the rebels' longing for an equitable, bygone past and their demand for future equity. The implicit desire for the past's reclamation constructs the context of Jack Cade's success, but it is not until Cade offers his audience a future, a utopic Land of Cockaigne, that they laud and accept him. '[V]ow[ing] reformation', Cade promises

> There shall be in England seven half-penny loaves sold for a penny; the three hooped pot shall have ten hoops, and I will make it felony to drink small beer. All the realm shall be in common, and in Cheapside shall my palfrey go to grass.   (4.2.55, 56–60)[65]

In a future mood evocative of Tamburlaine, and adding that 'There shall be no money' and 'all shall eat and drink on my score' (4.2.62–3), Cade rhetorically crafts an utterly unknown world, despite the familiarity of his cry for all to be in common.[66] His vision, moreover, arguably glances at mock fantasies like the polemicist Fielde's, whose imagined Catholics lamented just this sort of 'golden world [. . .] when we had 24 egges for a peny [. . .] then we had a mery world, and all things plenty'. Cade's appeal to a shared, imagined space – a collective unknown – and the suggestion that that space is not only reclaimable but close at hand foments action and rouses Cade's followers, silencing their caustic asides. It is these utopic, and admittedly carnivalesque, fundamentals of Cade's vision which are crucially persuasive, rather than Cade himself. While various critics argue for the persuasive power of carnival to account for Cade's attractiveness and power, 'carnival' is not enough to address the rebels' motives, which Shakespeare is at pains to set up from the beginning of 4.2. This play consistently thinks about the status of the poor in contrast with their rulers, as the episode of Simpcox and his wife illustrate. When the beadles chase Simpcox away, his wife pleads to an unforgiving Gloucester, 'Alas, sir, we did it for pure need' (2.1.147). The petition against Suffolk for enclosing the Melford commons and the Queen's subsequent tearing of the petitioners' complaints (1.3.22–3, 36–9), and Gloucester's reference to the 'needy commons' (3.1.116), further exemplify the play's awareness of the material consequences status difference creates.[67] 2 *Henry VI*'s audience would be familiar with mocking Catholicism's fantasised longing for the past, but irrespective of their social status playgoers would also understand the appeal of being offered a choicer alternative to their present lot. The tension thus created by the undesirable Cade and the attractiveness of his proposal provides a morally complicated scenario, in which the *ethos* of the rhetor conflicts with what he offers and in which nostalgia plays a crucial role in establishing such an offer's tantalising nature.

Ironically, Cade embodies the present's implicit superiority over the past and the future, as the 'before' he seeks to reconstruct assumes increasingly grotesque elements. He would have England revert to its feudal laws, as he plunges further into a bygone era:

> The proudest peer in the realm shall not wear a head on his shoulders, unless he pay me tribute; there shall not a maid be married, but she shall pay to me her maidenhead ere they have it; men shall hold of me *in capite*; and we charge and command that their wives be as free as heart can wish or tongue can tell. (4.7.99–103).[68]

Cade's correct use of current and historical legal terms like 'in capite' reveals how his own knowledge of history and law is extensive enough to pervert its course, and he may represent the same educated men he publicly denounces; he is no malapropistic Dogberry.[69] His use of 'tribute' further fashions himself as an absolute ruler capable of demanding a price for peace (glancing again at Tamburlaine, perhaps). His claim to the *droit de seigneur*, then, aggrandises such a statement which is grossly literal rather than historically accurate.[70] Furthermore, the speech marks a policy shift for Cade, as it turns away from his first appeal to the Kentish rebels, when he proclaimed his programme would improve both their lives and the 'threadbare' commonwealth, as Nick describes it (4.2.6). Cade's upside-down world destroys one English institution after another – from the aristocracy (whose members he seeks out and murders, and whose rituals are rendered meaningless when he knights himself), to the end of record-keeping and rejection of education, to the rule of law (upon Dick the Butcher's plea, Cade's 'mouth shall be the Parliament of England', 4.7.11). In Cade's accusations against Lord Saye (4.7.18–35), *2 Henry VI* affirms the danger of his future fantasies and the nostalgic desires that drive his followers. In one of the play's many moments of pitch-black comedy, Cade uses Saye's humanist commitment to demand his execution: in building a grammar school he 'hast most traitorously corrupted the youth of the realm' (4.7.24–5). He employs a nostalgic invocation of a time of ignorance – akin to the Protestants' derisive imaginings of Catholic longings – to accuse Saye, proclaiming that 'whereas before, our forefathers had no other books but the score and the tally, thou hast caused printing to be used, and, contrary to the King his crown and dignity, thou hast built a paper mill' (4.7.25–8).[71] Here, 'forefathers' links an ignorant past with nostalgic desire, and Cade's vision of the future now problematically resembles that past.

Ultimately, Cade's ambitions and his followers' hopes are thwarted by Lord Clifford's own strategy of nostalgic desire, one that articulates the past's promise of the future. Situating Henry V at the centre of that longing, Clifford persuades the rebels to put down arms against England and take them up against France, and he succeeds because his rhetoric reorients his auditors' nostalgic fantasies. Clifford's success may seem to be the state's unavoidable containment of subversion; Buckingham and he offer 'free pardon', and the lords employ other engines of persuasion such as flattery ('you are strong and manly' 4.8.8, 47).[72] However, it is not the state's authority alone that persuades the rebels, but rather what Clifford's rhetoric proposes to them. First offering the rebels a choice of two futures – the king's mercy or death – he finds it necessary to persuade them that mercy is indeed preferable to death, instructing them that 'Who hateth him [the king] and honours not his father, / Henry the Fifth, that made all France to quake, / Shake he his weapon at us, and pass by' (4.8.15–17). Clifford not only shames the rebels for potentially abandoning their national hero, he also suggests that they dishonour their own fathers. For a brief moment the audience also hears the ambiguity of 'who [...] honours not his father', and Clifford implies the significance of forefathers that *The Contention* makes explicit.[73] Ever the alert orator, Cade answers nostalgia with nostalgia, and in both *2 Henry VI* and *The Contention*, he invokes the idea of an 'ancient freedom' to persuade his followers to remain. Like Clifford, he too attempts to shame them, declaring: 'I thought ye would never have given out these arms till you had recovered your ancient freedom. But you are all recreants and dastards, and delight to live in slavery to the nobility' (4.8.23–5).[74] Once more the promise of a political inheritance is activated in the play, and Clifford himself continues this *topos*, again trotting out Henry V to win back the rebels. He asks:

> Is Cade the son of Henry the Fifth
> That thus you do exclaim you'll go with him?
> Will he conduct you through the heart of France
> And make the meanest of you earls and dukes?
> [. . .]
> Methinks already in this civil broil
> I see them [the French] lording it in London streets,
> Crying '*Vigliocco*' unto all they meet.
> Better ten-thousand base-born Cades miscarry
> Than you should stoop unto a Frenchman's mercy.
> To France! To France! And get what you have lost!
> Spare England, for it is your native coast.
> Henry hath money, you are strong and manly;
> God on our side, doubt not of victory. (4.8.30–3, 40–8)

Clifford relies on both the opportunity that the rebels' capture affords him and the proven power of evoking a legendary past to persuade the rebels to allegiance to the crown. His invocation of Henry V's fabled status-shifting, making 'the meanest' into 'earls and dukes', addresses the anxieties that fuelled Nick's nostalgic *paroemia*. Clifford's offer of honour and the reclamation of England's inheritance implicitly promises the rebels a preferable future, one that will allow them to live, through posterity, in the annals of the past. First, however, he must threaten an alternative future – one in which Frenchmen rule London – before promising a more desirable vision that turns on the question of what was 'lost'. Arguably *The Contention* makes more of this question of political inheritance, as the play draws towards its close with York's declaration of his own rightful inheritance: 'fortunate this fight hath bene, / I hope to us and ours, for Englands good, / And our great honour, that so long we lost, / Whilst faint-heart Henry did usurpe our rights' (TLN 2203–6). By destabilising the idea of reclaiming what is 'lost' and past practice's status as 'lost', *2 Henry VI* and *The Contention* stage a suspicion of nostalgic narratives.

Clifford glosses history to appropriate the fantasies which the rebels had allied with Cade's golden age future and the image of an England without economic constraint. He appeals not only to their ability to idealise the past and future to urge them to resurrect Henry and conquer France again, but to their sense of *duty* to the past – what Shakespeare in *1 Henry VI* casts as a particularly English characteristic.[75] Clifford's speech capitalises simultaneously on the politic opportunity to rally the rebels' discontent around a utopian ideal and on the personal motive for honour and, perhaps, equality. Following the rebels' final desertion of Cade (in a line absent from Q), he bitterly laments, 'The name of Henry the Fifth hales them to an hundred mischiefs, and makes them leave me desolate' (4.8.52–3).[76] The play's final invocation of its shadow figure is Cade's final acknowledgement that he has failed in his own struggle to rely on past fantasy to claim and determine the future.

In *2 Henry VI*, nostalgic discourse is designed to disclose its status as rhetoric and its inherently ambivalent, always-available nature. Clifford's persuasive speech reveals the commons' susceptibility to idealisations of the past in the future, in a manner similar to how Cade's money-less promised land of common property exploits nostalgic longing for a pre-lapsarian state. The allure of recreating a perfect past in the future is implied in Protestant polemicists' and dramatists' mocking texts, which sought to demonise any language of the 'old days', and old ways, of a potentially preferable, Catholic past and to evacuate any desirability from that past. These writers share with the Queen's Men, Marlowe and Peele a suspicion of nostalgia that, across their works, orients temporal awareness away from the past and towards the preferable Elizabethan present. Where these writers seek to disconnect the claims of that idealised past, Shakespeare demonstrates how central the idealised past is to imagining, and acting for, the future. The use of nostalgia by various characters in *2 Henry VI* reveals its dangerous fluidity, and consequently Shakespeare demystifies the *topos* of the proverbial 'merry world' or 'merry England', as the play dramatically employs this cultural commonplace to reveal the instability of such constructions. *2 Henry VI* illustrates how nostalgia may be appropriated not solely as the voice of the state, or as the voice of dissent, but as a rhetoric that highlights its own constructed nature. In doing so it offers a model of dramatic nostalgic discourse that had not yet been seen on the Elizabethan stage.

Notes

1. John Caius, *A boke, or counseill against the disease commonly called the sweate, or sweatyng sicknesse* (London, 1552), Dvii^{r-v}.
2. On Caius's confessional position, see Vivian Nutton, 'Caius, John (1510–1573)', *Oxford Dictionary of National Biography* (Oxford: Oxford University Press, 2004) [http://www.oxforddnb.com/view/article/4351, accessed 12 December 2009]. His invocation has been a favourite amongst

scholars writing on the 'merry world', who have been interested in Caius's remarks both as a response to Edwardian reforms and in their vague specificity – when precisely 'Englande' was 'merye' can only be conjectured. See Baldo, *Memory in Shakespeare's Histories*, p. 82, and Phillips, *Nostalgia in Print and Performance*, pp. 39–40.

3. Phillips, *Nostalgia in Print and Performance*, p. 24, and see pp. 31–59; Ronald Hutton, *The Rise and Fall of Merry England: The Ritual Year 1400–1700* (Oxford: Oxford University Press, 1994), esp. pp. 5–39; Duffy, *The Stripping of the Altars*; and David Knowles, *Bare Ruined Choirs: The Dissolution of the English Monasteries* (Cambridge: Cambridge University Press, 1976).

4. Recent scholarship has further complicated an already complicated history for *2 Henry VI* (F, 1623), the play also known as *The First Part of the Contention Betwixt the Two Famous Houses of York and Lancaster* (Q, 1594). Across the Q and F texts, the use of nostalgia establishes an image of the future that persuades individuals to political action. I will provide the Q readings in the chapter endnotes. The latest research argues that *2 Henry VI* is a collaborative text, for which we have evidence of Shakespeare, Marlowe and possibly another author (or authors). This evidence remains contested, as does the exact textual relationship between *The Contention* and *2 Henry VI* and the manuscripts that lie behind those texts. On the most recent developments in the authorship debate see: John V. Nance, '"We, John Cade": Shakespeare, Marlowe, and the authorship of 4.2.33–189 *2 Henry VI*', *Shakespeare*, 13:1 (2017), 30–51; Gary Taylor and Rory Loughnane, 'The Canon and Chronology', in *The New Oxford Authorship Companion*, ed. Gary Taylor and Gabriel Egan (Oxford: Oxford University Press, 2017), pp. 417–602, 493–6. For a newly revised date of *2 Henry VI* and *The Contention*, see Taylor and Loughnane, 'The Canon and Chronology', p. 493.

5. Shakespeare, Marlowe and others, *2 Henry VI*, ed. Rory Loughnane in *The New Oxford Shakespeare*, gen. ed. Gary Taylor et al. (Oxford: Oxford University Press, 2017), 4.2.6–7. All future citations of the play will be made in the text. The Q text reads: 'Twas never merry world with us, since these gentle men came up' (TLN 1556), in *The First Part of the Contention (1594)*, prep. William Montgomery, the Malone Society Reprints (Oxford, 1985). Segarra et al. assign this scene to Shakespeare in Santiago Segarra, Mark Eisen, Gabriel Egan and Alejandro Ribeiro, 'Attributing the Authorship of the Henry VI Plays by Word Adjacency', *Shakespeare Quarterly*, 67:2 (2016), 232–56. Marlowe uses the word 'merry' only three times (in *Dido Queen of Carthage*) and never in this proverbial manner. Louis Ule, *A Concordance to the Works of Christopher Marlowe*, The Elizabethan Concordance Series, ed. Jean Jofen (Hildesheim and New York: Georg Olms, 1979), p. 493. Shakespeare uses the 'merry world' proverb two additional times: in *Twelfth Night* at 3.1.98 and in *Measure for Measure* at 3.2.5.

6. In Q, Gloucester 'must unfold his griefe' (TLN 99).

7. Henry Peacham, *The Garden of Eloquence*, Dii^v. For Puttenham it is a 'Figure of False Semblant or Dissimulation', *The Art of English Poesy by George Puttenham: A Critical Edition*, ed. Frank Whigham and Wayne

A. Rebhorn (Ithaca, NY and London: Cornell University Press, 2007), pp. 271–3.
8. See William Barker, ed., *A Selection from Erasmus's Adages* (Toronto and London: University of Toronto Press, 2001); James Obelkevich, 'Proverbs and Social History', in *The Social History of Language*, ed. Peter Burke and Roy Porter (Cambridge: Cambridge University Press, 1997), pp. 3–72, at p. 4; R. S. Boggs, 'Proverb Lore', *South Atlantic Bulletin*, 3:4 (1938), 1 & 7.
9. Obelkevich, 'Proverbs', p. 56. 'It was never a merry world since $x \ldots$' is a formula R. W. Dent identifies in his *Shakespeare's Proverbial Language: An Index* (Berkeley and London: University of California Press, 1981), W.878.1, p. 259. Tilley's ground-breaking study locates seventy-two proverbs in *2 Henry VI*, but doesn't include 'merry world'; Morris Palmer Tilley, ed., *Dictionary of the Proverbs in England in the Sixteenth and Seventeenth Centuries* (Ann Arbor: University of Michigan Press, 1950), p. 806.
10. Obelkevich, 'Proverbs', p. 65; on 'we say', see Tilley, *Dictionary*, p. v.
11. Tilley, *Dictionary*, pp. vii, viii.
12. John Calvin, *Little booke of John Calvines concernynge offences*, trans. Arthur Golding (London, 1567), Diii^v. 'Atqui nunquam magis saevis belorum tempestatibus concussus orbit fuit: nunquam tam multiplici profundaque marlorum colluvie submersus', John Calvin, *De Scandalis* (1550), in *Joannis Calvini Opera Selecta, vol. II: Scripta Calvini ab 1542 usque ad annum 1564 editos continens*, ed. Petrus Barth and Guilelmus Niesel (Eugene, OR: Wipf & Stock, 2011), p. 183, ll. 5–7.
13. Calvin, *Little booke*, Diii^v; 'pax ubique et alta quies', Calvin, *De Scandalis*, p. 183, l. 8.
14. John Carr, *The ruinous fal of prodigality with the notable examples of the best aprooved aucthours which hath bin written of the same* (London, 1573), C^r.
15. The *OED* credits the play with the word's creation, and in the sense of 'scoffer', the word circulated in England through the early seventeenth century. Cf. 'hick'scorner, n.' and 'hick, n.' *OED Online*, June 2017, Oxford University Press. http://www.oed.com/view/Entry/86700?redirectedFrom=hick+scorner (accessed 10 July 2015). For dating, see Ian Lancashire, ed., *Two Tudor Interludes: The Interlude of Youth and Hick Scorner* (Manchester and Baltimore, MD: Manchester University Press/Johns Hopkins University Press, 1980), pp. 22–4; and Eleanor Rycroft, 'Morality, Theatricality, and Masculinity in The Interlude of Youth and Hick Scorner', in *The Oxford Handbook of Tudor Drama*, ed. Thomas Betteridge and Greg Walker (Oxford: Oxford University Press, 2012), pp. 465–81.
16. Captain Cox (fl. 1575) includes *Hick Scorner* in his collection of books; on 15 January 1582 *Hick Scorner* was licensed with other 'plaiebookes' to John Charlewood, in Edward Arber, ed., *A Transcript of the registers of the Company of Stationers of London, 1554–1640*, vol. ii, fol. 186^r–186^v. Rights for Charlewood's plays passed to his widow's new husband, James Roberts, on 31 May 1594; Lancashire, *Interludes*, pp. 5, 10. Geoffrey Bullough includes *Hick Scorner* as an 'Analogue' to *2 Henry IV* in *The Narrative and Dramatic Sources of Shakespeare*, IV (London: Routledge and Kegan Paul, 1962), pp. 267, 292–9; Rycroft, 'Morality, Theatricality,

and Masculinity', p. 471. On Protestant use of Catholic texts, see Gillian Woods, *Shakespeare's Unreformed Fictions* (Oxford: Oxford University Press, 2013), pp. 1–24.
17. Lancashire, *Interludes*, l. 329. Additional references will be made in the text.
18. This is the final refrain of *The maner of the world now a dayes*, a poem (or ballad) published c. 1590 but versions of which were in circulation in the late fifteenth century. See Lancashire, *Interludes*, pp. 204, 266.
19. On the Protestant construction of that longing, see Phillips, *Nostalgia in Print and Performance*, pp. 31–69. The uniformity of Catholic longing is part of the fantasy; on Catholic nostalgia see Keith Thomas, *The Perception of the Past in Early Modern England*, The Creighton Trust Lecture (London: University of London, 1983), pp. 11–13; Alison Shell, *Catholicism, Controversy and the English Literary Imagination, 1558–1660* (Cambridge: Cambridge University Press, 1999), p. 109ff.
20. Gracious Menewe, *A plaine subversyon* (Wesel, 1555), Ee.v[r]. James Frederic Mozley, in *Coverdale and His Bibles* (London: Lutterworth Press, 1953) suggests that Menewe is a pseudonym for Becon; Samuel Halkett and John Laing accept it in their *Dictionary of Anonymous and Pseudonymous English Literature*, rev. and enlarg. edn (Edinburgh and London: Oliver & Boyd, 1926–62), p. 332. Seymour Baker House makes no mention of 'Gracious Menewe' as one of Becon's pseudonyms, placing him in Germany at this time; S. B. House, 'Becon, Thomas (1512/13–1567)', *Oxford Dictionary of National Biography* (Oxford: Oxford University Press, September 2004; online edn, October 2009).
21. Becon and Foxe knew each other in exile, see House, 'Becon, Thomas'.
22. John Foxe, *Actes and monuments*, vol. 2 (London, 1583), XXXxii[r].
23. John Fielde, *A caveat for Parsons Howlet* (London, 1581), t.p.
24. Ibid., Dviii[v]–E[r]. My emphasis.
25. Fielde, *A caveat for Parsons Howlet*, E[r].
26. Henry Smith, *A fruitfull sermon upon part of the 5. chapter of the first epistle of Saint Paule to the Thessalonians* (London, 1591), C6[r]. Smith was lecturer of St Clement Danes, whose patron, William Cecil, Lord Burghley, was the brother of Smith's stepmother Margaret. Anthony à Wood reported that people stood in alleyways to listen to him. Gary W. Jenkins, 'Smith, Henry (c.1560–1591)', *Oxford Dictionary of National Biography* (Oxford: Oxford University Press, 2004) [http://www.oxforddnb.com/view/article/25811]. See also Patrick Collinson, *The Religion of Protestants: The Church in English Society 1559–1625* (Oxford: Oxford University Press, 1982), p. 231.
27. In the 1599 Geneva Bible, this is Jeremiah 44.17–19, the marginal note explicitly connecting the verse to Catholic practice: 'it seemeth that the Papists gathered of this place *Salve Regina*, and *Regina caeli latare*, calling the virgin Mary Queen of heaven, and so of the blessed virgin and mother of our Savior Christ, made an idol'.
28. William Burton, *Ten sermons* (London, 1602), K8[r]. Dent dates the sermon to 1594, *Shakespeare's Proverbial Language*, p. 259.
29. Cf. Shell, *Catholicism*, and Woods, *Shakespeare's Unreformed Fictions*.
30. Annabel Patterson, *Shakespeare and the Popular Voice* (Cambridge, MA: Blackwell, 1989), pp. 41–2, at 42.

31. Harding, *A confutation of a booke intituled An apologie of the Church of England* (London, 1565), G2ᵛ; cited in Jewel, *A defence of the Apologie of the Church of England* (London, 1567), Eᵛ.
32. Harding, *An answere to Maister Juelles chalenge* (Louvain, 1564), 'To the Reader', *iiʳ.
33. Jewel, *A defence*, Eiiʳ.
34. Jewel, *A defence*, Eiiʳ. For further discussion of this verse, see pp. 19–20.
35. John Guy, *Tudor England* (Oxford: Oxford University Press, 1988), p. 126; this citation is from *Letters and Papers Foreign and Domestic of the Reign of Henry VIII*, 21 vols (London, 1862–1910, 1929–32), 16 (1540–1), pp. 48–9.
36. Sir William Thomas, *A speech of William Thomas* (London, 1641), C2ʳ–C2ᵛ.
37. Baker, *A chronicle of the Kings of England* (London, 1643), Eee2ʳ.
38. For an extensive discussion of the problems of dating and ordering the three extant print editions of the interlude, see J. M. Nosworthy, 'Introduction', in R. Wever, *An Enterlude Called Lusty Juventus*, prepared for the Malone Society by Nosworthy (Oxford: the Malone Society, 1966/1971), pp. v–xxii.
39. Cf. John Doebler, 'Beaumont's *The Knight of the Burning Pestle* and the Prodigal Son Plays', *Studies in English Literature, 1500–1900*, 5:2 (1965), Elizabethan and Jacobean Drama, 333–44, 333–4.
40. P. M. King, 'Minority Plays: Two Interludes for Edward VI', *Medieval English Theatre*, 15 (1993), 87–102, 87–8.
41. R. Wever, *Lusty Juventus*, C.iii, ll. 655–62. Further references will be made in the text.
42. King, 'Minority Plays', 93.
43. Anon [Nicholas Udall?], *Respublica* (1553), in *Tudor Interludes*, ed. Peter Happé (Harmondsworth, 1972), 5.5.1–7.
44. The play is underlined in the manuscript. Shakespeare and others, *The Book of Sir Thomas More*, ed. W. W. Greg, The Malone Society Reprints, rev. Harold Jenkins (Oxford: Oxford University Press, 1911, 1961, 1990), Scene IX, ll. 918, 919–22 (manuscript fol. 14b), 31. Further citations will be made in the text. This scene is written by S (Scribe), identified as Anthony Munday, 'Supplement to the Introduction', p. xxxiv.
45. See Happé, ed., *Tudor Interludes*, pp. 417–18, n 14.
46. These scenes have been the recent focus of scholars' arguments concerning the play's authorship. Citing Segarra et al., Taylor and Loughnane attribute 4.2, 4.4, 4.6, 4.8, 4.9 to Shakespeare and 4.1, 4.3, 4.5, 4.7 to Marlowe; Taylor and Loughnane, 'The Canon and Chronology', p. 496. The lines I analyse remain attributed to Shakespeare, as are all the scenes relevant to my arguments.
47. 'Nick. [. . .] Twas never merry world with us, since these gentle men came up' (TLN 1556).
48. Craig A. Bernthal, 'Jack Cade's Legal Carnival', *Studies in English Literature 1500–1900*, 42:2 (2002), 259–74, 268.
49. Stephen Greenblatt, 'Murdering Peasants: Status, Genre, and the Representation of Rebellion', *Representations*, 1 (1983), 1–29, 23, 24; Nance, '"We John Cade"', 48; Bernthal, 'Jack Cade's Legal Carnival', 260.

50. Cf. TLN 1571–1601.
51. In Q, the lines comparable to those at 4.7 take place at TLN 1596–1601 (4.2).
52. Bernthal, 'Jack Cade's Legal Carnival', 260, 259.
53. Buchanan Sharp, *In Contempt of All Authority: Artisans and Riot in the West of England, 1586–1640* (Berkeley: University of California Press, 1980), pp. 38–9, p. 39 citing PRO, S.P. 14/28/64.
54. Thomas Cartelli, 'Jack Cade in the Garden: Class Consciousness and Class Conflict in 2 *Henry VI*', in *Enclosure Acts: Sexuality, Property, and Culture in Early Modern England*, ed. Richard Burt and John Michael Archer (Ithaca and London: Cornell University Press, 1994), pp. 48–67, p. 54.
55. Richard Grafton, *A Chronicle at Large* (1569) cited in Bullough, *Narrative and Dramatic Sources*, III, p. 128. Ball is 'John Wall' in Grafton's text.
56. Ibid., p. 129.
57. Holinshed, *Third Volume of Chronicles* (London, 1586), Rr.v^r.
58. Ibid., Ssi^r; Stow reports that he was excommunicated, *The Annales of England* (London, 1592), fol. 458.
59. Holinshed, *Third Volume of the Chronicles*, Ssi^r. Stow's disapproving account of Ball's sermon at Blackheath includes Ball's comparison between past and present as crucial argumentation for immediate political action and government overthrow; Stow, *Annales*, fol. 458, and cf. Froissart, *Here begynneth the first volum of sir Iohan Froyssart of the cronycles of Englande, Fraunce, Spayne, Portyngale, Scotlande, Bretayne, Flau[n]ders: and other places adjoynynge. Tra[n]slated out of frenche into our maternall englysshe tonge, by Johan Bourchier knight lorde Berners [. . .]* (London, 1523), ddd^{r-v}.
60. 'Stafford. [. . .] his father was but a Brick-laier. / Cade. And Adam was a Gardner, what then?' (TLN 1640–1). Shakespeare makes comic use of Ball's proverb in the Gravediggers' scene in *Hamlet*, ed. Ann Thomson and Neil Taylor (London, 2006), 5.1.29–33.
61. On the date of *Jack Straw*, see Forker, 'Marlowe's *Edward II*', p. 59.
62. Anon, *The life and death of Jack Straw* (London, 1594), A4^r–A4^v.
63. Greene, *A quip for an upstart courtier*, B2^r; he repeats the 'world was never' idea: 'the world was never in quiet devotion, neighbourhoode nor hospitality never flourished in this land, since such up start boies & shittle witted fooles became of the ministry', E4^v.
64. '*George*. I warrant thee, thou shalt never see a Lord weare a leather aperne now-a-daies' (TLN 1557–8). 'Now-a-daies' echoes many of the sources discussed (e.g. *Hick Scorner, Respublica*).
65. '*Cade*. [. . .] you shall have seven half-penny loaves for a penny, and the three hoopt pot, shall have ten hoopes, and it shall be felony to drinke small beere' (TLN 1589–92).
66. 'All [shall] eate and drinke on my score' (TLN 1594–5).
67. Simpcox's wife's line is absent from Q. Compare TLN 333–9, where it is Suffolk who tears the petition, and TLN 1043.
68. 'There shall not a noble man weare a head on his shoulders, / But he shall paie me tribute for it. / Nor there shal not a mayd be married, but he shal fee to me for her. / Maydenhead or else, ile have it my selfe, / Marry I will

that married men shall hold of me in capitie, / And that their wives shalbe as free as hart can thinke, or toong can tell' (TLN 1828–33).

69. From *tenere in capite*, to hold land 'in chief', that is 'directly from the Crown', 'in capite, adv.'. *OED* Online, June 2017, Oxford University Press. http://www.oed.com/view/Entry/301090?redirectedFrom=in+capite (accessed 19 October 2017).
70. Knowles, ed., *King Henry VI Part 2*, p. 326n.
71. Q valorises the 'score and tally' in three different forms, at TLN 1596–7, TLN 1614–15 and finally alongside Cade's vision that 'all things shall be in common, and in Cheapeside shall my palphrey go to grasse' (TLN 1771–2, 1773–4).
72. In Q, Clifford tells the rebels that the king 'mildly hath sent his pardon' if they abandon Cade (TLN 1865).
73. 'Why country-men and warlike friends of Kent, / What meanes this mutinous rebellions, / That you in troopes do muster thus your selves, / Under the conduct of this Traitor Cade? / To rise against your soveraigne Lord and King, / Who mildly hath his pardon sent to you, / If you forsake this monstrous Rebell here? / If honour be the marke whereat you aime, / Then haste to France that our forefathers wonne, / And winne again that thing which now is lost' (TLN 1860–9). Clifford's use of 'forefathers' and their French victories suggests Henry V's image and campaign.
74. 'Why how now, will you forsake your general, / And ancient freedome which you have possest? / To bend your neckes under their servile yokes, / Who if you stir, will straightwaies hang you up' (TLN 1873–4).
75. Cf. Jerome Mazzaro, 'Shakespeare's "Books of Memory": *1* and *2 Henry VI*', *Comparative Drama* (2001/2002), 393–414, 401, 402.
76. Both Q and F texts include references to Henry V that the other doesn't, but *2 Henry VI* invokes the hero's name more consistently than *The Contention*; see TLN 1658–62 and 4.2.131–3.

Chapter 3

In the Mean Season:
Richard II's Absent Hospitality

In his seminal *The Country and the City* (1973), Raymond Williams captures the impossibility of satiating the nostalgic in his image of an unending, time-travelling escalator. For every generation, its predecessor offers salvation, some respite from the perceived degeneration and decline of the present.[1] The escalator symbolises the sense of a ceaseless descent into the past to search for perfection, for refuge. Of equal importance and symbolism is the escalator's inherent rejection of return. As I emphasised in the Introduction, through various discourses early modern English culture articulated possibilities of reclaiming or renewing the past. These discourses arguably augment the rhetorical power of claims to return to an idealised past. While *The Country and the City* has informed theories of early modern hospitality, early modern discourses of hospitality themselves trouble the singular direction of Williams's striking metaphor. Felicity Heal's definitive study of early modern hospitality relies partly on Williams' recognition of a *mythos* emergent from the dichotomy of rural and urban, country and city. As Heal's analysis of early modern literature and ballads persuasively argues, this dichotomy is characterised as hospitable (country) and inhospitable (city). Furthermore, a second dichotomy appears alongside it: that of the hospitable past and the inhospitable present.[2] Such an opposition situates hospitality as both a product and inherent quality of an idealised past, and in so doing contributes to the creation of a 'myth of hospitality', the notion that there once was a space and time – a past England – when hospitality was readily available. What sets the nostalgic practitioners of Heal's 'myth of hospitality' apart from the individual on Williams's escalator is how their turn backwards is used to imagine both present and future. In the discourses of early modern England, the hospitable past could return.

Using the *ur*-narrative of hospitality, discourses of the hospitable countryside or the hospitable past could, and did, both censure 'the attitudes of [the] present-minded urban man' and effect a 'call to action', as such demands insisted that the gentry and nobility reproduce their ancestors' behaviour by providing hospitality.³ Latent nostalgia becomes essential to enacting change in the present: to persuade present landowners to be hospitable, the idealised actions of their personal pasts (via their forebears) must be invoked. Hospitality, in this view, operates as one type of English political inheritance. In light of Alexandra Walsham's work on the centrality of landscape to early modern constructions of history and memory, however, this potentially positive return becomes fraught with religious significance. As I discuss below, the iconoclasts' desire to eradicate the past through material destruction transformed the presence of pre-Reformation ruins, spaces associated with the positive practice of hospitality, into dangerous sites of popery.⁴ *Richard II* translates this potent duality inherent in calling up the idealised past – its potential for both hope and heresy – into an ambivalent nostalgia. Lost hospitality forms a crucial part of the play's nostalgic rhetoric, as the necessity of hospitality to England's well-being forms a cornerstone of that longing. As in *2 Henry VI*, in *Richard II* Shakespeare stages unequivocally the power of such longing and its attendant future fantasies, which together inspire the play's political action.

In 1596 the Privy Council issued a directive on hospitality as a means of 'stay[ing]' the ongoing dearth in England at the time, and the directives in place by 1595/96, when *Richard II* was first performed, together with England's larger socio-economic situation, offer an important discursive context for the play.⁵ First, the dearth itself would certainly have stimulated a collective consideration of the past and its superiority to the present time of famine. Second, the directive represents the crown's recognition that a structure of useful aid was lacking or, at the least, failing; the crown then identified hospitality as both a needful tradition and one that had deteriorated. In what follows, I argue that in *Richard II* England's absent hospitality provides a political ground for John of Gaunt's and the Duke of Northumberland's reclamatory nostalgia, which fuels the play's rebellion. Shakespeare, however, uses both that absent hospitality and its attendant nostalgia to place his tragedy in a 'mean season', a flawed in-between time that reveals the imperfection of past and future.⁶

This chapter's historicist analysis and attention to hospitality bring together two critical approaches to *Richard II* that have characterised recent work on the play and Shakespeare studies more broadly. Historical analyses have been interested in identifying contemporary political parallels between the Earl of Essex as Bolingbroke and Queen Elizabeth I as Richard, even before the 1601 revolt and Elizabeth's famous retort to William Lambarde, 'I am Richard II, know ye not that?' Additionally, the long-standing critical interest in sovereignty, and more recently in popularity, indicates the play's political stakes.[7] As Jeffrey Doty persuasively argues, the play offers a model of political critique for its audience, one that in effect asks an audience to 'analyse analysis', and I would add that the play's *argumentum in utramque partem* structure invites the audience to critique desire for an idealised past.[8] Critics of *Richard II* have often identified a sense of 'nostalgia' in the play: the celebration of a chivalric code that was praised (and lamented as lost) in Elizabethan England and Gaunt's famous 'Sceptr'd isle' speech are just two commonplace examples. But as this chapter argues, Shakespeare's dramaturgy renders such nostalgia both powerful, as it is deployed to call an idealised future into being, and transgressive.

Hospitality, too, has been increasingly of interest as a critical lens for Shakespeare studies outside of an exclusively historicist practice. Julia Reinhard Lupton uses James C. Gibson's theory of affordances as a means of thinking about hospitality phenomenologically, while Derrida's *Of Hospitality* is a springboard for other scholars interested in an exchange economy.[9] These theorists are more generally concerned with what hospitable practices signify by being (or not being) performed. I am concerned with how *Richard II* laments and stages absent hospitality as a symptom of England's fallen state. In this and in my attention to how the play's patterns of political thought rely on nostalgia, I demonstrate how *Richard II*'s political action depends on constructions of the idealised past. *Richard II* uses pervasive absent hospitality to signal England's degeneration and Richard's misrule. Absent hospitality signifies social and political failure in the play, and it rebounds throughout the drama in shadows of the Dissolution and images of grief, the latter used to highlight the injustices of England's king. Once more departing from critical understandings of nostalgia as oriented exclusively to the past, I argue that *Richard II*'s language of hospitality creates a hopeful nostalgia, one that the play itself will check by pursuing the desires such hope breeds.

Where *2 Henry VI* offered an image of peace and security with the quelling of rebellion, *Richard II* offers rather a 'mean season', an intermediate time of hardship that the play's conclusion does not entirely resolve, despite the fact that its nostalgic discourse suggests a way through that time. From the outset, Shakespeare uses forensic rhetoric – the rhetoric of investigation into the Duke of Gloucester's murder – to establish an idealised past juxtaposed with an oppressive present. Initial deliberation about that present, voiced by Gaunt and the Duchess of Gloucester, gives way to definitive judgement from Gaunt, York and

Northumberland about that present's decline into tyranny, as I discuss. Throughout, the rhetoric of the past's interest in the future reinforces the image of the present as post-lapsarian. Richard's tyranny brackets his present as a temporary 'meanwhile' bounded by an idealised past upon which the future depends. That future collapses, however, as the rhetoric of the perfect past is exchanged for Carlisle's fantasy of a monstrous future. That the hoped-for time to come is itself violent and uncertain casts doubt on the constructions of the past that seemed so convincing in their immediate context of an imperfect now. Within *Richard II*, the *topoi* of an absent or ironically invoked hospitality highlight both the disconnection of the idealised past from the fallen world of the present and Richard's role in denigrating his commonwealth through his 'wasted time'. Shakespeare employs the discourse of hospitality circulating at the time of *Richard II*'s composition, performance and publication to complicate and attenuate the desires on which it is founded.

Locating Elizabethan Hospitality

By November 1596, when *Richard II* had already been staged and was nearing its 1597 publication, England's economic situation was bleak. The dearth England was experiencing coincided with real agricultural prices rising and real wages falling (as they would continue to do so in the succeeding decades); further, from 1596 to 1598, '[p]erhaps two-fifths of the population' fell below the margin of subsistence'.[10] This situation had been deteriorating despite government attempts to cauterise it in previous years: in 1594, 1595 and 1596 the Privy Council issued orders 'for the reliefe and stay of the present dearth of graine'.[11] An overview of the orders for each year suggests that the dearth's severity increased over time, as directives and proscriptions became more detailed and restrictive. The 1594 and 1595 declarations focus primarily on who may buy and sell corn and order the creation of 'juries' in each parish to effectively conduct a census of corn: who uses it, who has it, who might have it, who makes malt with it, who sells it, who has made agreements to buy and sell it. The Privy Council ordered that 'where any Parish is not able to give sufficient relief to such their poore, that Parish to have the supply of such other parishes neere adjoyning, as have fewer poore, and are better able to give reliefe'.[12] However, just as communities were enjoined to provide poor relief, so too were they reminded of its limits. The poor who beg would not be 'suffered', and the Council warned that any township that failed to observe the order 'for the attaching & punishing of the said vagabondes' could be punished with a fine to the entire community.[13] Such policy continued the Henrician state's interest in controlling both the movements of the poor and the conditions of receiving succour. As Ilana Krausman Ben-Amos writes, '[a]lready in 1530 [. . .] some local courts issued orders that no hospitality was to be offered to those [beggars] travelling without a licence'.[14] 'Dearth' and 'hospitality' were vital elements in a government discourse aimed at maintaining social order at a time when hospitality practices themselves were in flux and were even disappearing.[15]

While the 1594 and 1595 declarations restated issues from the previous decade, they also added new requirements that dealt specifically with the scarcity of corn, which echoes as well throughout *Richard II*. These government measures largely concerned alehouses and other sites where corn in the form of malt would be produced or consumed. In 1594 the Privy Council ordered Justices of the Peace (JPs) 'to take viewe of the number of Ale-houses, vitailing houses, and toiling houses in every Towne, Parish, Village, and Hamlet within their Jurisdictions' and consequently to determine which of the said houses were necessary for the towns, parishes, villages and hamlets 'to continue'. The JPs were then responsible for identifying the superfluous houses, 'discharging' them, and permitting only a certain 'convenient number' to remain. 1595 saw a similar but more severe declaration: the Privy Council's concern about alehouses now extended not merely to their number, but to their geographic location. It ordered the Justices 'to allowe [. . .] no more then [sic] shalbe needfull, and those but in places necessarie' in the centre of the town or village.[16] The forced closure of various sites of pleasure, entertainment and to some extent hospitality reflects, perhaps, the programme of the restructuring of social manners that was happening in the 1580s and 1590s.[17] The Council likely believed that restricting the availability of ale and beer would restrict demand and check licentious behaviour in a time of dearth and famine, when the government was especially alert to the possibility of social unrest.

The directives proclaimed in November 1596 strongly suggest that the dearth had worsened by the time of its issuing, and the situation would only continue to decline. By 1598, not only individuals but entire families were seeking relief.[18] Two years prior, the Privy Council demanded the

> [1] observation of former orders against ingrossers, & regraters of corne. 2. And to see the markets furnished with corne. 3. And also against the carying of corne out of the realme. 4. And a prohibition to men of hospitalitie from remooving from their habitation in the time of dearth. 5. And finally a strait commandement to all officers having charge of forts to reside thereon personally, and no inhabitant to depart from the sea coast.[19]

The Council demands again the ban of exports of corn (as it did in 1594–5), but this proclamation explicitly encourages its citizens to inform on those they suspect of exporting, and it offers a financial incentive: informers on those found guilty would receive 'both the halfe of the value of the Corne transported, and the halfe of the fines imposed upon the offenders'.[20] The declaration that those stationed on the sea coast must remain implies a need not only for defence, but for military power to check the country's imports and exports.[21] The increasing extent and gravity of the government's directives suggests the dire situation in England by November, when the Privy Council ordered the practice of hospitality.

The fact that between Henry VIII's 1536 Poor Law and the crisis of the 1590s no Tudor government had issued an order of hospitality highlights not only that mandate's uniqueness and importance. In the government's reaching back to the past to influence contemporary practice, the directives imply the changed priorities of English society.[22] The 1596 Proclamation insists on ensuring hospitality as a viable social practice, demanding that those able to provide hospitality must remain where they are, and those who have left their estates must immediately return. It declares that

> her Majestie is particularly informed of some intentions of sundry persons of abilitie to keepe hospitalitie in their Countreys, to leave their said hospitalities, and to come to the Citie of London, and other Cities and townes corporate, thereby leaving the reliefe of their poore neighbours, as well for foode, as for good rule, and with covetous minds to live in London, and bout the Citie privately, and so also in other Townes corporate, without charge of company.[23]

In dictating the behaviour of those who provide or could provide hospitality in the country, the government politicises hospitality. It suggests that those who have left 'their Countreys' privilege themselves before the kingdom, suggesting that they wish to starve their 'poor neighbours', do not value social order ('good rule'), are avaricious in their actions, and lack Christian virtue through their 'covetous minds' and absent *caritas*. By the Council's account, self-preservation drives the nobility, and those able to provide were shirking their duties to their neighbours in both the intention to remove and the act of removing to London or elsewhere. Rejecting the duties of hospitality in favour of life in London was a self-interested calculation; the capital had more food and fewer hands that wanted to claim it, as the city had access to imported Baltic grain.[24]

Invoking hospitality in the time of dearth had political resonances beyond producing a moral dichotomy of 'good' and 'bad' practitioners and shaming the latter. The proclamation demonstrates again the Privy

Council's interest in maintaining order and stability at a time when the lack of food, especially affordable food, could incite political unrest. Food riots occurred 'spasmodically' in London, the southeast and the southwest in 1595; in the mid-1590s London was generally spared the starvation that afflicted regions north of the capital.[25] Heal argues that '[i]t was in this context [of anxiety about supply and the dangers of disorder] that the notion of hospitality was invoked, as a specific against dearth and as a means by which rural relationships might be stabilised'.[26] The interest in 'stabilisation' is explicit in the 1596 Proclamation, which states that one role of those who provide relief is 'good rule'. Social stability, good rule and the ability to provide: these are the qualities and outcomes of the envisioned practice of hospitality in the closing years of the sixteenth century. Regardless of how it chastises the nobility in the present, the Privy Council's proclamation produces implicitly an image of a future hospitable England. In the declaration, the queen 'chargeth all maner of persons, that shall have any such intention during the time of this dearth, not to breake up their households, nor to come to the said Citie, or other townes corporate'. Arguably, the government attempts to control future behaviour (the manifested 'intentions') and, moreover, to undo the inhospitable actions committed to this point; the proclamation continues by demanding that 'all others that have of late time broken up their households, to returne to their houses againe without delay'.[27] By interrupting nobles' intentions and furthermore reversing their present course of action, the government implies that a hospitable country is possible in the immediate future. That intimated future image drew some of its force from the discursive binary that idealised the hospitable, rural past over the inhospitable, urban present and that was circulating in sixteenth-century England and firmly in place by the seventeenth century. As noted above, this opposition was the product of grafting a temporal dichotomy (hospitable past and inhospitable present) onto a spatial one (hospitable country and inhospitable city). In producing these dichotomies, the period's civility literature and handbooks gradually marginalised the rural and the past as 'other'.[28] By making absent hospitality central to its nostalgic rhetoric, *Richard II* not only rejects that otherness, but in fact stages hospitality's (temporary) centrality in the political sphere of the mid-1590s. Nostalgia becomes fundamental to imagining not only the present state, but England's future as well.

Into this circulating discourse of a privileged past-ness and rural locale enters the hospitality that Elizabeth and her Council wished to re-establish, a hospitality that would reaffirm both sixteenth-century social hierarchy and Christian principles. Hospitality was an exchange between two social groups: the rich provided alms, food and shelter for those who sought it; in return, the poor accepted their landed neighbours' authority, and their acceptance of relief cast honour and an enhanced reputation back on their benefactors.[29] There existed as part of this exchange a silent transaction, one of exercised Christian duty. While the Reformation had irrevocably changed theology in England – particularly through the redefinition of the path to salvation through faith rather than faith and works – pre-Reformation practices, like the seven corporal works of mercy, remained influential in the late Tudor Church. These works demanded that Christians feed the hungry and provide drink to the thirsty, and the state used them in its ecclesiastical instruction to incline individuals to provide hospitality as an extension of charity, 'a civil obligation in the Christian commonwealth'.[30] Printed in 1596, *Three sermons, or Homelies to moove compassion towards the poore* cites the Gospel of Matthew, in which the works of mercy are found, throughout the first sermon, concluding with an explicit reference to the works and their role in gaining salvation. 'Come, yee blessed of my Father, inherite the kingdome prepared for you, from the foundations of the world: For I was hungred, and ye gave me meat &c', the author writes, and further includes the theological benefits of giving:

> Salomon saith: Cast thy bread upon the waters, for after many daies thou shalt find it. As if he shold say: bestow thy alms, where it may seem to be lost: yet doubt not of thy rewarde, for surely thou shalt not lose it.[31]

This verse's significance lies not only in the explicit parallel the author makes between casting bread away and its return. Undoubtedly, the literal image of giving away bread ('a dominant trope' in late Tudor discussions of hospitality) would have had a profound resonance for its readership and audience in 1596.[32] In these religious and political discourses, hospitality becomes a source of political and social stability, an idea refracted in *Richard II*, where hospitality is the sign of both preferable past and future – and is rendered unobtainable.

Despite these discourses, despite the circulating dichotomies that idealised the past and the rural as hospitable loci, hospitality as a practice was evidently absent in the 1590s. To the Elizabethan regime, this absence became an intolerable fault – or at least, it became intolerable when a breaking point was reached. Only in times of desperate socioeconomic crisis was government policy forced to reorient its focus to subjects and customs associated with the past, as Andrew McRae has persuasively shown.[33] That is, the invocation of past practice became a politically useful tool to influence individual and collective behaviour. The late-Elizabethan government's demands for hospitality reproduced the centralisation of eleemosynary practices that followed the 1536 Poor

Law and the Dissolution of the Monasteries. The 1536 law sought to resituate the provision of hospitality from the individual almsgiver at the door to a central public authority that would integrate poor relief into a governmental responsibility.[34] Implicit in this shifting of roles is the shifting of relationships, restructuring the personal bond between the alms-recipient and the provider into one where the state becomes the personal benefactor to the poor. The state becomes arch-host, an idea also suggested by *Richard II*.

That hospitality played an important social role in early modern England is clear not only from extant personal testimonies, but from the post-Dissolution response to hospitality as well.[35] Prior to the Dissolution, monasteries were an integral and assumed part of its practice, and it was the monasteries' attendant social utility that constituted their leaders' and patrons' arguments for their preservation. Some priors built almonry houses specifically for the giving of alms to those who came to the gate, while others fed their pilgrim and travelling guests alongside those present for a feast.[36] Abbots, priors and monks were also expected to entertain and fête their noble patrons, several of whom had duties over many religious institutions and who cultivated strong relationships with certain houses to which they gave their support. For example, the Howard family's monasteries stretched from Kent to Yorkshire; at the Dissolution, the Duke of Norfolk, Thomas Howard, was the patron 'of no fewer than nineteen houses of monks, canons and nuns'.[37] (Notably, one of Howard's predecessors to these houses and this rich tradition of patronage was Thomas Mowbray, the same Duke of Norfolk who is depicted in *Richard II*.) The hospitality of the religious did not go unnoticed by their denouncers, and even some of Thomas Cromwell's commissioners noted the reputation for hospitality of these institutions in their communities.[38] Nonetheless, the hospitable practices associated with them – 'parish handouts, monastic hospitality, and personal holiday and funeral almsgiving' – could not meaningfully reduce poverty in the period.[39] Even before the Reformation, hospitality represented an ideal rather than a material, permanent solution.

More ritual or cultural tradition than programme of relief, the practice of hospitality was still recognised by successive governments as an important custom. The invocation of the past associated with hospitality was a political tool, one that became especially important as the state took over the role of the monasteries following their dissolution and the centralisation of eleemosynary practices. Henry VIII sought to replace religious communities' hospitality in his 1536 Poor Law and through those who bought the abbeys and their lands from the crown, as the government 'insisted' that the farmers and new tenants provide hospitality as their predecessors had done (for example by providing alms and food).[40] The practice of hospitality, then, became displaced and adapted, as its spaces were repurposed as Anglican houses of worship or left as ruins, symbols of the deeply complex relationship with the past and present which offered a multitude of ways to be read. They could signify 'Tudor avarice and Cromwellian sacrilege or [. . .] Protestantism's conquest over Antichristian papistry', and even this latter symbol offered various readings, as the impulse to completely eradicate signs of popery existed alongside the desire to allow ruins to stand as testimony, both a sign of Protestant triumph and a warning against future error.[41]

Evidence from Shakespeare's plays and poems demonstrates the persistent place of England's pre-Reformation heritage in the late-sixteenth-century cultural imagination, suggesting hospitality's translation from social service to literary utility. Commonplace examples include the anachronistic presence of a ruined monastery in *Titus Andronicus* (c. 1591) and the hint of one in Sonnet 73. In Act 5 of *Titus*, the monastery becomes the site of an important plot development when a Goth warrior reports to Titus's son Lucius, commander of the Goth army, that 'from our troops I strayed / To gaze upon a ruinous monastery' and that he 'earnestly did fix mine eye / Upon the wasted building' when he heard a baby cry and discovered Aaron and his child.[42] The soldier's report repeats within the small space of three lines the interest of this building. It draws him from his own troops, fascinating him so that he 'earnestly did fix' his view on the building, its dilapidated state emphasised by 'ruinous' and 'wasted'. This unnamed character's brief narrative merges distant past, immediate past, and present, inviting the audience to imagine any one of the derelict monasteries that remained in London and across England. This experience of a post-Reformation monastery outside pagan Rome highlights how the historical space of hospitality still circulated in the late-Elizabethan collective imagination.[43] Similarly, Sonnet 73 draws on the image of ruin in its first quatrain:

> That time of year thou mayst in me behold,
> When yellow leaves, or few, or none, do hang
> Upon those boughs which shake against the cold,
> Bare ruined choirs where late the sweet birds sang.[44]

The speaker associates the decayed religious space, the 'choir', with both individual and collective degeneration, multiplying the image of decay through the implicit vision of the former choristers, invoked by the 'sweet birds' who replaced them and who now themselves are gone. The ruin, an 'emblem of ambiguity', requires a 'double vision' in the reader, to hold the past and present, speaker and structure, at once together.[45]

Shakespeare exploits such doubleness to privilege and amplify the grief of human passing; but that grief depends not so much on the loss of the past as on the hostility of the future. Indeed, Sonnet 73 offers an unhospitable future for the beloved, and the couplet announces inevitable separation: 'To love that well which thou must leave ere long' (l. 14). In Sonnet 64, Shakespeare teases out his interest in the linguistic potential of 'ruin', writing, 'Ruin hath taught me thus to ruminate' (l. 11). Here, 'ruin' expands into '*rumi*nate'; or, using the 1609 quarto spelling, 'Ruine' entirely encompasses '*rumi*nate'.[46] Both examples demonstrate Shakespeare's ability to see ruin paradoxically exceed its boundaries, to appear where it is unexpected – as it does in *Titus*. In these texts, the decayed spaces of hospitality become a site for Shakespeare to consider not simply those spaces' significance for the present, but what they suggest about the future.

The fact of the Dissolution's past-ness, its place in Henrician England, does not negate the break it still represented between past and present for Elizabethan England, as works by Shakespeare and other writers make clear. John Stow's *The Survey of London* (1598, 1603) provided in literary form the labyrinth of London's history and its present, as he remarks on the previous lives of well- and little-known London spaces. Walsham describes his *Survey* as 'suffused with sadness', but as I suggested in the Introduction, his matter-of-fact attitude towards the disappearance or replacement of monastic buildings still enables, even encourages, a multiplicity of readings.[47] Early in the *Survey* Stow uses a joke by Policronicon as evidence of the Saxons' use of wooden buildings:

> [*Policronicon*] sayeth that then had yee wodden Churches, nay wodden Chalaces and golden Priestes, but since golden Chalaces and wodden Priestes: And to knit up this argument, king *Edgar* in his Charter to the Abbey of Malmesbury, dated the yeare of Christ 974. hath wordes to this effect: All the Monasteries in my Realme, to the outward sight, are nothing but worme eaten and rotten tymber, and boordes, and that worse is, within they are almost emptie, and void of divine service[.][48]

Wooden priests and monasteries empty of 'divine service': this hardly sounds like regret on Stow's part. Yet elsewhere his history implicitly asks the reader to judge present conditions against the past, as when he recounts the history of Portsoken Ward, in which

> [K]ing *Edward* [. . .] (having before in a tempest on the sea, and perill of drowning, made a vow to build a Monasterie to the honour of God, and our Ladie of grace, if God would grant him grace to come safe to land) builded there a Monasterie, placing an Abbot, and Monkes of the Cistercian, or white order [. . .] This house, at the late general suppression was valued at 546.*l*. 10. d. yearely, it was surrendered in the yeare 1539. the 30. of *Henrie*

the 8. since the which time, the said Monasterie being cleane pulled downe by sir *Arthur Darcie* knight, and other, of late time in place thereof is builded a large Storehouse for victuale, and convenient Ovens are builded there, for baking of Bisket to serve her Majesties Shippes.[49]

Two elements of this cyclical history, which begins and ends at sea, are particularly striking. First, Stow refers to both the suppression and the new building of a 'Storehouse' as 'late', an ambivalent temporal term that suggests the Dissolution as both past and recent, reachable through Stow's accounts.[50] Second, Stow juxtaposes the holy origins of the monastery with its material worth, the fact that it was 'cleane pulled downe', and its new purpose. The material categorically replaces the spiritual, and the reader is left to determine the wisdom of these events.

In addition to Stow's well-known work, two very different manuscript sources provide further evidence of late Elizabethan interest in the Dissolution. Parliamentarian, scholar and co-author of *Gorboduc* Thomas Norton's 1581 letter to Francis Mylles – a secretary of Francis Walsingham – narrates events surrounding the Dissolution that he has 'understode by that at wh[ich] I have red & heard'.[51] Norton's letter possesses the tone of a concerned historian and subject as he presents Wolsey and Cromwell as the arch-instigators of the Dissolution and locates its cause not in religious but in political and financial motivations. His letter does not discuss the monasteries' hospitality or long for its return, and certainly he participates in perpetuating the focus on the 'Sodomies' of religious houses – a tenuous claim.[52] Still, Norton's interpretation of the contextual and causal events of the Dissolution recognises a rupture. Mylles's interest in the topic, and Norton's ready and eager response, suggest a renewed desire to uncover and understand the Dissolution in terms outside and in addition to the chronicles of the period. Similarly, the late sixteenth-century *Rites of Durham*, dated to 1593, describes the rites and customs of Durham Cathedral before the Dissolution, and its anonymous author briefly depicts the hospitality offered by Durham's monks, who with other Catholic religious orders were bound by their faith to open their doors to care for pilgrims, travellers, the poor, the sick and strangers.[53] Hospitality towards poor children and 'aged' women, while physically located on the margins of the abbey, is noted as part of the cathedral's rites and customs. Not overtly nostalgic in his tone, the author of *The Rites* demonstrates how Durham in particular functioned as a locus and image of hospitality, a focal point within the community as it reached out to all strata of society. Both Norton's letter and *The Rites of Durham* represent just two cases of how late Elizabethan individuals were thinking about and responding to a lacuna of knowledge. Of course, those most critically affected by the monasteries' closing were unlikely to be writing their history. The late sixteenth-century resurgence of an interest in hospitality on a legislative level as well as in a range of texts – personal letters, historical accounts, sermons – suggests a latent historiographical project which re-evaluates and prioritises hospitality based on ideas of the past that necessarily depend upon a pre-Reformation inheritance of the concept.

The latent nostalgia fomenting in the wake of failed harvests and diminishing and changing traditions of hospitality meant that for *Richard II*'s audience and readers, the play of a 'mean season' could refract their own time: a time of difficulty that looked back to a preferable past and forward to the future and the end of their hardship, which they hoped it would signify. But as this chapter argues, in *Richard II* Shakespeare is not interested in rehearsing a familiar complaint. He stages lost hospitality both to critique the idealised past and the idealising process, and to reveal the ethical and political consequences of nostalgic desire.

Inhospitable England

Queen Elizabeth's 1596 Proclamation recognises on a national scale the value of localised hospitality throughout the country, and consequently it stresses the duty of the individual, particularly the nobility, to the commonwealth. This context provides the backdrop to this chapter's analysis of *Richard II*, to which I now turn. Using nostalgic narratives of a lost home, nation and kingship, the play's absent hospitality illuminates that sense of duty and the serious political and social consequences that follow when it is neglected by the quintessential representation of nobility: the king.

The *topoi* of dissolution and desolation that articulate absent hospitality in *Richard II* create tangible representations of an immaterial past for an audience that would never have known pre- (or possibly post-) Reformation practices of hospitality. These representations become tangible through characters' evocation of images resonant in the mid-1590s; paradoxically, they remain immaterial because the consistent invocation of these images – as in Stow's *Survey* – reinforces their absence and their consignment to the unknown past. Consequently, the language and *topoi* of hospitality invigorate and command the sense of nostalgia produced in the play. Images of desolation and grief nurture the nostalgic longing for the past that Gaunt's and Northumberland's respective speeches generate, images that are questioned by the apocalyptic future prophesied by Carlisle at the play's end. In *Richard II*, nostalgia and its persuasive power rely on hospitality as that element of an idealised past that evokes individual experience and a personal sense of what has been lost. This conjunction of both individual and national loss initiates the act of idealising the past in *Richard II*, an act that casts a shadow across the play's present and invites dramatic political action.

To cast that shadow, the play's first act relies on a language of hospitality that within and without the play creates a morally problematic longing for the past. The unfolding plot that occurs through and around the arguments of the Duchess of Gloucester, her brother-in-law John of Gaunt and his son Henry Bolingbroke establishes King Richard as a selfish, wanton tyrant. The dramatic shape of *Richard II*'s first half encourages nostalgia as it aligns England's woes with its ruler and looks forward to a time ahead – the time of Bolingbroke's return from exile, perhaps even the time after Richard. Furthermore, the first act's forensic rhetoric encourages auditors to question how the play's characters craft images of the past and present, to analyse the analysis of the play itself, to return to Doty's phrase.[54] The opening scene's conflict between Bolingbroke and Mowbray remains mysterious enough to prevent auditors from uncovering, or re-covering, the past that Richard further attempts to shroud in Scene 3. Shakespeare's use of *argumentum in utramque partem* in the successive scenes demonstrates a dramaturgy deeply concerned with the past's construction and narrative's power to persuade, as Gaunt and the Duchess, and Gaunt and his son, deliberate the virtues of Christian patience in navigating present difficulty. What such rhetoric reveals about the past invites reflection on, and potential critique of, both the Ricardian present of the play and the Elizabethan present of the audience. In rhetorically shaping England's glorified past throughout *Richard II*'s first four scenes, the nobility lends that past a legitimacy with which the present is forced to contend.

From its first line, *Richard II* juxtaposes ways of thinking about time's passage, opposing the past's legitimacy and authority with the present. King Richard calls on 'Old John of Gaunt, time-honoured Lancaster' to bring forth his son Bolingbroke to respond to charges made against him.[55] Contrary to common critical interpretations of these epithets, the use of 'old' and 'time-honoured' immediately introduces to the play a historiographic dichotomy of negative and positive perceptions of the past.[56] The 'irreverence' with which Richard later uses the phrase 'aged Gaunt' (2.1.72) gestures to the phrase's negative use.[57] Bushy's announcement that 'old John of Gaunt' will soon be dead further confirms that in calling Gaunt both 'old' and 'time-honoured', a temporal opposition is established (1.4.54). The derisory invocation of 'old' and 'aged' by Richard and his flatterers suggests a second, supplementary dichotomy in the opposition of the old order that represents the good of the commonwealth and the 'liberal largesse' of Richard's regime (1.4.44). 'Old' communicates the passage of time, but the play doesn't inherently communicate a value in that passage. In contrast, Shakespeare's formulation 'time-honoured' states clearly both time's agency and its powers of improvement, as it implicitly gilds its object, John of Gaunt, honouring him. (Shakespeare's use of the adjective is unique in his own works and appears to be so in the literature of the period. Where 'time' and 'honoured' are paired in texts of late Elizabethan England, it is usually to clarify that at a specific time an individual was honoured.) Are old ideas, people and values 'time-honoured' and desirable? Or are they aged and irrelevant? As the play unfolds it asks its audience and readers to adjudicate representations of time – of past and present – through its insistent questioning of what is 'time-honoured'.

Howsoever King Richard jeers at what is old and 'past', *Richard II* constructs time in its incarnation as 'the past' as an ideal, invoking hospitality as a key aspect of that idealisation. The play's revealing second scene between the Duchess of Gloucester and her brother-in-law, without precedent in Shakespeare's historical sources, complicates almost immediately the sense of the past established in the previous scene. The Duchess attempts to persuade Gaunt to pursue justice for her murdered husband, and having glorified his ancestry and his immediate family through the image of the Tree of Jesse, she chastises his inaction and suggests his phlegmatic, passive state by demanding 'Hath love in thy *old* blood no living fire?' (1.2.10, my emphasis). Through that invocation of 'old', the Duchess affirms the juxtaposition of what is 'old' and what 'time-honoured', as she uses 'old' in explicit opposition to the idealising language with which she describes Gaunt's familial legacy, his father and particularly his brothers, who were 'vials' of 'sacred blood', and 'fair branches' (1.2.12, 13). The failure of past legacy to persuade Gaunt to action intimates that the values of the past have been corrupted, and when it is certain that the Duchess cannot convince Gaunt to act, her unattainable wishes reveal Richard's impact on the state of England. He has rendered it inhospitable. This becomes clear when she interrupts Gaunt's exit with a desperate invitation:

> Commend me to thy brother, Edmund York.
> Lo, this is all. Nay, yet depart not so!
> Though this be all, do not so quickly go;
> I shall remember more. Bid him – ah, what? –
> With all good speed at Pleshy visit me.
> Alack, and what shall good old York there see
> But empty lodgings and unfurnished walls,

> Unpeopled offices, untrodden stones?
> And what hear there for welcome but my groans?
> Therefore commend me; let him not come there
> To seek out sorrow that dwells everywhere. (1.2.62–72)

The Duchess's house does not, and cannot, afford hospitality.[58] Its unwelcoming environment is host only to ubiquitous 'sorrow' (l.72). Her initial lines express an anxiety to force Gaunt to stay just a few moments more. Struggling for a reason, the Duchess hurriedly issues an invitation before she realises its impossibility. The uncertainty of what to say encompassed in the notably unrhymed 'ah, what?' (l.65) exemplifies her harried state of mind, which undermines her genuine desire to provide hospitality. Dissolved and deserted, her household is 'unpeopled', its hallways 'untrodden' and hospitality a futile wish (l. 69). The palpable emptiness and definitive sense of abandonment that her words and couplets create evoke the image of 'cold, / Bare ruined choirs'. Like the monasteries, the only remnant of the Duchess's past is the structure that surrounds her, Pleshy itself; those elements which lent it beauty and warmth no longer exist. 'Unfurnished walls' (l.68) suggests that Richard's greed may even have demanded the tapestries from Pleshy's rooms, a parallel to the pillaging of the monasteries and a reading made more plausible by Richard's instinct to seize Gaunt's 'plate, his goods, his money and his lands' (2.1.210) just a few scenes later. Finally, the Duchess's lament that she has only 'groans' (l. 70) with which to welcome York points to an abrogated tradition represented in language's breakdown into mourning and lament. The fact that in her home she is rendered incapable of providing hospitality even to her family further illustrates England's woeful state as a commonwealth that denies individuals the opportunity to perform their Christian duty to each other. The Duchess's rhetorical economy evokes a powerful image of ruin through its imaginative lacunae and its dependence upon an audience's collective memory. Ironically, absence is used as a trope to provide rhetorical clarity for what is present: Richard's tyrannical behaviour. In narrating the misfortune that confronts her household, the Duchess's lament for lost hospitality confirms the king's negative impact on the commonweal, and it is the implicit and explicit argument that Richard is ruinous for England that structures the first half of *Richard II*.[59]

Pleshy's cold desolation becomes more substantial when compared with how the contemporary, anonymous drama *Thomas of Woodstock* (1591–5) represents the manor.[60] *Woodstock* has been recognised by many as a precursor to *Richard II*, and some critics have labelled it a prequel. While I remain unconvinced by the idea of *Woodstock* as an intentional 'prequel', the play does possess significant resonances and connections with Shakespeare's drama.[61] The *Woodstock* dramatist's occasional focus on Pleshy and its status as a site of hospitality in the play emphasises just how *Richard II* dwells on hospitality's absence. The play's protagonist 'Plain Thomas', stripped of his office as Protector and cast out of court with his brothers, welcomes to Pleshy his friends and his enemies, including a ridiculous courtier and the king and his favourites, disguised as maskers.[62] The *Woodstock* dramatist seems eager to depict the eponymous character's estate as a locus of beauty and good governance, and in the play Pleshy functions as a distinct contrast to Richard's court. Woodstock welcomes his brothers York and Lancaster 'with as true a heart / As Richard with a false, and mind corrupt, / Disgraced our names and thrust us from his court' (3.2.2–4). York confirms the contrast by describing Pleshy for the audience:

> This house of Plashy, brother,
> Stands in a sweet and pleasant air, i'faith:
> 'Tis near the Thames and circled round with trees
> That in the summer serve for pleasant fans
> To cool ye, and in winter strongly break
> The stormy winds that else would nip ye too.   (3.2.9–14)

Woodstock's home represents the manorial ideal, 'an idealised icon of rural peace and harmony', perfect in any season.[63] Its protective nature, evidenced by its trees to 'cool ye' in summer and in winter to shield from winds that would 'nip ye' (ll.13, 14), demonstrates the unbounded hospitality of Pleshy, and its constancy in the face of temporal change forms a crucial element of the estate's image. The opposition of such constancy with Richard's failings is put to humorous effect with the arrival of one of the king's courtiers in the same scene. Despite the envoy's rudeness and unwelcome message recalling Woodstock to court, the Duke invites him in for refreshment (3.2.127, 132–245). Furthermore, the play identifies 'Plashy' as the locus and source of hospitality for England, as it is from there that Woodstock can protect the people against the blank charters Richard issues and where the Duke may be 'Plain Thomas still' (3.2.241). That 'still' urges again the constancy exemplified by his hospitable locale, as it affirms Woodstock's role as the ideal gentleman, one in demand in late Tudor (as in medieval) England.

The 1596 Proclamation makes clear that the nobility were expected to provide hospitality, and Elizabethan texts illustrate and argue for ideal gentle behaviour. Thomas Smith's *A Discourse of the Common Weal of this Realm of England* (1581) stresses the significant role gentle families must have played in the sixteenth century in its dialogue concerning the causes of the present inflation and dearth, which Smith stages as a conversation between a knight, a Justice of the Peace, a merchant, a doctor, a husbandman and a capper.[64] While the characters never mention the abbeys' provision of hospitality, the capper does lament the absence of hospitality provided by gentlemen. Using a phrase familiar from Chapter 2, he grumbles that

> It was never merry with poor craftsmen since gentlemen became graziers; for they cannot nowadays [. . .] find their apprentices and servants meat and drink but it costs them almost as double as it did before hand.[65]

As with certain 'never merry' incarnations discussed previously, here the phrase bewails the suffering of labourers and peasants that results from the gentry's mounting greed, which the practice of enclosure exemplifies (gentlemen are now 'graziers'). Smith's characters then debate the role of the court in contributing to the absence of hospitality, as the nobility's presence was demanded in London.[66] In his discussion of the duties of a gentleman and his hospitality, Smith outlines the character that Thomas of Woodstock embodies: the dutiful lord who, keeping an open house, welcomes all and in that act of welcome stabilises the state.

Ultimately the Duke's hospitality is his undoing, and the *Woodstock* dramatist suggests both the monarch's role in eradicating the practice and hospitality's failure to guarantee virtue in the realm. The lack of hospitality is particularly associated with Richard, as Woodstock reports that Queen Anne's 'charity hath stayed the commons' rage / That would ere this have shaken Richard's chair / Or set all England on a burning fire' (4.2.58–60). The Duke, troubled by the queen's illness and the sky's portents, asserts nonetheless his faith in the future, that he may yet 'see / This state attain her former royalty' (4.2.75–6), a remark that expresses an idea so crucial to Shakespeare's own use of nostalgia, the notion of reclaimable honour. To combat woe, Woodstock calls up lights and music for the maskers at the gate, for 'all are welcome' (4.2.69–70, 98, 100). The players, however, are King Richard and his flatterers, come to kidnap Woodstock and send him to his death. The *Woodstock* dramatist thus depicts the downfall of Pleshy that Shakespeare asks his audience to imagine in *Richard II*, and that play's image becomes all the more emotionally evocative if they know the 'Plashy' of *Woodstock*. In depicting hospitality as Woodstock's source both of his excellence and of his ruin, the drama suggests the futility of this practice and its inevitable destruction as a consequence of court vice. Given the Elizabethan government's centralised role in dictating and attempting to resuscitate hospitality as a practice, *Woodstock*'s depiction of it in monarchical hands offers a glancing critique of the ruling elite.

These dramas' contrasting visions of Pleshy's hospitality intensify a process of fiction-making in Shakespeare's play, as *Woodstock*'s mimetic representation of what hospitality could be is supplanted by *Richard II*'s rhetoric of absence and what was. The anonymous drama relies upon multiple scenes and characters to create in Pleshy the hospitable ideal, the destruction of which the audience then witnesses. By contrast, in the Duchess of Gloucester's rhetorical economy and formulation of Pleshy's inhospitable nature as a question, Shakespeare implies concrete, past events by using *hypophera*, the answering of a question oneself has asked.[67] Her 'Alack, and what shall good old York there see / But empty lodgings and unfurnished walls, / Unpeopled offices, untrodden stones [. . .]?' depends upon the audience's piecing together of vivid images obscured by an ignorance of how exactly the picture of a desolate Pleshy came about (1.2.67–9). The audience, then, must participate in fiction-making as they imagine the time between Woodstock's murder and the Duchess's grief (an ability not dependent upon their having seen *Woodstock*). Such participation is part of Shakespeare's complex construction and questioning of nostalgia in *Richard II*. The audience must themselves call up nostalgia, they must here provide what constitutes the idealised time and place – the England before Woodstock's murder, before hospitality was rendered impossible and absent.

To this point, I have stressed Shakespeare's dramaturgical insistence on the imperfection of the play's present. By depicting the aristocratic need of hospitality throughout *Richard II*'s first act, Shakespeare both affirms the essential relationship between true nobility and hospitality while also insisting on Richard's lack of nobility through his active role in eradicating a 'hospitable' England, as the dramatic history of Pleshy exemplifies. The Duchess of Gloucester's arguments demonstrate that her inability to provide hospitality results directly from Richard's actions, and the king's interference in a legal trial results in another interruption: Bolingbroke's banishment from England. He is forced to leave '[his] mother and [his] nurse that bears [him] yet' (1.3.307, my emphasis). Ironically, Bolingbroke frames his response to banishment in terms of 'an enforced pilgrimage', as he names his exile, a punishment which renders Richard's unwelcome intervention the act of a poor host (1.3.264). Richard forces him from the place that still succours him, and Bolingbroke must turn away from that hospitable source and become a pilgrim, a representative of another group affected by hospitality's alteration in post-Reformation England.[68] Richard has made Bolingbroke a pilgrim who must seek hospitality outside his native country, and the scene's repeated use of the pilgrim image – time also makes a 'pilgrimage' with Gaunt (1.3.230) – affirms Richard's role in creating an inhospitable England. Following Gaunt's death, to which Richard himself has mockingly made a 'pilgrimage' (2.1.154), the king will even make Bolingbroke a 'vagabond' (2.3.120). Bolingbroke's 'pilgrimage' drives Gaunt to an early grave, and these stock images of those craving hospitality at Richard's hand – the sick, the pilgrim – affirm Shakespeare's initial characterisation of Richard as a disinterested tyrant. He consistently acts in a way detrimental to his kingdom, and Shakespeare consistently binds that hostile behaviour to absent hospitality.

To complete the conditions for a politically charged nostalgia, Shakespeare uses Gaunt's deathbed 'Sceptred isle' speech to further disclose the time's dire situation by comparing past and present. Gaunt's monologue revels in its *sententiae* and its apostrophe of England, and likely it was partly for these reasons that it was circulated and celebrated in late-Elizabethan England through Robert Allott's *England's Parnassus* (1600). I contest, however, the unmitigated nostalgia and the death of the old order that critics often associate with this speech, as Gaunt does not initially seem nostalgic. Certainly the speech idealises England, and that idealisation further establishes and articulates a nostalgia that depends upon the construction of a past, paradisal image. However, Gaunt's rhetorical repetition of 'this' (sixteen times), insists emphatically that the England of which he speaks is *now*, in the present:

> This royal throne of kings, this sceptred isle,
> This earth of majesty, this seat of Mars,
> This other Eden, demi-paradise,
> This fortress built by Nature for herself
> [...]
> This happy breed of men, this little world,
> This precious stone set in the silver sea,
> [...]
> This blessed plot, this earth, this realm, this England,
> This nurse, this teeming womb of royal kings,
> [...]
> This land of such dear souls, this dear dear land[.]
> (2.1.40–3, 45–6, 50–1, 57)

Here, Shakespeare uses form to reinforce his focus on space: the iambs stress the land images ('earth', 'seat', 'world', 'stone', 'sea', 'plot', 'earth', 'realm', 'Eng*land*'), the metre reinforcing the ideal *place* of England. Gaunt's gendering of England as the metaphorical nurse and mother of her sovereigns (an echo of Bolingbroke at 1.3.307) points most clearly to his idea that, as he speaks, she remains capable of preserving and producing kings.[69] Against this spatial construction, Shakespeare's Richard will relocate England's reproductive capacities in the monarch, creating himself mother and nurse. Returning from Ireland two scenes later, he greets the land, 'As a long-parted mother with her child / Plays fondly with her tears and smiles in meeting, / So weeping, smiling, greet I thee, *my* earth' (3.2.8–10, my emphasis). Gaunt offers a contrasting image of England's rulers: they are 'Feared by their breed' and 'Renowned for their deeds' (2.1.52, 53). His use of the adjectival past participle in 'feared' and 'renowned' perpetuates the notion that these images still characterise England while suggesting that this characterisation of kings is past. The speech first establishes a sense of what remains and what is present before Gaunt explodes that notion in his condemnation of Richard.

His rhetoric shatters the intimate image of king-bearing England and her 'dear souls' when he makes the suggestion of the past an explicit argument in his speech. Having established the many virtues of England, he pronounces the country's reality:

> This land of such dear souls, this dear dear land,
> [. . .]
> Is *now* leased out [. . .]
> Like to a tenement or pelting farm.
> England [. . .]
>   is *now* bound in with shame,
> With inky blots and rotten parchment bonds.
> That England that was wont to conquer others
> Hath made a shameful conquest of itself.
> (2.1.57, 59–61, 63–6, my emphasis)

Several specific rhetorical shifts mark the change of how Gaunt conceptualises present and past England as his speech climaxes and concludes, highlighting his grief at England's 'conquest'. His interjection 'now' explicitly condemns the present: now England is no longer a 'demi-paradise'. The duke's previous description and praise are no longer representative, for the country is not simply *shamed*, which would imply the consequence of past action; rather, it is 'bound in with shame', a continuous, circuitous image that has no apparent end for Gaunt. His rhetoric's logical conclusion is that 'this England' of fifteen lines prior is now 'That England', and accordingly the present tense has become the past. England 'that was wont to conquer others' now conquers 'itself'. Even that 'itself' possesses critical undertones, for it eradicates the 'herself' implied in the constructed image of England as nurse and mother. A self-perpetuating England has been replaced by a self-consuming one. The suspicion and critique of the present that Shakespeare slowly crafts through the first act finds its obvious, but not final, embodiment in Gaunt's rhetoric.

The lament for the England that did not seek to vanquish its own subjects is briefly but explicitly nostalgic, as Gaunt's speech articulates his sense of England's intrinsic nature. He juxtaposes the past with the present and thus condenses the lengthier argument he has been making, that the England that was is not the England that is, and that discrepancy he locates in Richard's (mis)rule. Consequently, the creation of past and present in this speech – a moment of temporal rupture that Shakespeare will restage in *Julius Caesar* – allows the audience's own feeling of nostalgia for a loss of all that Gaunt has previously described. His lament that England is 'bound' evokes the rotten 'bonds' that have created Richard 'Landlord' (2.1.113) and which, as a singular image, also evoke notions of duty: a king bound to his country, a subject bound to country and king.

Gaunt's invocation of 'Landlord' announces implicitly that the king is no longer a noble host, and by circulating the tropes of fasting and dearth the play also attaches Richard to the creation of an inhospitable England. Again, these tropes were connected to the ongoing dearth-hospitality crisis in the mid-1590s. At the same time that the Privy Council was policing the corn market to secure fair prices and demanding that 'men of hospitalitie' leave London, they were also creating fasting days. In 1595, as in the decade before, orders for fasting accompanied orders for public prayer to be said on Wednesdays and Fridays. While fasting in Elizabethan England continued to be a Catholic practice, 'among its distinctively protestant features was the sense that fasting should always be related to some particular cause or affliction'.[70] Fasting as a public practice represented the junction of 'prudential and providential' governance.[71] As part of secular policy, it was a means of conserving food. As a religious practice, it acknowledged the role of sacrifice with prayer in imploring God to come to England's aid. Together, fasting and hospitality were represented by religious and civic leaders as practices essential to the care for the commonwealth. In 1595, citizens in the diocese of Norwich were 'enjoined by their ministers to practice "hospitality", to refrain from all "excess in diet", and to have patience not to "give ear to mutinies"'; Heal notes the 'undifferentiated charity' instigated by Elizabeth.[72] Fasting and charity formed two elements of self-denial, which was lauded as a virtue opposed to vanity – the vice that Shakespeare's play and *Thomas of Woodstock* associate with Richard II.

Having articulated so clearly and devastatingly the break between past England's fecundity and the present's degeneracy, Gaunt attacks Richard with the language of 1590s London. His punning on his name must have resounded powerfully with an audience embroiled in policies and proclamations compelling them to abstain. Dying, Gaunt describes to Richard 'how is't' (2.1.72) with him:

> Within me Grief hath kept a tedious fast,
> And who abstains from meat that is not gaunt?
> For sleeping England long time have I watched;
> Watching breeds leanness, leanness is all gaunt.
> The pleasure that some fathers feed upon
> Is my strict fast – I mean my children's looks,
> And therein fasting hast *thou made me* gaunt.   (2.1.75–81, my emphasis)

In the same way that the Duchess, deprived of her husband, is deprived of the possibility of hospitality, so too Gaunt, deprived of his 'pleasure' – his son – is forced into a strict abstinence. In the world outside of *Richard II*, Gaunt's fasting would be associated with government-solicited collective action performed for the benefit of the kingdom. Gaunt's 'watching' connotes that his own fast, a consequence of his constant service to 'sleeping England', is born of worry for the realm. Its ruler lingers over 'sleeping England' like an external threat, an unwelcome guest. As Richard implicitly made Gaunt lean through watching a troubled state, so he made him gaunt through Bolingbroke's banishment. The negative consequences of Gaunt's fasting highlight England's need, again affirming the troubled state of the present in the past and problematising any Elizabethan impulse to idealise a past marked by clear misrule. Echoing the present's problems in the theatrical past, Shakespeare produces a multi-layered vision of temporal desire that finds no analogue in Williams's escalator: the past longs for the past and, as will be clear below, the future.

A Sovereignty in Time

Sovereign or landlord, Richard fails to make, or to keep, England hospitable, and the kingdom's hostility to its inhabitants breeds a desire for a preferable past that catalyses political revolution. Having witnessed Richard's illegal seizure of Gaunt's goods and lands, Lord Northumberland echoes Gaunt as he peers into the future and woefully pronounces England 'this declining land' (2.1.240). Such a succinct phrase does a lot of rhetorical work, as it establishes again the image of the preferable past alongside a fear for the future. Shakespeare uses Northumberland and the Lords Ross and Willoughby to detail and summarise the king's abuses that signal this decline: commons taxed grievously, nobles fined, new financial 'exactions [...] devised' without restraint against subjects of the realm (2.1.249; cf. 246–50).

Willoughby's despairing 'But what, i'God's name, doth become of this?' disrupts the lords' succinct evidential statements and laments the absent redress of these wrongs, providing Northumberland with the perfect opportunity to launch his rebellion (2.1.251).

That idea of 'opportunity' is crucial at this point in the play, and the success of Northumberland's speech relies on two temporal ideas that have been essential to establishing nostalgia as a persuasive and potent rhetoric in *Richard II*. First, Northumberland relies on *kairos* in both speech and action, as he seizes the moment of the king's departure from Ireland and Bolingbroke's return from exile to urge his fellow nobles to rebel. Second, he argues for the idea of an English inheritance, a legacy known and owed. As I claimed previously and as we shall see in the next chapter, Shakespeare's use of ideas of political inheritance forms the cornerstone of his nostalgic rhetoric. The concept of an owed political inheritance is bound to the idea of cyclical history, and it both articulates and enables the belief in the reclamation of the past in the future.

To muster support for his rebellion, Northumberland declares:

> If, then, we shall shake off our slavish yoke,
> Imp out our drooping country's broken wing,
> Redeem from broking pawn the blemished crown,
> Wipe off the dust that hides our sceptre's gilt
> And make high majesty look like itself,
> Away with me in post to Ravenspurgh.   (2.1.291–6)

A 'blemished crown', a dusted, gilded sceptre, and 'high majesty' that does not 'look like itself' are all images of inherent, but past, goodness that must be recovered: a crown burnished, a sceptre dusted off, majesty made recognisable. The image of dust alone, of the accumulation of filth, suggests that the passage of time has marred, rather than honoured, the crown under Richard's watch. Northumberland creates the powerful image of tainted kingship, and he presents the imperative 'Away with me' as the only means to reclaim the past for the future. Indeed, his argument frames defection to Bolingbroke as the exclusive recourse to correcting present ills. Northumberland's nostalgic overtones make his longing for an idealised past not a hopeless lament, but a well-armed leap into the future.

Significantly, he grounds this call to arms in the discourse of seizing the moment, of *kairos*. Highlighting the importance of *kairos* (or *occasio*) to understanding sixteenth-century Renaissance political thought, Joanne Paul illustrates the political implications of *kairos*'s function as a rhetorical theory. As 'an understanding of how and, more importantly, when to speak in a given context', it 'has a fundamental role to play in Renaissance political counsel'.[73] Accepting *kairos* as part of political counsel invites a re-evaluation of precisely what Northumberland performs rhetorically in this galvanising speech. What further underscores the opportunistic nature of this moment is its timing: Northumberland knows that Richard sails for Ireland, and consequently that this is the occasion to seize and to change the political future. Shakespeare stages the power of that reclamatory, kairotic rhetoric through Ross and Willoughby's immediate, unconditional departure with Northumberland.

Shakespeare's use of *kairos* in this speech highlights how early modern temporal ideas inform his conceptualisation of nostalgic discourse. That an individual might seize time and control it disrupts the play's conventional ideas of time as exclusively linear and inevitably past or passing. Kairotic rhetorical theory allows an individual to respond to the 'character of the times' by responding to that precise moment instead of to universal moral codes. As Machiavelli noted, *kairos/occasio* represents a rare moment to operate within chronological time, and this is precisely what Northumberland advises.[74] Here, nostalgia both outlines a lost, and due, political inheritance, and voices the possibility of reclaiming that inheritance. The Duchess and Gaunt have already suggested that inheritance in their respective invocations of a preferable past. However, their rhetorics fail to persuade their auditors to action because they fail to look beyond the immediate temporal comparison and consider its implications for the future. In contrast, Northumberland's speech punctures Gaunt's earlier reflections on how shame binds England by offering to break that implicit imprisonment. As I argued above, Gaunt's speech moves England from present to past in the course of his speaking; he provides no explicit image of the future. Northumberland, by contrast, builds on Gaunt's past ideal and England's present desolation, offering to make the kingdom hospitable again and escape its present shame. That Northumberland's discourse refuses to rely exclusively on the construction of a past ideal to supplant the failing present demonstrates that in Shakespeare's use, the rhetoric of the idealised past must have some investment in the future to succeed. Its use must be more than a temporary salve of lament. It must look to perform an act of recovery.

Remarkably, hospitality becomes one means of enabling that recovery, that reclamation of tainted kingship. As acting regent during Richard's Irish foray, the Duke of York confronts Bolingbroke, Northumberland and their supporters at Berkeley Castle, and he rails against his nephew. York is 'no traitor's uncle' (2.3.88). He repeats a Duchess of Gloucester-style prolonged departure, eventually taking his leave of the rebels – before immediately offering them shelter: 'So fare you well /

Unless you please to enter in the castle / And there repose you for this night' (2.3.159–61). Considering the political and legal ramifications of England's temporary regent offering refuge to a banished man and his armed supporters, this hospitable proposal is surprising, but it communicates York's own 'shifting allegiance'.[75] Shakespeare foregrounds this shift in 2.1, with York's rejection of Richard's preposterous temporal logic. Richard's tyranny and Bolingbroke's claims persuade York to act for the latter, who lacks a home because Richard has denied him his inheritance.[76] In an England without Richard, hospitality is finally available, but with a price. Offering hospitality – an indicator of social cohesion and order – becomes complicated by its object, rebels who 'wound' the kingdom (3.2.7). York's subversive act inverts the social order in accepting rebellion; still, this subversion rejects the inimical status quo, and thus implicitly favours social harmony. Hospitality becomes an ambivalent practice here. That ambivalence signifies both how far the idealised space and time of hospitable England has receded, and how imperfect the present is as even the act of hospitality, the signifier of the perfect past, is implicated in treason.

By crafting Richard's role in creating an inhospitable commonwealth and thus creating a need to reclaim an idealised past, Shakespeare encourages and provokes repulsion to the king. The play, however, qualifies that affect as its unravelling *pathos*, elicited by Richard's fall, recasts him first as a pilgrim and then as a sorrowful – if potentially vengeful – maker of dearth. In Act 3 Richard becomes the object of the inhospitable England that he himself has made, and he now relies on others for succour. He wishes to be a beggar or a pilgrim, offering

> [. . .] my jewels for a set of beads,
> My gorgeous palace for a hermitage,
> My gay apparel for an almsman's gown,
> My figured goblets for a dish of wood,
> My sceptre for a palmer's walking staff,
> My subjects for a pair of carved saints
> And my large kingdom for a little grave. (3.3.147–53)

Like his reversal of fortune as a whole, Richard's rhetoric here disrupts the sympathy for his victims that Shakespeare steadily crafts through the play's first half. Accordingly, the rhetoric of a lost hospitality that had functioned as a source of nostalgia and a lament for England under Richard's rule now appears to be a lament for England, regardless of ruler. This multivalent discourse of lost hospitality reveals that England has become inhospitable to both ruler and ruled, its inherent nature – if it ever had one, Shakespeare asks us to wonder – denigrated first by corrupt kingship and then by rebellion. Shakespeare's insistence that England is now hospitable to no one iterates the idea of the 'mean season' that I read into this play. The only accessible locus of good is in the distant past, which as *Richard II* demonstrates is unknown even in that past's representation.

A scant eight lines following his pilgrim speech, Richard affirms England's pervasive hostility as he recoils from the inhospitality he suffers and imagines punishing his country. He declares to the Duke of Aumerle, 'We'll make foul weather with despised tears; / Our sighs and they shall lodge the summer corn / And make a dearth in this revolting land' (3.3.161–3). The king's vengeful wish for scarcity puns on the word 'lodge', and so even – or especially – in his bitterness he participates in the play's discourse of hospitality. While the primary sense of 'lodge' here signifies 'to beat down crops' through rain or wind (Richard's respective tears and sighs), the more common use, particularly by Shakespeare, of 'lodge' as a home or storehouse produces a secondary understanding which imagines Richard's fecundity (the tears and sighs) as paradoxically hoarding, 'lodging', the corn and thus creating a 'dearth' for his countrymen.[77] This second available sense creates not the absent hospitality that the rest of the play constructs, but rather a pernicious present hospitality. The image of storing food to intentionally harm the kingdom contrasts sharply with the social benefit that hospitality was supposed to produce. Moreover, Richard's threat of 'dearth' would have rung sharply in the ears of mid-1590s Elizabethans. 'Famine' was something that mostly happened elsewhere or in the past, something beyond the government's control; 'dearth' signified a dearness, one half of the common 'dearth and scarcity' that dogged England in these years.[78] With this threat Richard reprises his role as inhospitable king, as the failed host who interrupts events over which he presides (the trial), arbitrarily gives and takes time (to Bolingbroke) and illegally seizes what is not his (Bolingbroke's inheritance). Now, threatening to 'make a dearth', he jeopardises the sympathy won when he said he would 'with rainy eyes[,] / Write sorrow on the bosom of the earth' (3.2.146–7). Richard's tears possess a spiteful, violent power that seeks to make his rebellious subjects suffer, and these lines' multifaceted representation of hospitality encapsulate Richard's own complexity. He is both the tyrant still actively pursuing destructive policies towards his kingdom, and the repentant man who will finally recognise his waste of Time (5.5.49).

Reflecting on the dissolution, desolation and dearth that constitute the *topoi* of hospitality in *Richard II*, one little wonders that grief's prosopopoeic presence in the play is invariably connected to a language of absent or ironic hospitality. As the affect of loss, grief is the Duchess's sole 'companion' at Pleshy (1.2.55); Bolingbroke is its 'journeyman' (1.3.274); it keeps a 'tedious fast' in Gaunt (2.1.75); it is the Queen's guest 'in reversion' (2.2.38; cf. 2.2.7–9); and, 'hard-favoured', it lodges in Richard, himself a 'beauteous inn' (5.1.14, 13). The Duchess's and the Queen's respective implicit and explicit 'welcomes' to grief as a guest, grief's explicit physical existence *within* both Gaunt and Richard, and the fact that this 'guest' affects characters across political lines, intimate that larger concerns for the state underlie grief's presence. The drama's 'principal voice', grief in fact seems to be the only guest in this play.[79] As it is an unwelcome one, its ubiquity only further underlines the absence and impossibility of hospitality in *Richard II*. The play's connection between grief and injustice produces a powerful lens through which to consider how the play exposes the consequences of absent hospitality: this absence represents a failing commonwealth, a failure evident through the rule of a tyrant who willingly perpetuates that lack.

These elements together – tyrannical rule, a failing commonwealth, and its marker absent hospitality – incite grief at the loss of an idealised past, and that grief urges the reclamation of a time that is believed to have existed and is now (temporarily) lost. Shakespeare's early work offers a precedent in associating grief with the pursuit of an absent justice, and he repeats this association in *Richard II*.[80] While spectators bear witness to Richard's lack of interest in due process, the Duchess of Gloucester's grief represents a desperate search for unattainable justice. Gaunt counsels the Duchess to have patience and depend upon intervention from God, 'the widow's champion', but she demands revenge: 'To safeguard thine own life / The best way is to venge my Gloucester's death', she tells him (1.2.35–6). Redressing the Duke's murder is an act of reclaiming Gaunt's own self, as Gaunt is 'slain in him [Gloucester]' because of the blood that binds them (1.2.25). The stakes of the Duchess's plea are represented in Gaunt's grief for a greater loss, one compounded by his brother's murder and his son's banishment: the loss of England to a 'Landlord', tyrant king (2.1.113). The expression and recognition of loss inevitably create a dichotomy of a positive past and a negative present, and the temporal difference articulated in that dichotomy affirms the possibility of reclamation. More than the longing for the past's return, it is the language of that return's possibility that defines Shakespeare's use of nostalgia in *Richard II*.

As *Richard II* starts to complicate its initial construction of the present's inferiority to the past, a reorientation occurs in the tragedy's focus on Richard and on the future. The play stages Richard's failure to recognise the past as a model for behaviour and the determinant of his own inheritance, his 'fantasy of a continuous present' wherein Richard's connection of affect and legal possession fails to consider time.[81] In fact it is not until Richard recognises a rupture in his present – Bolingbroke's 'usurping steps' – that he can begin to consider temporality (3.2.17), and he begins to fixate on the future, threatening Northumberland and Bolingbroke with an image of violence to come. From the walls of Berkeley Castle, Richard warns:

> But ere the crown he [Bolingbroke] looks for live in peace,
> Ten thousand bloody crowns of mothers' sons
> Shall ill become the flower of England's face,
> Change the complexion of her maid-pale peace
> To scarlet indignation, and bedew
> Her pastor's grass with faithful English blood.
> (3.3.95–100 and cf. ll. 85–90)

While the rebels seek to reclaim the past in the interest of the future, here Richard denies that that future will fulfil their fantasies of 'high majesty'. Rather, their actions curse future generations, and the glorious England they wish to re-establish will be stained with the blood of its own, creating a new generation of the grieved who will seek a new (violent) path to reclamation. But Richard has made his politics in the present and consequently failed to comprehend the temporality inherent in law that gives him the authority to make those politics.[82]

The nostalgia that bred the rebels' future-oriented acts, when thrust into that future, collapses, and its failure to revive the desired 'high majesty' demonstrates again how Shakespeare's dramaturgy insists not only on the fallibility of any time – past, present, future – but on the limits of temporal desire. Where Gaunt emphasised the nation's glorious past and grieved for the loss of England's virtue at the hands of Richard, Bolingbroke's acts of reclamation, his ascendancy to the throne, incite the Bishop of Carlisle's bloody predictions for England's reckoning. Threatening that 'future ages [shall] groan for this foul act' (4.1.139), he echoes not only the Duchess of Gloucester's 'groans' of welcome (1.2.70), but also the maternal image of England discussed above. Carlisle imagines not simply a general anguish, but labour pains, an origin point for a new, unwelcome England. Anticipating the Duchess of York's plea to her husband ('Hadst thou groaned for him / As I have done, thou wouldst be more pitiful', 5.2.102–3), Carlisle predicts that Bolingbroke's actions will give birth to future violence.[83] Shakespeare binds the bishop's future prophesy with past and present as Carlisle recalls both Richard's and Gaunt's language in his warning that

> [I]n this seat of peace tumultuous wars
> Shall kin with kin and kind with kind confound.

> Disorder, horror, fear and mutiny
> Shall here inhabit, and this land be called
> The field of Golgotha and dead men's skulls.
> O, if you raise this house against this house,
> It will the woefullest division prove
> That ever fell upon this cursed earth. (4.1.141–8)

The bishop repeats Richard's compassing of future civil war and the generations that will cry against their ancestors for planting such a seed, as he imagines that 'child, child's children, cry against you, "Woe"!' (l. 150). Like Gaunt, Carlisle invokes 'this land' – yet the image he crafts is not of an 'other Eden', but of 'Golgotha'. 'This land' both cites and attenuates Gaunt's lines ('this land of such dear souls, this dear dear land', 2.1.57), while 'This seat of peace' inverts Gaunt's 'seat of Mars' (2.1.41), and the bishop re-imagines 'this earth of majesty' as 'this cursed earth' (2.1.41). That Carlisle is absent for Gaunt's speech highlights all the more how Shakespeare rewrites Gaunt's sense of a lost past to deny its availability now or in the future. For the bishop, there is no past. Fearing the consequences of tyranny and misrule for England, both Gaunt and Carlisle react to their respective presents: the former's speech functions as an elegy, the latter's as a lament for the future, and together they confirm the play's temporal status as a 'mean season'. Both men envision desolation and thus participate in the rhetoric of absent hospitality that *Richard II* offers and aligns with the neglect of the kingdom. The seeds of Carlisle's threatened 'Disorder' and 'mutiny' have already been sown through that neglect, that absence of the noble care on which hospitality depends.

As a final image to insist on hospitality's absence in England under the new order, Shakespeare uses Bolingbroke to return to the imagery of forced pilgrimage that attached to his exile in 1.3. His promise to 'make a voyage to the Holy Land' (5.6.49) is not explicitly called a pilgrimage, but this vow may signify just that, rather than the failed 'crusade' of the *Henry IV* plays.[84] While Bolingbroke can now command others like Exton to 'wander' '[w]ith Cain' (5.6.43), regardless he must also, like his Act 1 self, seek hospitality outside his country 'To wash this blood off from my guilty hand' (5.6.50). Bolingbroke does not possess the power to make England hospitable, and it cannot offer him the forgiveness or the clear conscience he needs. His recognition of the pilgrimage's significance (whether in earnest or as politic strategy) represents in the final instance the inability to practice hospitality at home.

For Elizabethans of the 1590s, the idea of hospitality remained starkly present, not only in places of its former practice, but in government demands, contemporary prose and drama. *Richard II*'s insistent absent hospitality, its language of fasting and dearth, anchor the play's medieval world in sixteenth-century problems and policies. Hospitality's absence in the mid-1590s echoes throughout the play, as the *topoi* of desolation and dissolution recall a ruined tradition that the government sought to reinstate, to return to. In offering a vision of a medieval England that should be a space of hospitality and is instead hostile to that practice, the play interrogates how the idealised past, or any past, is constructed.

Simultaneously, *Richard II* stages the power that construction possesses when bound to a tantalising future: it inspires rebellion, it sets into motion the deposition of a tyrant king. In rendering the 'present', fourteenth-century England inhospitable, *Richard II* offers nostalgic narratives of a more distant, perfect past that suggest both that past's accessibility and its status as a natural right of England. As I have argued, Gaunt's speech, like the play as a whole, claims that hospitality provides the conditions of national stability because it relies on the practice of true nobility. Hospitality, in this view, operates as one type of English political inheritance. While the play stages the failure to reclaim that inheritance, and indeed questions the reality of such an inheritance, it still positions nostalgia as the successful rhetorical engine of that reclamatory act. In its representation of a 'mean season', *Richard II* argues that there was no perfect, hospitable past, and consequently there can be no perfect, hospitable future.

Notes

1. Williams, *The Country and the City*, pp. 9–12.
2. Felicity Heal, *Hospitality in Early Modern England* (Oxford: Clarendon Press, 1990), p. 112.
3. Heal, *Hospitality*, p. 113.
4. See Walsham, *The Reformation of the Landscape: Religion, Memory, and Identity in Early Modern Britain and Ireland* (Oxford: Oxford University Press, 2011), especially chapters 2–4.
5. Critics still debate the precise dating of *Richard II*. While its language groups it with *A Midsummer Night's Dream* and *Romeo and Juliet* (1594/1595), Chris Fitter has argued for 1596, linking Shakespeare's construction of Bolingbroke and his handling of source material to Essex and events of that year. See Fitter, 'Historicising Shakespeare's *Richard II*: Current Events, Dating, and the Sabotage of Essex', *Early Modern Literary Studies*, 11:2 (2005), 1.1–47. http://purl.oclc.org/emls/11-2/fittric2.htm
6. My use juxtaposes our contemporary understanding of the phrase with the sense it obtained in the early modern period, as 'coming or occurring between two points of time or two events' ('Mean', adj.^{2}, 2. *OED* (Oxford: Oxford University Press, draft revision March 2009)). Connoting an 'unpleasant time', the phrase 'mean season' operates in a somewhat

punning way, as the notion of 'season' – a bounded period of time – activates that temporal quality already present in the sense of 'mean' as an intermediate. The phrase was used in texts across the sixteenth century – from Robert Greene to translations of Tacitus – and was used metaphorically (for example, in Menewe's *A plaine subversyon*, Aii^v).

7. Cf. Stephen Orgel, 'Prologue: "I am Richard II"', in *Representations of Elizabeth I in Early Modern Culture*, ed. Alessandra Petrina and Laura Tosi (New York: Palgrave Macmillan, 2011), pp. 11–43; Fitter, 'Historicising Shakespeare's *Richard II*'; Jeffrey S. Doty, 'Shakespeare's *Richard II*, "Popularity", and the Early Modern Public Sphere', *Shakespeare Quarterly*, 61:2 (2010), 183–205; Joseph Campana, 'The Child's Two Bodies: Shakespeare, Sovereignty, and the End of Succession', *ELH*, 81:3 (2014), 811–39.
8. Doty, 'Shakespeare's *Richard II*', 192.
9. Julia Reinhard Lupton, 'Making Room, Affording Hospitality: Environments of Entertainment in *Romeo and Juliet*', *Journal of Medieval and Early Modern Studies*, 43:1 (2013), 145–72; Lupton, 'Macbeth's Martlets: Shakespearean Phenomenologies of Hospitality', *Criticism*, 54:3 (2012), 365–76; Lupton, 'The Affordances of Hospitality: Shakespearean Drama between Historicism and Phenomenology', *Poetics Today*, 35:4 (2014), 615–33; David Ruiter, 'Shakespeare and Hospitality: Opening *The Winter's Tale*', *Mediterranean Studies*, 16 (2007), 157–77; Daryl W. Palmer, *Hospitable Performances: Dramatic Genre and Cultural Practices in Early Modern England* (West Lafayette, IN: Purdue University Press, 1992).
10. Guy, *Tudor England*, p. 404. On wages, see Larry Patriquin, 'The Agrarian Origins of the Industrial Revolution in England', *Review of Radical Politics*, 36:2 (2004), 196–216, 210.
11. England and Wales, Privy Council, *The renewing of certaine orders devised by the speciall commandement of the Queenes Majestie, for the reliefe and stay of the present dearth of graine within the realme* (London, 1594).
12. Ibid., Biiii^v.
13. Ibid., C^r.
14. Ben-Amos, *The Culture of Giving: Informal Support and Gift-Exchange in Early Modern England*, Cambridge Social and Cultural Histories series, ed. Margot C. Finn, Colin Jones and Keith Wrightson (Cambridge: Cambridge University Press, 2008), p. 314.
15. See Margo Todd, *Christian Humanism and the Puritan Social Order* (Cambridge: Cambridge University Press, 2003), pp. 135–7; Ben-Amos, *The Culture of Giving*, p. 141 on the presence of charitable giving despite drastic changes in the hospitality tradition.
16. England and Wales, Privy Council, *A new charge given by the Queenes commandement, to all justices of peace, and all maiors, shiriffes, and all principall officers of cities, boroughs, and townes corporate, for execution of sundry orders published the last yeere for staie of dearth of graine, with certaine additions nowe this present yeere to be well observed and executed* (London, 1595), C3^v.
17. Heal, *Hospitality*, p. 133.
18. Guy, *Tudor England*, p. 404.

19. England and Wales, *The Queenes Majesties proclamation* ... (London, 1596), t.p. See also England and Wales, *By the Queene. A proclamation for the dearth of corne* (London, 1596).
20. Ibid., [p. 2].
21. Heal, *Hospitality*, p. 118.
22. See Heal, *Hospitality*, p. 99.
23. England and Wales, *The Queenes Majesties proclamation*, [p. 2].
24. Guy, *Tudor England*, pp. 404–5.
25. Ibid.
26. Heal, *Hospitality*, p. 118.
27. England and Wales, *The Queenes Majesties proclamation*, [p. 2].
28. Heal, *Hospitality*, pp. 112 and cf. pp. 111–22, 113.
29. Heal, *Hospitality*, p. 19, cf. pp. 19–22, and see Ben-Amos, *The Culture of Giving*, pp. 126–34.
30. Ole Peter Grell, 'The Protestant Imperative of Christian Care and Neighbourly Love', in *Health Care and Poor Relief in Protestant Europe 1500–1700*, ed. Andrew Cunningham and Ole Peter Grell, Studies in the Social History of Medicine (London: Routledge, 1997), pp. 42–63, p. 49. Cf. Heal, *Hospitality*, pp. 122–5; Duffy, *The Stripping of the Altars*, pp. 357–62.
31. Anon, *Three sermons, or Homelies* (London, 1596), B^v. The author cites Ecclesiastes 11.1.
32. Heal, *Hospitality*, p. 129.
33. McRae, *God Speed the Plough: The Representation of Agrarian England, 1500–1660* (Cambridge: Cambridge University Press, 1996), pp. 58–9, 60.
34. McRae, *God Speed the Plough*, p. 98.
35. Cf. Thomas Norton's letter to Francis Mylles, Folger Shakespeare Library MS X.c.62; Anon, *Rites of Durham* (1593), ed. J. T. Fowler, Publications of the Surtees Society, 107 (Durham, 1903); Margaret Aston, 'English Ruins and English History: The Dissolution and the Sense of the Past', *Journal of the Warburg and Courtauld Institutes*, 36 (1973), 231–55, 243; and Schwyzer, *Literature, Nationalism, and Memory*, p. 73.
36. Heal, *Hospitality*, p. 230.
37. Karen Stober, *Later Medieval Monasteries and their Patrons: England and Wales, c. 1300–1540* (Woodbridge, UK: Boydell, 2007), p. 171.
38. Duffy, *The Stripping of the Altars*, p. 384, and Heal, *Hospitality*, pp. 231–2.
39. Todd, *Christian Humanism*, p. 136.
40. Heal, *Hospitality*, p. 233.
41. Walsham, *Reformation of the Landscape*, pp. 276, 114, 116, 296, 147.
42. *Titus Andronicus*, in William Shakespeare, *The Oxford Complete Works*, gen. eds Stanley Wells and Gary Taylor (Oxford: Clarendon Press, 1988; reissued 1998), 5.1.20–1, 22–3.
43. On the play's Reformation references and its alignment of the Goths with Reformation reformers, see Jonathan Bate's edition of *Titus Andronicus*, Arden Third Series (London and New York: Routledge, 1995), pp. 19–21.
44. Sonnet 73, *Oxford Complete Works*, ll.1–4.
45. Philip Schwyzer, *Archaeologies of the English Renaissance* (Oxford: Oxford University Press, 2007), pp. 75, 99 and cf. pp. 75–107.
46. Helen Vendler notes how it also contains 'ruinate', *The Art of Shakespeare's Sonnets* (Cambridge, MA: Harvard University Press, 1997), p. 301.

47. Walsham, *The Reformation of the Landscape*, p. 275.
48. Stow, *Survey*, pp. 7–8. All further references will be made in the text.
49. Ibid., pp. 125–6.
50. On the complexity of late, see Schwyzer, '"Late" Losses', 97–114.
51. Norton, Letter to Francis Mylles, Folger Shakespeare Library MS X.c.62, 1ʳ.
52. Norton, Letter to Francis Mylles, Folger Shakespeare Library MS X.c.62, p. 1ᵛ. Cf. Knowles, *Bare Ruined Choirs*, pp. 182–90.
53. The author might be the house's last Register, George Bates; J. T. Fowler's edition of the *Rites* tacitly supports this claim, first voiced by Cambridge antiquarian Thomas Baker in his 1740 manuscript of the text, *Rites of Durham*, ed. J. T. Fowler (Durham: For the Society by Andrews & co, 1903), p. xiv.
54. Cf. n 8 above.
55. William Shakespeare, *King Richard II*, ed. Charles R. Forker, Arden Third Series (Walton-on-Thames, 2002; repr. 2004), 1.1.1. All references are to this edition and will be made in the text.
56. Cf. Forker's note to 1.1.1, pp. 179–80; David Norbrook, 'A Liberal Tongue: Language and Rebellion in *Richard II*', in *Shakespeare's Universe: Renaissance Ideas and Conventions: Essays in Honour of W. R. Elton*, ed. John M. Mucciolo, with the assistance of Steven J. Doloff and Edward A. Rauchut (Aldershot, UK: Scolar Press, 1996), p. 43; Phyllis Rackin, 'The Role of the Audience in Shakespeare's *Richard II*', *Shakespeare Quarterly*, 36:3 (1985), 262–81, 264–5; George Gopen, 'Private Grief into Public Action: The Rhetoric of John of Gaunt in "Richard II"', *Studies in Philology*, 84:3 (1987), 338–62, 340; and David Bergeron, '"Richard II" and Carnival Politics', *Shakespeare Quarterly*, 42:1 (1991), 33–43, 38.
57. Norbrook, 'A Liberal Tongue', p. 43.
58. For a discussion and definition of 'afford' and 'affordances' see Lupton, 'Making Room, Affording Hospitality', 147.
59. See also Molly Smith, 'Mutant Scenes and "Minor" Conflicts', in *Richard II: A Feminist Companion to Shakespeare*, ed. Dympna Callaghan, 2nd edn (London: Wiley & Sons, 2000/2016), pp. 281–93, p. 285; Lynne Magnusson, 'Shakespearean Tragedy and the Language of Lament', in *The Oxford Handbook of Shakespearean Tragedy*, ed. Michael Neill and David Schalkwyk (Oxford: Oxford University Press, 2016), pp. 120–33; Jennifer C. Vaught, *Masculinity and Emotion in Early Modern English Literature* (Aldershot, UK: Ashgate, 2008) pp. 88–105, p. 90.
60. Peter Corbin and Douglas Sedge, eds., 'Introduction', in Anon, *Thomas of Woodstock* (Manchester: Manchester University Press, 2002), p. 4.
61. The play's early editions make the connection explicit in the title; cf. Anon, *A Tragedy of King Richard the Second, Concluding with The Murder of the Duke of Gloucester at Calais*, ed. J. O. Halliwell (London, 1870); and Anon, *The First Part of the Reign of King Richard the Second or Thomas of Woodstock*, ed. Wilhelmina Frijlinck (London: the Malone Society, 1929). The play's Elizabethan dating has been challenged by Macdonald P. Jackson, who post-dates it to *Richard II* and claims it for Anthony Munday, 'Shakespeare's *Richard II* and the Anonymous *Thomas of Woodstock*', *Medieval and Renaissance Drama in England*, 14 (2001), 17–65, and

idem, 'The Date and Authorship of *Thomas of Woodstock*: Evidence and its Interpretation', *Research Opportunities in English Renaissance Drama*, 46 (2007), 67–100. Certain concordances and echoes are evident between the plays, but the differences in overall tone, style and even arguments – not to mention the stark absence of Mowbray, which is significant in light of the plotting and depiction of Woodstock's murder – suggest we should consider this play much more *Thomas of Woodstock* than 1 *Richard II*. Recent productions of *Richard II* suggest that the Woodstock story is not essential to understanding the play: Rupert Goold's film adaptation (2012) and Shakespeare's Globe's 2015 stage production both cut Act 1, Scene 2 entirely, where Gaunt and the Duchess discuss explicitly Richard's involvement in the Duke of Gloucester's death, which *Thomas of Woodstock* depicts.
62. Cf. 3.2 and 4.2 in Anon, *Thomas of Woodstock*, ed. Peter Corbin and Douglas Sedge. Further references will be made in the text.
63. Corbin and Sedge, *Thomas of Woodstock*, p. 109, note to 3.2.9–14.
64. Dated to the 1540s but not published until 1581, this text was long attributed to William Stafford and then to John Hale, but Mary Dewar has attributed it to Smith (cf. Dewar, ed., *A Discourse of the Common Weal of this Realm of England* (Washington: Folger Shakespeare Library, 1969).
65. Dewar, ed., *A Discourse*, p. 20.
66. Ibid., pp. 21–2.
67. For the definition of *hypophera* and other forms of *interrogatio*, see Warren Taylor, *Tudor Figures of Rhetoric*, ed. Warren Shibles (Whitewater, WI: The Language Press, 1972), p. 103.
68. The presence of pilgrimage on stage was not without loaded meaning, as criminality was associated with the practice of pilgrimage in Elizabethan England. See Walsham, *Reformation of the Landscape*, pp. 103, 106, 82–3.
69. Gaunt's reference contains echoes of the Bastard in *King John*, the 'sister play' of *Richard II*, Lander and Tobin, eds., *King John* (London: Bloomsbury, 2018), p. 315n. In that play Philip also makes use of an anaphoric 'now' at 4.3.142–56, and he attacks the rebelling nobles with 'You bloody Neroes, ripping up the womb / Of your dear mother England' (5.2.152–3), where Salisbury had previously referred to himself and his fellow nobles as 'the sons and children of this isle' (5.2.25).
70. Collinson, *The Religion of Protestants*, p. 261, but see pp. 60–3.
71. Paul Slack, 'Dearth and Social Policy in Early Modern England', *Social History of Medicine*, 5:1 (1992), 1–17, 7.
72. Slack, 'Dearth and Social Policy', 6–7; Heal, *Hospitality*, p. 128, and cf. pp. 127–8, and see Steve Hindle, 'Dearth, Fasting and Alms: The Campaign for General Hospitality in Late Elizabethan England', *Past and Present*, 172:1 (2001), 44–86.
73. Paul, 'The Use of *Kairos* in Renaissance Political Philosophy', 43–78, 44.
74. Paul, 'The Use of *Kairos* in Renaissance Political Philosophy', 57.
75. I am grateful to an anonymous reviewer for *Parergon* who pointed out this moment and used this apt phrase to describe York's attitude.
76. In addition to Richard's seizure of Gaunt's wealth at 2.1, Bolingbroke accuses Bushy and Green of having 'Disparked my parks, and felled my

forest woods, / From my own windows torn my household coat, / Razed out my imprese . . .' (3.1.22–5).
77. 'lodge, v.' *OED Online*, July 2018, Oxford University Press. www.oed.com/view/Entry/109703 (accessed 27 October 2015). Shakespeare's use of the paradox of abundance producing famine is of course familiar from his Sonnet 1.
78. See Slack, 'Dearth and Social Policy', 7–9.
79. Charles R. Forker, 'Marlowe's *Edward II*', p. 84; see also Peter Sacks, 'Where Words Prevail Not: Grief, Revenge, and Language in Kyd and Shakespeare', *ELH*, 49:3 (1982), 576–601; Zenón Luis-Martínez, 'Shakespeare's Historical Drama as "Trauerspiel: Richard II": And After', *ELH*, 75:3 (2008), 673–705; Smith, 'Mutant Scenes'; Virginia Carr, 'The Power of Grief in *Richard II*', *Études Anglaises*, 31:2 (1978), 145–51.
80. Grief is then linked to the theme of *terras Astraea reliquit*, Sacks, 'Where Words Prevail Not', p. 579. *Titus Andronicus* provides a striking example of this argument; in Act 4 Titus and his kinsmen shoot arrows over the palace, and he quotes Ovid as he continues his vain pursuit: '*Terras Astraea reliquit*: be you remembered, Marcus, / She's gone, she's fled' (4.3.4–5), and his thinking about Astraea persists in the ensuing lines.
81. Bradin Cormack, 'Shakespeare Possessed: Legal Affect and the Time of Holding', in *Shakespeare and the Law*, ed. Paul Raffield and Gary Watt (Oxford and Portland, OR: Hart Publishing, 2008), pp. 83–100, p. 87.
82. Cormack, 'Shakespeare Possessed', p. 89.
83. These maternal associations also recall the Queen's metaphorical delivery of woe in 2.2, where she imagines herself 'a gasping new-delivered mother' of her soul's 'prodigy' (2.2.65, 64), and the 'groan' that is her final word at her leave-taking of Richard (5.1.100).
84. Charles Forker, ed., *Richard II*, p. 483 n to 5.6.49.

Chapter 4

The Lessons of Nostalgia in *Julius Caesar* and *Sejanus*

So have I seene, when Cesar would appeare,
And on the Stage at halfe-sword parley were,
Brutus and *Cassius*: oh how the Audience,
Were ravish'd, with what wonder they went thence,
When some new day they would not brooke a line,
Of tedious (though well laboured) *Catilines*,
Sejanus too was irksome, they priz'de more
Honest *Iago*, or the jealous Moore.
And though the Fox, and subtall Alchimist,
Long intermitted could not be quite mist.[1]

With these lines, the poet and translator Leonard Digges (1588–1635) provided posthumous commendatory verses to the 1640 edition of Shakespeare's *Poems*, lines which echo his earlier laudatory poem for the First Folio and repeat his allusion there to *Julius Caesar*'s 'parley' scene. But these later verses specifically add an element of comparison which asserts Shakespeare's superiority as a poet, and which stresses the longing attendant on that superiority. Jonson himself perhaps makes a sly comparison in *Epicene or The Silent Woman* (1609), when Truewit threatens Morose that a wife may 'censure poets and authors and styles, and compare 'em, Daniel with Spenser, Jonson with t'other youth', where that 'youth' may refer ironically to a middle-aged Shakespeare.[2] Historically, such comparison as a method has often either opposed the two playwrights or urged Jonson's reliance on Shakespeare. Percy Allen's wildly speculative 1928 account of *Sejanus* argues that Jonson modelled his play on 'his master' Shakespeare, compared to whom he falls flat; Lynn Meskill more recently argues that Jonson must have felt 'a threat to [his] authorship' from the unknown collaborator referred to in his quarto.[3] However bardolatrous (and dated) Allen's claims are, such value judgements can and have created a narrative of one-way influence that doesn't necessarily see exchange or development, only uninspired dependence. Increasingly, however, critics have argued that Shakespeare and Jonson stage a dialogue or, failing that, a set of shared concerns: from *Othello* and *Volpone*, to *Othello* and *Every Man in his Humour*, to *Sejanus*'s influence on *Measure for Measure*, *King Lear* and *Coriolanus*, 'there is little proof of enmity and considerable evidence of artistic cooperation'.[4]

Looking closely at *Julius Caesar* (1599) and *Sejanus* (1603/05), their material and thematic connections certainly encourage this line of thinking about the plays' relationship more as a 'conversation' than a contention.[5] *Sejanus* was first performed just a few years after *Julius Caesar*, and evidence suggests that it was the first Roman play produced on the public stage after *Caesar*'s success at the Globe.[6] Jonson likely worked on *Sejanus* for a year or two before its first production in 1603, and the commendatory poem of 'Ev. B' in the 1605 quarto seems to corroborate this, noting that the play cost Jonson 'so much sweat, and so much oyle'.[7] By this time Jonson had joined the Chamberlain's Men – in 1599, when *Caesar* and *Every Man Out of his Humour* were first performed – left for Blackfriars and the Children of Queen Elizabeth's Chapel, and joined again. *Sejanus*, Jonson's first play for the newly minted King's Men, was not a success, and to say so is a gross understatement.[8] Endeavouring to rehabilitate *Sejanus* in his unique and highly stylised 1605 quarto, Jonson revealed the stage version's collaborative nature: 'A second Pen had good share' in writing the drama, and critics from the eighteenth century to the *New Oxford Shakespeare* have suspected that this collaborator was Shakespeare, one of the play's 'principall Tragoedians' and of course the King's Men's principal playwright.[9] *Sejanus* seems to pick up where *Julius Caesar* left off, as it 'in effect depicts the consequences of the transition from republic to empire which was the subject of *Julius Caesar*, and in doing so it overturns the assumptions which govern Shakespeare's play'.[10] Shared interests in secrecy, lying, the slippery nature of language, the legitimacy of the theatre, republicanism, tyranny – rather than proving Jonson's dependence on Shakespeare, such an overlap demonstrates a willingness to continue the 'conversation' Donaldson aptly observes.

While scholars have acknowledged the plays' shared interests in the power of language to (re)construct the political world, their shared used of nostalgic discourses as part of that power has to this point gone unnoticed. This chapter examines how Shakespeare and Jonson employ nostalgia only to reject it both as a manipulative rhetorical instrument and a means of affective and philosophical consolation. In Chapters 2 and 3, I argued that Shakespeare stages nostalgia as a potent, ambivalent political rhetoric, one that emerged from a culture which viewed certain forms of nostalgia suspiciously. In his English histories, political factions recognise the rhetorical power of idealising past and future, and they harness that power as a political strategy. Similarly, *Julius Caesar* demonstrates Shakespeare's interest in nostalgia as a successful mode of oratory, and one dependent on its future orientation for that success. Jonson, in contrast, highlights nostalgia's failure to offer an active philosophical refuge, and he argues that it is Neostoicism, not the idealised past, that offers the key to political survival. Howsoever Jonson, like Shakespeare, places nostalgia in the mouths of opposing factions (Arruntius and Latiaris), Jonson stages nostalgia as an impotent discourse when voiced by the Germanicans and a potently devious tool in the hands of Tiberius and his flunkies. By dramatising how language is manipulated for political gain, the plays re-present early modern England's anxieties about language's ability to conceal and perpetuate evil, which Shakespeare would explore elsewhere in tragedies like *Othello* (possibly influenced by *Sejanus*). Moreover, in *Julius Caesar* and *Sejanus*, nostalgia draws attention to how history is constructed and its particular use as a rhetoric interrogates the individual's role in history's inevitable rhythms. Nostalgia and language manipulation highlight historiography's centrality to both tragedies, and the deliberate, selective construction of history becomes, for good or ill, a mode of individual political action – one with topical relevance since the 1599 Bishops' Ban that made printing 'Englishe historyes' a criminal act.[11] This shared interest in and suspicion of language, and consequently of nostalgia, reinforces the dialogue between these two plays even as it will demonstrate how Jonson's use of nostalgia responds to and refuses Shakespeare's seemingly ambivalent use of it.

Nostalgia also highlights the historical models present within and across these plays, models linked, as I discuss below, to Tacitean concepts of history. In both plays, a political cycle seems to operate in the underlying plot structures. *Julius Caesar* depicts the rise and fall of a single man through the play. Pompey, we are told, has been defeated and forgotten by the Romans; Caesar is bound for kingship, then assassinated; Brutus seems poised to be named 'Caesar' but falls to Antony and Octavius. As the play closes we know – and an early modern audience knew – that Antony, too, at his height will fall to the future Caesar Augustus. *Julius Caesar* ends with the anticipation of an emperor/tyrant, and it is with a tyrannical emperor that *Sejanus* begins and ends, the play offering a mimetic illustration of how totalitarian power – rather than Fortune – effects the rise and fall of individuals. Simultaneously, the invocation of an idealised past affirms the idea of cyclical history, of events building towards a crescendo that will diminish only to be repeated, and in this way it disrupts the notion of teleological history. In *Julius Caesar*, competing narratives of Rome and of its citizens, and the declaration of the individual's ability to shape the future and its retelling as history (as Brutus and Cassius proclaim), become together the signs of the postlapsarian state. History's conflicts highlight its existence. It is a recognisable turn, one evident in *2 Henry VI* and *Richard II*, which used idealised constructions of the past as the basis for political action to gain a utopian state. By contrast, in *Sejanus* Jonson insists on the irretrievability of the past that seems so tantalisingly close in Shakespeare.

Both playwrights construct respective Romes that display the instability not only of language, but of interpretation; the language that articulates a perfect past becomes evidence of just how fallen the present is. That Shakespeare and Jonson make the act of interpretation within their plays – through politician, poet or historian – crucial to their dramaturgy reinscribes how distant Rome and its implicit cognate – early modern London – are from a perfect future. Any longing for reunion, for a return to an ideal point of origin, necessarily implies a drastic alteration in the role of language. As *Julius Caesar* and *Sejanus* both make clear, words are divorced from the stable meaning that they possess before the Fall. Both Romes are characterised by the danger of language's porousness, its openness to interpretation, and as such reveal Tacitean anxieties about the use of language as a mask.

Digges's poem, while attempting to distinguish Shakespeare from Jonson, strongly intimates the anxiety of discursive flexibility shared by both men. The text compares Sejanus, the flatterer so dangerously, jealously close to power, both to Iago – Shakespeare's most dangerous, jealous character – and to Othello, who proved equally, if tragically, jealous. Writing that '*Sejanus* too was irksome', Digges concludes that the audience 'priz'de more / Honest *Iago*, or the jealous Moore'. Why make this comparison? Digges had many other Shakespearean tragedies to choose from; perhaps he simply needed an end rhyme (he was equally uninventive with those preceding). At first glance, these plays seem to have very little in common beyond an Italian setting: one is a tragedy of state; the other seems to be a comedy-romance until the plot twists darkly to a love tragedy. But *Othello* and *Sejanus* were performed within a year of each other, and Shakespeare could have been writing his Mediterranean tragedy as Jonson was finishing his Roman play.[12] Digges therefore may have been remembering comparisons made at the time, when he would have been studying at Oxford. Both plays have at their centre sociopathic villains fed by hatred; both enact the fall of favourites – Tiberius's Sejanus and Venice's beloved Othello, and Othello's favoured, 'honest' ensign. The comparison of

Iago and Sejanus highlights particularly the early modern anxiety about rhetoric and language that lies at the heart of both plays: that language could mask the true nature of an individual; that it could be used to advance oneself while inciting psychological torture, domestic violence and murder; that it could enable the destruction of the best of the best society. These possibilities are performed by both plays, and all return to a central concern binding Jonson and Shakespeare across these dramas: language makes complete knowledge of another impossible, even in the exhibitionist realm of drama. We never learn Iago's answer to Othello's 'Why'.[13]

I have extracted from Digges's brief comparison one example of how Jonson and Shakespeare are bound through their interests in a corrupt language. By focusing on nostalgia as a manifestation of that language, I argue that both playwrights reveal nostalgia's inadequacy to reclaim the past in the future and to provide a solution to tyranny. In *Julius Caesar* and *Sejanus*, Shakespeare and Jonson reject the image of an idealised ancient Rome and challenge once more the seemingly innocuous desire for a perfect past.

Tacitus and the Playwrights: Creating Suspects of History

This shared interest in degenerate language likewise aligns both plays with the historian of their moment, Tacitus, whose *Annals* and *Histories* Jonson lamented were in the pockets of 'ripe statesmen [...] growing in every street'.[14] Scholars have justly focused on the poet's knowledge of Tacitus – Jonson himself provides the evidence in his quarto annotations to *Sejanus*, whose vigilantly cynical view of the political process under Tiberius Caesar demonstrates a Tacitean influence. But the Roman historian was also known to Shakespeare, who likely had read, or was reading, Tacitus around the time he was writing *Julius Caesar*.[15] This influence and familiarity were co-emergent with Tacitus's rise as a historian of interest in late Tudor England and particularly at the turn of the seventeenth century, and Jonson and Shakespeare stage not only Tacitean concerns with historiography and the historian's intentions and purposes in writing history, but also urgent political questions such as obedience under tyranny. As the sixteenth century drew to a close, Tacitus's reputation moved away from the 'mixed' reception it had received throughout Western Europe earlier in the century, and he became fashionable and popular, if still controversial, for his 'master[y] of politics' and his historical parallelism; that is, comparing past to present.[16] Tacitus intrigued late Elizabethan society not only with his masterly style, but because he offered 'a framework [of political action] freed from the providentialist bias of popular histories', narratives of how '"the autonomous politic will"' might '"dominate events by its command of the politic arts"'.[17] Statistics alone indicate Tacitus's status-shift: between 1550 and 1600, four editions of Tacitus's works (the *Agricola, Annals, Histories*) were printed in England; between 1600 and 1649, at least 67 editions of the *Annals* and *Histories* were published.[18] As noted, his popularity irked Jonson, whose Jack Daw describes him as 'an entire knot, sometimes worth the untying, very seldom' (*Epicene*, 2.3.55-6) and later swears an oath by him: 'As I hope to finish Tacitus, I intend no murder' (4.5.45). Justus Lipsius, who published his own edition of Tacitus in 1575, was instrumental in this positive shift in Tacitus's English and European fortunes. Lipsius made apparent just how relevant Tacitus's age was to the courts of early modern Europe. In the prefatory matter to his *Sixe bookes of politickes or civil doctrine*, Lipsius explains that of all the Greek and Roman authors cited in the volumes,

> *Cornelius Tacitus* hath the preheminence, being recited extraordinarily, because he alone affoordeth more matter, then all the rest. The reason hereof consisteth in the wisedome of the man, both because he is very sententious, as likewise because *Lipsius* had bene very conversant with him: by which meanes he offred him selfe without call.[19]
>
> [*Inter eos eminet Corn. Tacitus extra ordinem dicendus: quia plus unus ille nobis contulit, quàm ceteri omnes. Caussa in Prudentiá viri est, & quia creberrimus sententiis: atque etiam, quia familiaris nobis, & offerebat se non vocatus.*][20]

Tacitus's 'wisdom' ('Prudentia') lends him 'more matter' (suggesting perhaps to Shakespeare that Tacitus's works possess 'less art'). In ten years, between 1594 and 1604, Lipsius's *Sixe bookes* went through fifteen Latin editions – one new edition every eighteen months.[21] Additionally, through Sir Henry Savile's English translation of the *Histories* (1591) and Richard Greneway's 1598 translations of the *Histories* and *Annals*, Tacitus's work was consumed by the period's (for Jonson, pseudo-) intellectuals – most notably the Earl of Essex and his followers. Savile, who had previously tutored the Queen in Greek, dedicated his work to her, and his dedication, like Greneway's to Essex (to whose circle Savile, and perhaps Jonson, belonged), indicates the audience for which these translations were intended.[22] And while Tacitus remained in the literati's pockets, he also remained legible – through Jonson and Shakespeare's respective works – on the public stage.

At the heart of Tacitean historiography lay the practice of comparing times past to the present, the *similitudo temporum* that formed an essential element of humanist scholarship. Throughout his *Annals* Tacitus makes clear his project of explaining the past to the present and future, and as he details and suggests societal decline he also considers history's cyclical possibilities. Reflecting on the return under Vespasian of a more restrained code of living in Rome and the movement away from 'spendthrift epicureanism', Tacitus ponders what the source of such an alteration might have been. He writes,

> But the main promoter of the stricter code was Vespasian, himself of the old school in his person and table. Thenceforward, deference to the sovereign and the love of emulating him proved more powerful than legal sanctions and deterrents. Or should we rather say there is a kind of cycle in all things – moral as well as seasonal revolutions? Nor, indeed, were all things better in the old time before us; but our own age too has produced much in the sphere of true nobility and much in that of art which posterity well may imitate. In any case, may the honourable competition of our present with our past long remain!
>
> [*Sed praecipuus adstricti moris auctor Vespasianus fuit, antiquo ipse cultu victuque. Obsequium inde in principem et aemulandi amor validior quam poena ex legibus et metus. Nisi forte rebus cunctis inest quidam velut orbis, ut quem ad modum temporum vices, ita morum vertantur; nec omnia apud priores meliora, sed nostra quoque aetas multa laudis et artium imitanda posteris tulit. Verum haec nobis in maiores certamina ex honesto maneant.*][23]

The sardonic tone of Tacitus's reflection on his own time's 'true nobility' and 'art' is difficult not to hear, following hard as it does on the heels of the triumph of 'deference' and 'emulation'. Equally striking, he suggests that personal power – 'deference to the sovereign and the love of emulating him' – enacted a change in civil society that the law could not effect. But he then offers a second explanation for the transformation: that in fact the passage of time possesses an innate structure beyond the annual change and return of seasons. Intimating time's power over the law and the Roman emperor, Tacitus proposes that humanity's moral codes wax and wane, imbuing an otherwise fatalistic text with a glimmer of hope. Even as he undermines the absolute possibility of personal power with which this excerpt begins, Tacitus makes a further critical turn and rejects the implicit sameness of his 'moral revolution' theory. Past and present, present and future, have always been understood in relation to the other, thus signifying their inherent difference. Recognising temporal difference and similitude, Tacitus seemingly rejects nostalgia and argues that the inevitable comparison of past and present, the 'honourable competition' should remain. In doing so he creates a certain historical ambivalence as he juxtaposes two possible explanations for the unfolding of human history: Tacitus places the certainty of inevitable return and its correlating lack of agency against the surety of innovation, of difference across time and civilisations.²⁴ He offers a classical model of historical comparison that would become essential to humanist practice, one which at moments sounds distinctly like an Ovidian idea of degeneration.

While historians of political thought have registered Tacitus's cultural and political importance throughout this period, the exact dramatic appeal and power of a Tacitean conception of history remains under-examined.²⁵ Tacitean history presents a degenerate modernity, one debased from its upstanding republican past, and both Shakespeare and Jonson depend upon those ideas in their respective dramas.²⁶ Tacitus's image of decline enables and encourages nostalgia, and that nostalgia appeals to the ideas of renewal and reclamation inherent in Polybian cyclical history. The cyclical pattern of history draws on shared, idealised versions of the past, countering the recognition of decline with the representation of a grand rise. Across the plays, as I have noted, a political and moral cycle seems to occur. In *Julius Caesar*, the play's nostalgic discourse, fuelled by anxiety for the future and confidence in the republic's return, is curtailed by the Tacitean image of decline embodied by Brutus's death. *Sejanus* takes up this lament as it stages the argument that nostalgia provides no fruitful consolation in a time of moral decline. Tacitus's importance for both authors appears particularly in the fatalism of their final rejections of nostalgia.

But to arrive at that final rejection, *Julius Caesar* and *Sejanus* rely on precisely constructed histories in their use of nostalgia, on accounts of the past that must inspire confidence in dramatic auditors. That confidence in the idealised past as a model for the present – and thus for the future – elicits action from *Caesar*'s conspirators and manifests as asides and resignation from *Sejanus*'s Germanicans. In these Roman plays, the success of nostalgic rhetoric depends upon how characters construct the past, and that construction is rarely univocal, of shared intention, and without a competing history. By attending insistently to how narratives of the past are composed, Shakespeare and Jonson appear dedicated to creating suspects of history both on stage and off stage. That time and again in early modern drama – and in these plays particularly – we are witness to characters' recreations of people and events, recreations evoked with political aims, suggests the stage's conscious and unconscious role in exposing the literate and illiterate public to the possibility of history's conflicting claims.²⁷ Shakespeare and Jonson make nostalgic rhetoric part of these conflicts, and consequently they dramatise the role idealising processes can play in seeking, and laying claims to, political power.

The Engine of Nostalgia in *Julius Caesar*

From their respective first scenes, *Julius Caesar* and *Sejanus* situate nostalgia as a central mode of dramatic discourse. Shakespeare in particular uses Act 1 to invoke an idealised past through memories of past action and personal history, employing the tribunes and Cassius as instruments of nostalgic remembrance.[28] *Caesar* opens by establishing nostalgia – or rather, its absence – as the site and cause of conflict between the plebeians and their tribunes. Learning that the citizens 'make holiday' to celebrate Caesar, the tribune Murellus rages:

> Wherefore rejoice? What conquest brings he home?
> What tributaries follow him to Rome
> To grace in captive bonds his chariot wheels?
> [. . .]
> Knew you not Pompey?[29]

His questions announce the plebeians' hypocrisy and their mutable politics: in the current of action, the people forget their past loyalty to Pompey. Murellus reminds them that 'Many a time and oft' they waited 'with patient expectation / To see great Pompey pass', that they had 'made an universal shout' for him, before he disperses them 'tongue-tied' in their 'guilt[y]' forgetfulness (1.1.36, 40–1, 43, 61). In his chastisement, in his implicit use of nostalgia to shame the plebeians, Murellus supplants present actions with past deeds, reminding them of – and creating – an image of welcome for a deserving hero: the people climbed to the chimney tops with babes in their arms, they made the Tiber 'tremble' with their noise (1.1.38–9, 44). This scene's nostalgic rebukes in defence of Pompey introduce the tension in Rome's power structure, as the play reveals that the tribunes do not in fact represent the beliefs of the people, who align themselves with Caesar. From the first, then, the play alerts its audience to memory's selective nature. The plebeians' act of 'remembering' Caesar's triumph is also, as Murellus articulates, a cruel act of forgetting, of 'social amnesia'.[30] Significantly, the ease with which a lacuna forms in the citizens' recollections of Pompey will be repeated with Caesar, at Brutus's speech following the assassination. Murellus's successful reprimand of the plebeians – he deplores their 'ingratitude' – soon becomes another example of forgetfulness (1.1.54). In the following scene, their memory of Pompey has vanished once more as Caesar fulfils their wish and rejects kingship. Shakespeare's dramatisation here of the memorialising process, of remembrance and forgetting, signals and seemingly mirrors history's cycle. One conqueror, one 'strong man' is easily replaced with another.[31]

As Shakespeare keeps Caesar off stage, he uses Cassius to illustrate nostalgia's inherent place in the enactment of historical cycles. Cassius performs the classic set-up of the idealised past, as he voices to Brutus his discontent with the status quo: many of the best Romans are 'groaning underneath this age's yoke' (1.2.61, 63). He intimates that one Brutus may replace another, declaring:

> O, you and I have heard our fathers say
> There was a Brutus once that would have brooked
> Th'eternal devil to keep his state in Rome
> As easily as a king.   (1.2.159–62)

From their fathers Cassius and Brutus have learned, inherited, the republican tradition, one that equates kingship with the devil's rule, and one that consequently drives out kings – and devils. Cassius formulates the attitudes and actions of the past as a political inheritance that he then links directly to his friend. 'There was a Brutus *once*' locates in Marcus Brutus his responsibility to his ancestor, and it hints at his need, and Rome's need for him, to imitate that ancestor to retain the reputation in posterity that Lucius Junius Brutus possesses. This reminder of Rome's tradition of republicanism serves not only Brutus, but his auditors as well, as the threat of Caesar announces Rome's degeneracy.[32] Cassius's explicit appeal to Brutus's *Romanitas* is fuelled by his hope that Brutus will 'embrace his ancestral heritage as a mandate for present action', and his nostalgic reflection is the climax of a lengthy attempt to persuade Brutus to act against Caesar.[33]

Playing the Tacitist, Cassius relies on the paradoxical constructions of his time as particularly, uniquely corrupt and Caesar as particularly common in that time. Caesar is 'such a thing as I myself', Cassius laments, that he would not be '[i]n awe of', and he fashions Caesar as weak and inconstant in anecdotes in which a 'tirèd' Caesar nearly drowns and then with 'coward lips' cries out of illness '[a]s a sick girl'; he is a man 'of such a feeble temper' (1.2.98, 117, 124, 130, 131). Incredibly, such a man 'doth bestride the narrow world / Like a Colossus' and this fact only amplifies Cassius's conviction of Rome's weakness, its crisis of values like masculinity (1.2.136–7). Moreover, it affirms his faith in a preferable past, for 'Men at *sometime* were masters of their fates. / The fault, dear Brutus, is not in our stars, / But in ourselves, that we are underlings' (1.2.140–2, my emphasis). He reiterates this idea in his cry,

>   Age, thou art shamed—
> Rome, thou hast lost the breed of noble bloods.
> When went there by an age since the great flood,
> But it was famed with more than with one man? (1.2.151–4)

Cassius's totalising narrative here renders even himself degenerate. More importantly, he again insists on Caesar's rise as a singular feature of this particular historical moment. He retells the recent past and present to make Caesar's ascent a symptom of the time's decline. His proposition of historical consistency 'since the great flood', that great men can and have thrived simultaneously, urges once more the proximity of the preferable past, a proximity crucial to his final appeal to Brutus's personal history and Rome's republican tradition. In connecting the faults of Rome with its support of Caesar and by nostalgically concluding these arguments, Cassius further develops his initial argument that acting against Caesar is an act for Roman welfare. As Warren Chernaik argues, 'In Act I, nearly all mention of "Rome" or "Roman" has persuasive intent, used by enemies of Caesar to evoke a tradition of republican independence and self-reliance, while pouring scorn on those who fail to live up to these ideals.'[34] Cassius knows the persuasive influence that arguing for Rome's interest will have on his friend, who declared at the outset of Cassius's speech: 'If it [what Cassius would impart] be aught toward the general good, / Set honour in one eye and death i'th' other, / And I will look on both indifferently' (1.2.87–9). In Cassius's anecdotes, laments and exclamations, Shakespeare deploys once more a familiar formula, one we've already seen with characters like Nick the rebel and John of Gaunt: nostalgia begins with characters who offer identifiable critiques – class conflict and inequality, weak leadership, the advancement of the undeserving – and these work to convince on- and off-stage auditors of the fallibility and need for change in the present (dramatic) world.

Cassius's strategies exemplify the power of nostalgic rhetoric on which the action of this play's first half will turn, as Shakespeare shows how nostalgia works on political fantasies of the future. Brutus concedes:

>   What you have said
> I will consider: what you have to say
> I will with patience hear, and find a time
> Both meet to hear and answer such high things.
> Till then, my noble friend, chew upon this:
> Brutus had rather be a villager
> Than to repute himself a son of Rome
> Under these hard conditions as this time
> Is like to lay upon us. (1.2.168–76)

Already the past's bright example illuminates the future, as Brutus doubts what is to come, the 'hard conditions as this time / Is *like* to lay upon us'. Their exchange makes clear that the Republic is dead. Nostalgia in *Julius Caesar* articulates the difference between the political structure of the past and that of the present, and the invocation of Junius Brutus communicates a personal and political inheritance, that the time of the Republic waits to be regained for 'this time'. As the play's action unfolds, Shakespeare reveals how Cassius's persuasive use of historical reconstruction and the idealised past act upon Brutus's imagination. Reading aloud the abstract and vague 'instigations' Cassius has thrown through his window, Brutus must 'piece out' the second line: 'Shall Rome, et cetera' (2.1.49, 51). Of equal importance to Cassius's 'manipulation' that critics observe in this scene is how Shakespeare stages the power of nostalgic suggestion and desire as an essential element of that manipulation, as Brutus expands the narrative of Lucius Junius which Cassius began.[35] He muses,

> Shall Rome stand under one man's awe? What Rome?
> My ancestors did from the streets of Rome
> The Tarquin drive, when he was called a king. (2.1.52–4)

Repeated three times in as many lines, 'Rome' is central to Brutus's crisis of action, and in seeking out his course, he finds refuge and resolution in the past, in his familial, and Rome's own political, inheritance. By analogising Caesar to Tarquin, Shakespeare suggests the cyclical history that convinces Brutus that the Republic can be reclaimed. Brutus reads in his ancestors, in his personal history, the lesson of how to act when faced with the threat of singular rule: republicans expel kings. The future that Brutus envisions, in which Caesar claims the throne, cannot be separated from his awareness of the republican past. His future-thinking contradicts Maurice Hunt's claim that Brutus's 'hypothetical thinking displaces ruminating on actual affairs, such that the former seems the latter to [him]'.[36] Rather, the idealised past and the hypothesised future are part of 'actual affairs', because they cannot be dissociated from them. As Shakespeare and then Jonson make clear, present political action is intimately bound up with history and its promised future.

Central to Brutus's actions is the '*mythos* of the republic', which lies equally behind both Cassius's invocation and Brutus's musing on his ancestor. This idea 'impels Brutus to lead the conspiracy against Caesar', as Coppélia Kahn argues, and her term aptly summarises how the conspirators selectively imagine the Republic.[37] In their fantasies of this past and future *res publica*, the conspirators reveal their nostalgic thinking and its attenuated nature, as Brutus and Cassius imagine only the republic's inception rather than its life after that point of origin, of re-establishment. That repeated return to the point of origin obsesses them, as they make clear upon Caesar's death:

> CASSIUS   How many ages hence
> Shall this our lofty scene be acted over
> In states unborn and accents yet unknown?
>
> BRUTUS   How many times shall Caesar bleed in sport
> That now on Pompey's basis lies along,
> No worthier than the dust?   (3.1.113–18)

The future's absolute foreignness – its 'states unborn and accents yet unknown' – offers no bar to the political inheritance that the murderers offer. This moment cuts them off from their past, as Brutus and Cassius project their actions as their own moment of reclamation, a new origin point from which they already envision and desire the future's repetition of their act. What lies beyond that reclamation point is unclear because that point itself is irrelevant; they themselves are the new Lucius Junius Brutus, the new inheritors.

What makes Marcus Brutus a conspirator, in the end, cannot be divorced from his locating right action in a nostalgic past and his faith that the past can be reclaimed, remade in the future. Having reflected on the 'instigations', Brutus declares 'O Rome, I make thee promise, / If the redress will follow, thou receivest / Thy full petition at the hand of Brutus' (2.1.56–8). However conditional the future seems ('If . . . will follow'), Brutus's commitment is clear in his granting Rome's 'full petition'. This moment, when Brutus has convinced himself that he acts for Rome and for the republic of his ancestors, when Cassius's nostalgic narrative has fully persuaded him of the value of his actions, is the moment when he becomes a conspirator. Brutus had previously concluded that 'It must be by his death' and coupled that assertion with pro-Caesar counter-arguments, but Brutus needs historical precedent to confirm his uncertainties, and he finds it in Junius Brutus (2.1.10, 11–12, 19–21). Shakespeare dramatises again the power of nostalgic rhetoric through Brutus's acknowledgement that he has been Cassius's instrument – the latter has 'whet [him] against Caesar' (2.1.61). By confirming the success of Cassius's historiographical strategies which culminate in these patricians' explicit desire for an idealised past, Shakespeare stages the self-conscious awareness of nostalgia's power. He grounds the definitive political action of *Julius Caesar* in the interpretation of the past, and the downfall of Brutus and Cassius results from their failure to recognise that the power structures of the past cannot be reclaimed and reapplied to the present, one of the play's several hermeneutic failures.[38]

Brutus's idealistic myopia in particular enables the event of Antony's eulogy, which Shakespeare uses to articulate a counter-nostalgia opposed to the *mythos* of the conspirators. Bifurcating the play's action, Caesar's death allows the audience to experience the effects of nostalgia as they take hold, as Caesar himself is transformed from threatening tyrant to selfless Roman. Indeed, Antony's speech employs nostalgia at another 'beginning' to provoke political action, a repetition of the rhetorical strategy with which Cassius whets Brutus. Shakespeare constructs a series of anecdotes used to persuade the plebeians of Caesar's good intentions and then crowns Antony's rhetoric with nostalgic historiography, as Antony recalls Caesar's deeds in order to question Brutus's accusations of his 'ambition' and to reaffirm the people's love for Caesar. In his account, Caesar filled Rome's 'coffers', wept for the poor, rejected kingship. 'You all did love him once, not without cause', he cries, and his arguments echo those memories of Pompey invoked at the play's outset (3.2.80–9, 94). Most importantly, the promise of the will and Antony's rhetorical manipulation of that entire subject create a myth of Caesar himself, one Shakespeare develops from Plutarch.[39] Antony's myth of Caesar, like that of the Roman republic, relies on present and future desires. He manipulates time in the present by rhetorically building suspense, as he mentions the unmentionable 'testament' and then projects an image of the future by telling the people how they will remember Caesar. 'Treat[ing] him as a holy martyr', the people

> would go and kiss dead Caesar's wounds,
> And dip their napkins in his sacred blood,
> Yea, beg a hair of him for memory,
> And, dying, mention it within their wills,
> Bequeathing it as a rich legacy
> Unto their issue.   (3.2.124–9)[40]

The enfoldedness of time here produces a sense of eternity fitting for a would-be god, for a myth: from the present moment, Antony looks into the future and prophesies how the future-plebeians will memorialise the past, and moreover how they will bequeath to *their* future the significance of Caesar in their future-past. The 'rich legacy' implies this practice of inheritance, this continuity, down through the generations. Where the republican tradition was the inheritance of the conspirators, Antony establishes the idea of Caesar himself as inheritance, once more creating a new origin point for his audience from the point of no return that Caesar's murder establishes.

With Antony's funeral speech, Shakespeare not only repeats Cassius's strategy of future anticipation to elicit action, but he makes Antony similarly gifted in historicising, and in doing so he once again exposes the constructed-ness of the idealised past and its attendant longed-for future.[41] Antony uses nostalgic collective memory to construct an object of longing for the people as they hear Antony detail Caesar's death, the play's creation of 'then' and 'now'. Exhibiting Caesar's cloak for the audience, Antony evokes a shared memory of Caesar in his assured statement, '*You all* do know this mantle', before drawing the crowd further into the story of the cloak by narrating its history (3.2.158, my emphasis). The first time Caesar wore it – surely information previously unknown to the audience – ''Twas on a summer's evening in his tent, / That day he overcame the Nervii' (3.2.160–1). In this fabricated, serene vision of Caesar, Antony positions him in an idyllic time ('summer's evening') and having just vanquished his enemy, a detail that reminds the crowd of Caesar's military prowess and victories for Rome. These details are Shakespeare's invention, and they exemplify how he crafts personal memory in this speech.[42] Antony himself immediately disrupts this nostalgic reflection, which excludes any of Caesar's less-desirable qualities, with memories of violence. He juxtaposes his own 'memory' with another historical fiction: that of the conspirators' individual stabs.

> Look, in this place ran Cassius' dagger through.
> See what a rent the envious Casca made:
> Through this, the well-beloved Brutus stabbed[.]   (3.2.162–4)

Antony speaks with the confidence of a modern novel's omniscient narrator, of a witness to the murder. Shakespeare's audience knows otherwise, and they observe how Antony personalises Caesar's wounds to arouse pity, outrage and ultimately action from the on-stage spectators. In binding the conspirators to their individual acts of violence, Antony writes over the arguments Brutus made for 'lov[ing] Rome', as these details depict and enable the imagining of Caesar's death in the *sensus communis* of the Roman audience. Coupling the creation of that violent image with the use of one word, 'traitor', further eradicates Brutus's claims to selfless action. Antony continues:

> For when the noble Caesar saw [Brutus] stab,
> Ingratitude, more strong than traitor's arms,
> Quite vanquished him [. . .]
>   Look you here,
> Here is himself, marred as you see with traitors.   (3.2.172–4, 184–5)

Having subtly created an image of Caesar at peace and victorious, Antony's invocation and reconstruction of violent action against Caesar and his explicit use of 'treason' (3.2.180) cement his argument: the conspirators acted not for Rome, as Brutus claimed, but rather against the state and its people. Forgetting their previous cries to make Brutus Caesar – a Shakespearean invention – and their certainty of Caesar's tyranny, Antony's audience now proclaims the day's woefulness, Caesar's nobleness and the need for revenge (3.2.43, 61, 186–7).[43] It is the second plebeian's exclamation 'We will be revenged!' that the entire crowd augments in their cry 'Revenge, about, / Seek, burn, fire, kill, slay! / Let not a traitor live!' (3.2.188–90). Antony's speech succeeds where Brutus's fails because he uses nostalgia to affectively bind his auditors to Caesar, to affirm their imagined community, and then uses the past to cement the division between the people and the conspirators. Failing to learn from the nostalgia lessons he knows 'whetted' him, Brutus cannot connect the crowd to the past which moved him to action; how can they have a 'place in the commonwealth' when Brutus himself cannot construct it – rhetorically or in reality (3.2.36–7)? Brutus's speech suggests that the people desire a commonwealth, but there is no evidence for this, only evidence that they do not want a king. His inability to recognise that future promise will spur the people to the action he wishes for – the creation of the Republic – is a failure of self-recognition, a failure to identify what motivated himself to action, and thus a political failure. Nostalgia, fuelling and fuelled by idealising historiography and anticipatory futures, calls the Romans to violent, political action of unforeseen consequences.

Following the outbreak of war, the battle scenes and the past's literal haunting of Brutus, the play's conclusion asks spectators to return to the problem of nostalgia and historical construction. As the play's star rhetorician, this return depends unsurprisingly upon Antony, who declares over Brutus's body:

> This was the noblest Roman of them all:
> All the conspirators save only he
> Did that they did in envy of Great Caesar [...]
> His life was gentle, and the elements
> So mixed in him that nature might stand up
> And say to all the world, 'This was a man.'   (5.5.67–9, 72–4)

Antony's first 'all' remains ambiguous: he seems to announce Brutus's pre-eminence over all Romans, until the word's repetition in the succeeding line qualifies that superiority to the group of conspirators. And yet, Antony suggests, the particular place of 'nature' in Brutus sets him apart from all others who would claim to be men. Shakespeare even intimates that the crisis of masculinity Cassius saw in Caesar's rise finds its true climax here, with the death of the manliest of men. In titling Brutus 'the noblest', Antony makes death the great equaliser. As the audience may recall, Brutus is not the first man Antony elegises in this way. Speaking to the murdered Caesar, he proclaims, 'Thou art the ruins of the noblest man / That ever livèd in the tide of times' (3.1.260–1). Plutarch notes that Brutus and the conspirators were officially accused 'of killing the noblest person in Rome', but these elegies are Shakespeare's inventions.[44] They trouble how the audience should interpret idealising rhetoric even as they watch what is being memorialised. With these superlatives Shakespeare keeps consigning nobility to the past, moving further into the Tacitean degenerate present from which the conspirators wished to escape. In idealising men whose characters the play has consistently problematised and questioned, Shakespeare shows for a final time in *Julius Caesar* the discrepancy between the idealising process and its object. He affirms the distance between the promise of political inheritance and reality.

Republican Refuges: Nostalgia and Neostoicism in *Sejanus*

While *Julius Caesar* so definitively links nostalgic rhetoric to political action, the political conditions of *Sejanus* – the seeds of which we see at *Caesar*'s close – make such action impossible. In *Sejanus*, nostalgia articulates the basis for Neostoic resignation to inaction and it becomes the means by which the Germanicans are condemned, in doing so offering a reproof to those tempted by an idealised past. While *Caesar* makes nostalgia an element of critical dramatic moments from the play's outset, Jonson's drama articulates nostalgia as an obvious lament for the present, but one cut off from the possibility of persuasion to radical political action. In *Sejanus*, rhetoric and history make clear the past-ness of the past, and they fuel a Rome of unfulfilled hopes. Jonson's republicans, in contrast to Shakespeare's, are resigned to this fact. Tellingly, Jonson consistently places republican reflections at his play's margins, away from the power centres of Tiberius and Sejanus. In Jonson's dramatic world, political actors are separated irrevocably from their would-be political inheritance: Cassius and Brutus are not re-enacted, as they themselves imagine in Shakespeare's play, but are confined to a historical narrative which is itself destroyed. Imperial Rome is the limit of the past, and in creating such a world, however rooted in its historical sources, Jonson offers Neostoicism as a means of navigating the desire at nostalgia's heart. Simultaneously, Jonson reveals the painful futility of idealising the past. His Roman tragedy is not exclusively a response to Shakespeare, but it is difficult not to see how *Sejanus* takes up problems articulated in its predecessor and reworks and rethinks them, in particular offering a Lipsian Neostoic rejection of nostalgia. From *Julius Caesar* Jonson develops a suspicion of, and alertness to, nostalgia's mechanisms, its capacity for persuasion. But he puts such suspicion to work in a circumscribed, tyrannical world, and this itself might tell us something about Jonson's view of his time and its political climate. If Shakespeare reveals how nostalgic desires are produced and manipulated, then Jonson presents Neostoicism as a means of managing those desires when they cannot be accommodated, when they seem to have no referent. In so doing, nostalgia and its essential longing offer another facet to Jonson's thinking about language's malleability. For as Lorna Hutson argues, the play dramatises 'the thrilling and horrible efficiency with which words can be detached from their point of origin, and reiterated to bring about their original speaker's destruction'.[45]

Sejanus's Neostoicism responds to and participates in a trend in political thought at the turn of the seventeenth century, one that offered a means of navigating the vicissitudes of a corrupt, turbulent political world. Blossoming in response to violence and religious conflicts across continental Europe in the late sixteenth and seventeenth centuries, Neostoicism found its English adherents through translations of Justus Lipsius's *Six bookes of politickes or civil doctrine* and *Two books of constancie* (1594 and 1595 respectively). The former text provided 'applications of Neostoic ideas in terms certain to galvanize the attention of an English readership worried about religious division and fearful of the prospect of civil war', while the latter argued for the cultivation of constancy to weather unstable times.[46] Constancy, as Lipsius writes, '*is a right and immoveable strength of the minde, neither lifted up, nor pressed downe with externall or casuall accidentes*'.[47] Lipsius stressed constancy's foundation in 'judgement' and 'sound reason', and like many of his humanist contemporaries he provided classical exempla to inspire and inform contemporary behaviour. He writes:

> [W]hen *Pisistratus* had brought the citie of *Athens* under his obedience, *Solon* seeing that all his labour for defence of the common libertie was in vaine, came and laide downe his sword and Target before the Senate doores, crying out, *O my countrie, I have by word and deede defended thee whiles I could*. And so going home he was quiet afterwards. So do thou: yeeld to God, and give place to the time. And if thou be a good citizen or commonwealths-man preserve thy selfe to a better and happier end. The liberty which now is lost, may be recovered againe hereafter; and thy decayed country may flourish in another age: why doest thou loose al courage & fal into dispair?
> (I.XXII, sig. I^r)

Offering a Polybian confidence in a state's future rise, through the voice of Charles Langius, Lipsius counsels that the 'good citizen' must preserve himself, offering confidence in the future: lost liberty 'may be recovered'. But what sounds like a prescription of hope against despair is not so straightforward, for early in his dialogue Lipsius warns against such feeling. He praises the motto, 'Nec spe, metu', 'Neither with hope, nor with feare' and translates its 'lofty poesie' used 'in the armes and targets of some men of our time' to a more universal application, for if practiced by the individual, 'Thou shalt be a king indeed free indeed, only subject unto God, enfranchized from the servile yoke of Fortune and affections' (I.VI, sig. C3^{r-v}). Early modern drama stages the proximity of hope and fear to nostalgia and to regime change, and it is not surprising that in the *Six bookes of politickes*, Lipsius rejects innovation in government. Change inevitably signified political and emotional turmoil. Nevertheless, Michel de Montaigne, who praises Lipsius as 'the most learned man left' (the phrase itself implying learning's inevitable decline), seems to recognise the difficulty of avoiding change, and concludes that 'Nothing keeps changing so continuously as the Law', and acknowledges that in 'political matters' 'we may wish to do without constancy'.[48] While critics have stressed Montaigne's commitment to custom and tradition, his writing reveals his deep discomfort with custom and with law when he perceives it to be opposite to justice. Ancient traditions may legitimate governments, but humanity is not to be trusted either with making those governments or the laws, as the latter 'are but an uncertain sea of opinions deriving from peoples or princes, who will paint in as many different colours and present it, reformed, under as many different faces as they have changes of heart'.[49] This conviction intimates why Lipsian Neostoicism is so appealing to Montaigne.

Like Neostoicism, nostalgia appears invested in maintaining the status quo and the 'legitimacy' of past traditions. However, as I've shown throughout this book, Shakespeare's dramatic nostalgia depends upon hope and fear, both of which Lipsius rejects in *Two bookes of constancie*, as he rejects nostalgic discourse and the desire for an idealised past. Using nostalgia's inherent mode – 'COMPARISON' (*similitudo temporum* again) – Charles Langius states that he 'wil proove evidently that there is nothing grievous or great in all the evils which doo nowe abound every where, if we compare them with those of olde time' (II.XX, sig. P3^r). To young Lipsius's lament that 'as all rivers runne into the Sea: so it seemeth that al misfortunes are fallen upon this present age', Langius replies:

> Thou sayest this age is the unhappiest that ever was. This hath bin an old lay long ago used. I know thy gra[n]d father said so, and likewise thy father. I

know also that thy children and childrens children wil sing the same note. It is a thing naturally given unto men to cast their eies narrowly upon al things that be grievous, but to wink at such as be pleasant. As flies & such like vile creatures do never rest long upon smooth & fine polished places, but doo sticke fast to rough and filthie corners: So the murmuring mind dooth lightly passe over the consideration of all good fortune but never forgetteth the adverse or evil. (II.XX, sig. P3^v)

Langius sounds positively weary at his protégé's confidence in historical decline. Through statistical analysis and, as here, the argument that nostalgia is common to all men at all times, Lipsius via Langius argues with his interlocutor (his younger self) that the present offers reasons to be joyful.

Contrary to his influence on Jonson, Lipsius's writings do not seem to influence *Julius Caesar*, and whatever Stoicism Shakespeare's Brutus displays at Portia's death or at the prospect of his own, his actions and indulgence in nostalgia highlight the discrepancy between him and Jonson's Neostoics. For concomitant with the longing for an idealised past is an anxiety and an awareness that action, change, is necessary to maintain that tradition. *Julius Caesar* depicts how reverence for a romanticised ancient tradition is used to prevent the return of a past aberration: kingship. Such a return would upset the (lost) republican order. Preservation thus requires political action and revolution in the present. Such action depends, as we have seen, on hope for and fear of the future if change does not occur; tyranny will prevail, as the rebels of *Richard II* and *Julius Caesar* dread. In *Sejanus*, however, Tiberius's opposition, the Germanicans, lack the possibility for radical action, which Silius blames on everyone: from the Republic's demise, 'We since became the slaves to one man's lusts, / And now to many'.[50] The senator Arruntius is the play's primary nostalgic, and he and others construct the past as the source of legitimacy and stability in government. Yet if 'to be a Roman insurgent is to be always nostalgic', then Jonson stages the foolishness of that impulse for the insurgency, as he creates antinostalgic sentiment in the play.[51] Susceptibility to nostalgia exposes an individual to the dangers of imperial interpretation (witness Cordus), and it tempts one into 'treason' (witness Sabinus). While Jonson initially depicts nostalgia as a means of expressive survival in Tiberius's Rome, he reveals that imperial powers weaponise such longing, proving the justness of Arruntius's anxieties when he asks:

> May I pray to Jove
> In secret, and be safe? Ay, or aloud?
> With open wishes? So I do not mention
> Tiberius, or Sejanus? Yes, I must,

> If I speak out. 'Tis hard, that. May I think,
> And not be racked? What danger is't to dream?
> Talk in one's sleep? Or cough? Who knows the law? (4.300–6)

From coughing to thinking, Arruntius fears the consequence of any sound he makes in or outside his body. Against such worry, Neostoicism functions as a Tacitean 'middle way' – between '"defiant obstinacy and crooked subservience"'.[52] The play seems to create this 'middle way' for its readers and spectators, as 'Jonson engages his audience's sympathy for "the old liberty" of republican Rome, while inviting us to envy the chilling statecraft which defeats it'.[53] This conclusion however suggests that Jonson creates a conflict of desires in the play, and that a longing for the 'old liberty' gives way to Tiberius's attractively vicious regime; how else could it 'invit[e. . .] envy'?

Rather, Jonson presents a choice of strategies against the emperor's tyranny: nostalgia; suicide; Neostoicism. Unlike the rhetorics of nostalgia in Shakespeare's drama, Jonson makes it painfully clear that this discourse does not in fact constitute the first steps of oppositional action, howsoever that the desire for action remains evident in the rhetoric of those who long for the republican past. The Germanicans' sidelined conversations reflect and repeat oppressive 'custom' that seems to prevent them from acting against Tiberius and his titular minion. If, as Chapter 2 argued, the ventriloquised nostalgic discourse of lost Catholicism remained so appealing and so problematic in late Elizabethan England, then its use by what some have seen as stand-ins for the loyalist Catholic community – the Germanicans – in a play written by a recently converted Catholic might make Jonson's own positions on how to live under oppression more clear.[54] Neostoicism, the play instructs, must offer a superior path, a refuge, to the frustrated desires, hopes and anxieties attached to nostalgia. We can only see Neostoicism as a shelter, however, through Jonson's use of nostalgia as its opposite, the seeming emotional refuge that in fact fails its practitioners.

Like Shakespeare, Jonson prioritises discontent in his drama by establishing clear factional lines from *Sejanus*'s first scene, as the Germanicans voice their longing for Brutus and Cassius and their commitment to the *res publica*. However, Jonson prioritises equally how circumscribed his republicans are in their imperial setting. Arruntius rejects Sabinus's claim that 'these our times / Are not the same', and with both Tacitus and Shakespeare's Cassius he declares that it is rather the men who falter: 'The men, / The men are not the same; 'tis we are base, / Poor, and degenerate from th'exalted strain / Of our great fathers' (1.85–6, 86–9).[55] Arruntius's repetition – 'men', 'are not the same' – emphatically rejects a conflation between individuals and their time, insisting rather that people decline – and the time with them. Here, Jonson repudiates the archetypal formula of nostalgia that laments 'these times', rather recasting the problem as located in individuals, in human nature. For spectators and readers, it is too early in *Sejanus* to recognise the irony of these lines, which suggest a political agency that the play will deny. The problem with 'men' in Jonson's dramatic world, as Arruntius argues, is that they lack any interest in self-sacrifice for Rome:

> Where is now the soul
> Of god-like Cato? [. . .]
> Or where the constant Brutus, that (being proof
> Against all charm of benefits) did strike
> So brave a blow into the monster's heart
> That sought unkindly to captive his country?
> Oh, they are fled the light. [. . .]
> And not a spark of their eternal fire
> Glows in a present bosom; [. . .]
> There's nothing Roman in us; nothing good,
> Gallant, or great. Tis true, that Cordus says,
> "Brave Cassius was the last of all that race".[56]
> (1.89–90, 93–7, 99–100, 102–4)

For the audience familiar with Lipsius's *Two bookes*, the insistence on men changing and Rome changing with them might recall the book's argument that God fits a state to its citizens' nature, 'All which peradve[n]ture he wil change in time, if those people alter their dispositions' (II.9, sig. M^r). In locating present faults and his own discontent within the individual rather than within the 'age', Arruntius prioritises that individual's role in shaping his society. He identifies in individual action the responsibility for public grief or public good, and this is the responsibility which *Julius Caesar* depicts and, questionably, enacts.

In equating Rome with the Republic, Arruntius creates not only identity crises – if the Republic does not exist true Romans cannot exist – he also creates the temporal ruptures so conducive to nostalgia. The rupture between then and now was not, as for Brutus and Cassius, the rise of Caesar, but rather the conspirators' deaths that marked the end of what Arruntius might style (with Tacitus and Sallust) a Roman Golden Age. Jonson uses Arruntius's speech not only to establish Rome's political climate, but to emphasise how partial nostalgic historiography – here, bordering on hagiography – tells partial truths: Arruntius never discusses Rome's descent into civil war following Caesar's assassination. Jonson could rightly assume that his audience knew what violence resulted from Brutus's and Cassius's actions, and this meta-dramatic awareness implicitly disrupts Arruntius's praise of the chief conspirators and his vision of an idealised republican past. But unlike Shakespeare in *Julius Caesar*, it is not so much the falseness, the constructedness of the idealised past that Jonson is concerned with in *Sejanus*. It is rather the *futility* of the ideal past, as Jonson provides no anticipatory future to accommodate nostalgic discourse. Rather, the republicans' nostalgias reveal their status as 'passive sufferers': they witness Tiberius's and Sejanus's evils without expectation of correction.[57] Throughout his speech, Arruntius seems to echo his hero of *Julius Caesar*, until Drusus's entry to the scene completes the dramatic pattern that the play will produce. The republicans fall silent and 'stand aside' until he exits (SD 1.105). From the first 100 lines, Jonson depicts the opposition as political ideologues who, unwilling and unable to act against the state, themselves prove that 'Brave Cassius was the last of all that race'.

Silius's and Sabinus's respective glorifications of the dead military leader Germanicus serve simultaneously as riposte and ratification of Arruntius's lament, and their praise argues that absent Roman virtue has not, in fact, been absent so long. That Sabinus and Silius locate in Germanicus those qualities of republican Romans suggests both the proximity of past virtue and its irreclaimable loss. Germanicus possessed

> Pompey's dignity,
> The innocence of Cato, Caesar's spirit,
> Wise Brutus' temperance, and every virtue,
> Which, parted unto others, gave them name,
> Flowed mixed in him. He was the soul of goodness[.]   (1.150–4)

That such a man had lived in their time and yet was ruined by Rome's imperial powers demonstrates that the republicans recognise the pointlessness of bold political action.[58] Their epideictic rhetoric affirms Arruntius's melancholic appraisal of the state of things. With Germanicus's death, 'It is as though a whole heroic world has been extinguished [. . .] What remains is dark and small'.[59] In a crucial dramatic development, Jonson's tragedy rejects any possibility of reclamation that, as I have argued, Shakespeare always proffers. There is no sense of a political inheritance in the future of Jonson's Rome. That is not to say that Shakespeare dramatises a lasting hopefulness of nostalgia; quite the contrary. But the fact that Jonson refuses to stage any sense of political drive, any impetus, connected to this idealised world, announces a new dramatic framing for nostalgia, one which makes it inevitable but not actionable. One that makes it, in fact, quite modern. *Sejanus* announces the futility of desiring Germanicus's 'heroic world', for the men that could have reclaimed it no longer exist, and neither do the ideals which inspired them. The temporal breach, Jonson insists, is irreparable.

However distant the past might be, fear of temporal comparison persists, and *Sejanus* depicts how that fear both extends to the potentially legitimising power of nostalgia and fuels Tiberius's tyranny. In Actus Tertius the past is made a source of controversy, as Afer brings Cremutius Cordus to trial for writing his *Annals*, which chart Rome's history from its republican days to the play's present. For Tiberius, the act of writing history becomes an act of treason, and what the state reads as nostalgia consequently becomes radicalised, the hermeneutic process now politicised. Jonson uses Cordus's prosecution to effectively stage a trial of a critical historical (and Tacitean) method: the comparison of past and present. What was 'ancient tradition' the state now interprets as a dangerous longing for political change. The state arraigns the 'factious and dangerous' Cordus for the 'crimes' of 'bit[ing] the state' by 'comparing men / And times', in particular praising Brutus and naming Cassius '"the last of all the Romans"' (3.380, 384, 390–1, 391, 392). By having Afer assert that Brutus was 'an enemy to his country', Jonson introduces a competing historical narrative to Arruntius's earlier lament, and that introduction itself illuminates the question of historical practice that this trial stages (3.397). Afer's judgement both confirms the loss of the ideal (Brutus) and suggests that the ideal never existed. And while Jonson clearly sympathises with, and manipulates audience sympathy for, the Germanicans, the trial also reflects the early modern fear that history could be read 'wrongly'.[60] The play refutes the absoluteness of the idealised past even as it sympathises with its proponents. This ambivalence Jonson could have developed from Shakespeare, but Neostoic principles likewise would have encouraged a rejection of nostalgia. Regardless, Jonson's is not a whole-hearted ambivalence, but one created with one eye on the Privy Council and contemporary society and one on his historical sources. Jonson clearly wants to stage tyranny's ability to construct history, as he shows when the state rejects Cordus's presentation of facts and eradicates those facts' perceived subversion through the annihilation of contrarian ideas. In his defence, Cordus can only assert that his act of writing was not a participatory act of rebellion. He aligns himself with those of his profession who have shared his aims, and he argues that his work is 'aimed [. . .] free' and far from 'the time's scandal' as he writes of, rather than participates in, those events for which he has been doomed (3.446, 447). Behind Tiberius's suppression of the *Annals* is the emperor's interpretation that writing reinscribes, re-enacts, the act enclosed in the text. The suppression recognises the power of *similitudo temporum* in historical writing.

Cordus's trial in this light becomes representative of Jonson's own ideas about political action: as he wrote to Henry Savile, the translator of the *Annals*, '"Although to write be lesser than to doo, / It is the next deed, and a great one too"'.[61] *Sejanus*, following its sources, erases that writing through a mass book-burning that once again affirms the fallen-ness of Jonson's Rome, and the play's audience would certainly have heard in that event an echo of Elizabethan London's 1599 book-burning. Nostalgic reflection on the past – indeed, any reflection on the past – *literally* cannot exist in Tiberius's Rome. It can exist only in the speech of the Germanicans, and as the play winds towards its gruesome end that speech becomes increasingly compromised and marginalised.

If, as Tom Cain argues, Jonson would have thought of himself as a historian in writing *Sejanus*, and if, as Philemon Holland argued, 'the larger humanist *utilità* of Roman history was [...] to illuminate general "faults" of the times rather than specific "men"', then *Sejanus* raises a crucial question for this study: is nostalgia itself a 'fault' of the time?[62] While Shakespeare's Elizabethan plays took pains to exploit nostalgia's cultural impact and illustrate its use and power as a political rhetoric, Jonson's attitude towards nostalgia already presumes the fault that Shakespeare's plays establish. As a decidedly anti-Neostoic attachment to memory and affection, nostalgia for Jonson offers a fruitless mode of survival, one that can be manipulated to the persecution of the historian, as seen with Cordus, or co-opted by a tyrant's *agent provocateur*. Depicting Latiaris's betrayal of Sabinus, Jonson uses imitation and invention to illustrate unequivocally how nostalgia both operates as a dangerous, tantalising response to injustice and as fuel for discontent. Seeking Sabinus's undoing, Latiaris feigns the malcontent, bemoaning Rome's state of affairs and calling for violent political response:

> Methinks the genius of the Roman race
> Should not be so extinct but that bright flame
> Of liberty might be revived again,
> Which no good man but with his life should lose,
> And we not sit like spent and patient fools,
> Still puffing in the dark at one poor coal,
> Held on by hope, till the last spark is out.
> The cause is public, and the honour, name,
> The immortality of every soul
> That is not bastard or a slave in Rome
> Therein concerned. Whereto, if men would change
> The wearied arm, and, for the weighty shield
> So long sustained, employ the ready sword,
> We might have some assurance of our vows.
> [...]

> The rock and our hard steel
> Should meet, t'enforce those glorious fires again
> Whose splendour cheered the world, and heat gave life
> No less than doth the sun's. (4.142–55, 158–61)

Like Shakespeare's Cassius, Latiaris utilises images of oppression, enslavement and weakness to set up his call to arms. His performative, future-oriented nostalgia, captured in the image of the 'bright flame of liberty' which 'might be revived again', offers the promise of renewal and reclamation 't'enforce those glorious fires again / Whose splendour cheered the world'. Latiaris not only interrogates the utility of hope in such circumstances, by suggesting its futility, but he offers in its place the promise of violence – and that violent political action is the only proper response to protect the state, the 'public cause'. His is a call to action that does not wait, as Lipsius would suggest, for liberty to be restored, but insists it can be made. As Cassius and Antony did with their respective auditors, so too Latiaris weds past, present and future visions of Rome to appeal to and draw out Sabinus's as-yet concealed desire to remove Tiberius.

In a crucial difference with *Julius Caesar*, readers and audience members *know* that Latiaris attempts to inveigle Sabinus. Jonson presents the speech as dramatic irony, as he stages the spies' plot to trap the senator. This irony removes any ambivalence about how the play uses nostalgia, staging plainly its dangerous purpose and how a susceptibility to its longing compromises good men. As Tiberius's 'Tyrants' arts' (1.1.70) expand, the seemingly innocuous refuge of nostalgia, with which the play began, becomes unequivocally a means of entrapment. Moreover, by using the deceptive, vice-like character of Latiaris to voice nostalgia, Jonson recalls sixteenth-century interludes like *Lusty Juventus* and *Respublica* that employed vices to lament a lost, idealised past, and therein demonstrates his awareness of nostalgic rhetoric's power to 'whet' an auditor. But unlike those interludes, and unlike Shakespeare's Rome, for Jonson the idealised past is a thorny, threatening place when desired.[63] Tacitus records Latiaris's betrayal of Sabinus and Sabinus's outburst, but Jonson provides no marginal notes to this speech, which is wholly his invention. He consciously uses nostalgia as a mode of rhetorical manipulation and persuasion, perhaps following Shakespeare's method with Cassius and Brutus; or rather, I would argue, using an audience's familiarity with Cassius's persuasions to interrogate them unequivocally and, in a Lipsian vein, reject them.[64] To Latiaris's initial complaints Sabinus states that those tyrannised by Tiberius (the Germanicans) 'must be patient' (4.127), and he argues against resistance:

'A good man should and must / Sit rather down with loss than rise unjust', a passage flagged for potential commonplacing not only by its rhyming couplets but by the gnomic pointing of the quarto (4.165–6). Sabinus's restraint here is Jonson's particular creation; in Tacitus he weeps and laments.[65] Latiaris pierces this Neostoic front through his nostalgic discourse and his additional lament that present Romans fare worse than their historical counterparts, for they are 'slaves and bond / To Caesar's slave' (4.171–2). These speeches encourage Sabinus's recounting of Sejanus's and Tiberius's malevolent practices, which leads to his arrest. By giving the audience foreknowledge of Latiaris's intentions, Jonson offers this scene as a lesson in nostalgia's power and malleability. Without the courage of his Neostoic convictions, for Sabinus nostalgia becomes a fatally attractive, even self-destructive, discourse.

Jonson cements almost immediately the importance of those convictions as a means of survival and philosophical sanctuary, as just twenty-seven lines after Sabinus's exit he stages Lepidus's Neostoic counsels to the nostalgic Arruntius. Lepidus and Arruntius are, to the latter, 'almost all the few / Left to be honest in these impious times' (4.278–89). Lepidus, ignoring the final phrase, rejoins: 'What we are left to be, we will be, Lucius, / Though tyranny did stare as wide as death / To fright us from it' (4.280–2). His insistence on their constancy now and in the future in spite of fear summarises powerfully the Lipsian-Neostoic approach that he will then explain to Arruntius, who would know his 'arts' of survival:

> Arts, Arruntius?
> None but the plain and passive fortitude
> To suffer, and be silent; never stretch
> These arms against the torrent; live at home,
> With my own thoughts, and innocence about me,
> Not tempting the wolf's jaws: these are my arts.   (4.293–8)

Lepidus offers a potent image of withdrawal: arms 'never stretch[ed]', 'passive', belonging only to his own society, he suggests, never with those arms 'tempting' the violence outside his 'home'. Arruntius's interest in this programme stems from his desire for security, but his 'study' is short-lived as, following Nero's arrest, Arruntius can see only Tiberius's evil. Lepidus's counsel to look on Tiberius with 'Zeal, / And duty; with the thought he is our prince' (4.371–2) falls on outraged ears; Tiberius is rather 'our monster' (4.373). Jonson thus extends his argument against nostalgia into his dramaturgy, as he structurally asserts Neostoicism as a right and proper refuge. However garrulous Arruntius remains in his asides and comments through the remainder of the play, he never again voices a nostalgic thought. His prophesy that Macro 'will become / A greater prodigy in Rome than he / That now is fall'n' (5.761–3) is not in the vein of *Richard II*'s John of Gaunt or Bishop of Carlisle, used to curb competing temporal discourses. Rather, it reaffirms the bleak outlook which the play has cultivated and to which, as Jonson through Lepidus has insisted, subjects must respond with Stoic constancy.

In analysing *Julius Caesar* and *Sejanus* together, I have argued that two of the most important writers of their age use Rome to interrogate nostalgic rhetoric's power – and its ethics. Both tragedies use nostalgia to foreground their political action and political discourses, and both present a Tacitean representation of a degenerate present and an idealised past. Howsoever that idyll offers hope, impetus and community, Shakespeare and Jonson employ it to ends that implicate nostalgic rhetoric in conspiracy and violent civil war, as in *Julius Caesar*, and foolish complaint and self-sabotage, as in *Sejanus*. *Julius Caesar* stages a clear trajectory of conspiracy stemming from an anxiety for the future, an invocation of the idealised past, and a confidence in that past's reclamation. This clear causality contrasts markedly with *Sejanus*, where brief bursts of explicit nostalgia are subsumed by a Neostoicism that perpetuates an atmosphere of hopelessness and political resignation. As *Julius Caesar* makes clear, the political action that nostalgia sets in motion leads to civil war and eventually manifests the conspirators' primary fear: a single ruler of Rome. This circumstance then renders hope itself pointless, as Jonson's *Sejanus* brutally demonstrates. The tension created by nostalgia's mobilising energies in one play and its emphatically impotent and self-destructive tendencies in the other suggests an irresolvable negotiation of how past and future fantasies can construct the present in Rome's cognate, early modern London. Both dramatists' nostalgic rhetoric seems to respond to the uncertainty created around England's future under an ageing, heirless monarch, and which remained even with the accession of a new king. Together, the plays argue that regardless of nostalgia's rhetorical power, its weakness lies in its inability to guarantee the stability in language, memory or society that those who invoke it so often seek.

Notes

1. Leonard Digges, 'Upon Master William Shakespeare, the Deceased Authour, and his Poems' in *Poems: Written by Wil. Shake-speare. Gent.* (London, 1640) but written for the First Folio, cited in Gurr, *Playgoing in Shakespeare's London*, pp. 234–5. Digges's nephew Dudley, son of Sir Dudley Digges, was a friend of Jonson's who wrote 'An Elegie on Ben.

Johnson' in *Jonsonus Virbius, or the Memorie of Ben: Johnson Revived*, The English Experience no. 258 (Amsterdam and New York, 1970), pp. 22–4; cf. Mark Bland, 'Ben Jonson and the Legacies of the Past', *Huntington Library Quarterly*, 67:3 (2004), 371–400, 371–2.
2. Ben Jonson, *Epicene or The Silent Woman*, in *The Alchemist and Other Plays*, ed. Gordon Campbell (Oxford: Oxford University Press, 1995/2008), 2.2.101–2, cf. p. 467 n.
3. Percy Allen, *Shakespeare, Jonson, and Wilkins as Borrowers: A Study in Elizabethan Dramatic Origins and Imitations* (London: Cecil Palmer, 1928), p. 134, but see especially chapter VI. Lynn S. Meskill, 'The Tangled Thread of Authorship: Shakespeare's *Julius Caesar* and Jonson's *Sejanus, His Fall*', in *Medieval and Early Modern Authorship*, SPELL: Swiss Papers in English Language and Literature 25, ed. Guillemette Bolens and Lukas Erne (Tübingen: Narr Verlag, 2011), 75–91, 78.
4. Russ McDonald, *Shakespeare and Jonson/Jonson and Shakespeare* (Lincoln, NE and London: University of Nebraska Press, 1988), p. 4. See also Andrew Hadfield, 'Jonson and Shakespeare in an Age of Lying', *The Ben Jonson Journal*, 23:1 (2016), 52–74, which examines *Othello* and *Volpone*; Maurice Hunt, 'Jonson vs. Shakespeare: The Roman Plays', *The Ben Jonson Journal*, 23:1 (2016), 75–100; Tom Cain, 'Introduction', p. 197, in Ben Jonson, *Sejanus His Fall*, ed. Tom Cain in *The Cambridge Edition of the Works of Ben Jonson*, ed. David Bevington, Martin Butler and Ian Donaldson, vol. 2, 1601–6 (Cambridge: Cambridge University Press, 2012); Robert C. Evans, *Habits of Mind: Evidence and Effects of Ben Jonson's Reading* (Lewisburg, PA and London: Bucknell University Press/Associated University Presses, 1995), p. 160.
5. Ian Donaldson, '"Misconstruing Everything": *Julius Caesar* and *Sejanus*', in *Shakespeare Performed: Essays in Honour of R. A. Foakes*, ed. Grace Ioppolo (London: Associated University Presses, 2000), pp. 88–107, 88.
6. For an overview of Roman plays staged in early modern England, see Warren Chernaik, *The Myth of Rome in Shakespeare and his Contemporaries* (Cambridge: Cambridge University Press, 2011), p. 87. There are no surviving public Roman dramas between *Julius Caesar* and *Sejanus*. Cf. Chambers, *The Elizabethan Stage*, 4 vols, IV, appendix I, and Gurr, *Playgoing in Shakespeare's London*, pp. 47–63.
7. Ben Jonson, *Sejanus his fall* (London, 1605), A3^v. For Jonson's work on *Sejanus* before its performance, see Philip J. Ayres, ed., *Sejanus His Fall* (Manchester and New York: Manchester University Press, 1990), p. 9.
8. Ev. B's poem refers to 'the People's beastly rage', and Jonson refers disparagingly to 'such Auditors', that is, the public, who cannot delight in classic forms required of tragedy; cf. Jonson, *Sejanus*, A3^v, ¶2^r.
9. Jonson, *Sejanus*, ¶2^v; for the play's list of roles, see Ben Jonson, *The workes of Benjamin Jonson* (London, 1616), Oo3^v. Shakespeare likely played Tiberius. On the collaboration, see Barton, *Ben Jonson, Dramatist*, p. 94, and cf. pp. 92–4, and William Shakespeare and Ben Jonson, 'The Tragedie of Seianus', ed. Gary Taylor, in *The New Oxford Complete Works, Critical Reference Edition*, vol. 1, pp. 1229–30, at p. 1229.
10. Anthony Miller, 'The Roman State in *Julius Caesar* and *Sejanus*', in *Jonson and Shakespeare*, ed. Ian Donaldson (London: Macmillan in association

with Humanities Research Centre, Australian National University, 1983), p. 180.
11. Cited in Richard A. McCabe, 'Elizabethan Satire and the Bishops' Ban of 1599', *The Yearbook of English Studies*, Literature and its Audience, 11 (1981), 188–92, 188. Printed histories had to be '"allowed by somme of her majesties privie Counsell"', p. 188.
12. The New Oxford team dates *Othello* to October 1603–October 1604, with a 'best guess' of 'early 1604', Taylor and Loughnane, 'The Canon and Chronology', p. 553, cf. pp. 553–4. Ian Donaldson observes *Every Man In*'s echoes in *Othello*, in *Ben Jonson: A Life* (Oxford: Oxford University Press, 2011), p. 131.
13. Shakespeare, *The Tragedy of Othello; or, the Moor of Venice*, ed. Gary Taylor in *The New Oxford Shakespeare: Modern Critical Edition*, 5.2.298.
14. Epigram 95, 'To Sir Henry Savile', cited in McCrea, *Constant Minds: Political Virtue and the Lipsian Paradigm in England, 1584–1650* (Toronto: University of Toronto Press, 1997), p. 162.
15. Cf. Hebert Benario, 'Tacitus, Germanicus, and Henry V', in *Notes and Queries*, 57:3 (2010), 372–3, which notes the echo of Germanicus's anonymous nighttime visitation to his troops in Henry V's similar action on the eve of Agincourt. G. R. Price had already observed the connection in 'Henry V and Germanicus', *Shakespeare Quarterly*, xii (1961), 57–60. For the passage in question, see Tacitus, *The Annals*, II.401–3 (cf. 401–5) in Tacitus, *Tacitus: in five volumes/III, The Histories: books IV–V*, trans. Clifford H. Moore, and *The Annals: books I–III*, trans. John Jackson (London: Heinemann, 1931).
16. Peter Burke, 'Tacitism', in *Tacitus*, ed. T. A. Dorey (London: Routledge and Kegan Paul, 1969), pp. 149–71, p. 149, 151; cf. also Burke, 'Tacitism, Scepticism, and Reason of State', in *The Cambridge History of Political Thought*, ed. J. H. Burns (Cambridge: Cambridge University Press, 1991), pp. 479–98; Donaldson, *Ben Jonson*, p. 187.
17. John Guy, *Tudor England*, p. 415, possibly citing M. E. James, but the citation is unclear.
18. Burke, 'Tacitism, Scepticism, and Reason of State', pp. 484–5.
19. Justus Lipsius, *Sixe bookes of politickes or civil doctrine*, trans. William Jones (London, 1594), sig. A[v^v].
20. Justus Lipsius, *Politicorum, sive, Civilis doctrinae libri sex, qui ad principatum maximè spectant* (London, 1590), sig. B4^r.
21. Burke, 'Tacitism, Scepticism, and Reason of State', p. 485; McCrea, *Constant Minds*; R. V. Young, ed. and trans. *Justus Lipsius' Concerning Constancy*, Medieval and Renaissance Texts and Studies 389 (Tempe: ACMRS (Arizona Center for Medieval and Renaissance Studies), 2011).
22. David Womersley, 'Sir Henry Savile's Translation of Tacitus and the Political Interpretation of Elizabethan Texts', *The Review of English Studies*, 42:167 (1991), 313–42, 313; Donaldson, *Ben Jonson*, pp. 120, 122.
23. Tacitus, *The Annals*, III.LV, pp. 611, 610.
24. The Greek historian Polybius, who became increasingly of interest to early moderns from the late sixteenth century onwards, emphasised recurrent cycles of rise and decline in successive nations or rulers, and so offered a cyclical concept of history not entirely at odds with Tacitus's concept

of 'moral revolution'. See Polybius, *The hystories of the most famous and worthy cronographer Polybius discoursing of the warres betwixt the Romanes & Carthaginenses, a riche and goodly worke, conteining holsome counsels & wonderfull devises against the incombrances of fickle fortune*, trans. Christopher Watson (London, 1568). The translator's inclusion of 'an abstract, compendiously coarcted out of the life & worthy acts, perpetuate by our puissaunt prince king Henry the fift', t.p., shows his not-uncommon interest in drawing parallels between ancient and English history. Readers of Lipsius would also have come across references to him in his works, for example *Two bookes of constancie*, trans. Stradling (1595). See Peter Burke, 'A Survey of the Popularity of Ancient Historians, 1450–1700', *History and Theory*, (1966), 135–52.

25. One recent exception is Peter Gibbard's 'Ben Jonson's *Sejanus* and the Middle Way of Annals 1–6', *Studies in English Literature, 1500–1900*, 56:2 (2016), 307–25, and his *Republicanism, Tacitism and Style in English Drama: 1585–1608*, PhD dissertation, The University of Sydney, 2014.
26. Chernaik, *The Myth of Rome*, pp. 22, 81.
27. On early modern drama and literature's creation of sceptical spectators, cf. Annabel Patterson, *Reading Holinshed's Chronicles* (Chicago and London: University of Chicago Press, 1994); Hutson, *The Invention of Suspicion*; Sherman, *Skepticism and Memory*; and Karremann, *The Drama of Memory*.
28. The Folio text, the play's first printing, breaks the text into 'theatrically effective' acts, a practice which began after 1609, Sarah Neville, 'Introduction', in William Shakespeare, *Julius Caesar*, ed. Sarah Neville, in *The New Oxford Shakespeare: Modern Critical Edition*, vol. 2, p. 2933.
29. All citations of *Julius Caesar* are from Sarah Neville, ed., *Julius Caesar*, in *The New Oxford Shakespeare: Modern Critical Edition*, 1.1.31–3, 36. All further citations will be made in the text.
30. Peter Burke cited in Anthony B. Dawson, 'The Arithmetic of Memory: Shakespeare's Theatre and The National Past', *Shakespeare Survey*, 52 (1999), 56.
31. Coppélia Kahn, *Roman Shakespeare: Warriors, Wounds and Women* (New York and London: Routledge, 1997), p. 85.
32. Robert S. Miola, '*Julius Caesar* and The Tyrannicide Debate', *Renaissance Quarterly*, 38 (1985), 271–89, 276.
33. Kahn, *Roman Shakespeare*, pp. 81, 82.
34. Chernaik, *The Myth of Rome*, p. 79.
35. William Shakespeare, *Julius Caesar*, ed. David Daniell, Arden Third Series (London: Thompson Learning, repr. 2006), p. 200 n, and Edward Pechter, '*Julius Caesar* and *Sejanus*: Roman Politics, Inner Selves and the Powers of the Theatre', in *Shakespeare and his Contemporaries: Essays in Comparison*, ed. E. A. J. Honigmann (Manchester and Dover, NH: Manchester University Press, 1986), p. 62.
36. Hunt, 'Jonson vs. Shakespeare', p. 90.
37. Kahn, *Roman Shakespeare*, p. 77.
38. On such failures see Donaldson, '"Misconstruing Everything"', p. 88.
39. Plutarch writes that Antony 'framed his eloquence to make their [the

common people's] harts yerne the more', Sir Thomas North, trans., *The lives of the noble Grecians and Romanes, compared together by that grave learned philosopher and historiographer, Plutarke of Chaeronea: translated out of Greeke into French by James Amiot, abbot of Bellozane, Bishop of Auxerre, one of the Kings privie counsell, and great Amner of France, and out of French into English, by Thomas North* (London, 1595), p. 1062.

40. Daniell, ed., *Julius Caesar*, p. 260 n.
41. What I call 'historicising' other critics have called 'fiction-making': Daniell's edition explains that 'Antony did not join Caesar in Gaul until three years later. This is a fiction about himself and Caesar, like those of Cassius' "memories"', *Julius Caesar*, p. 262 n. But Daniell is applying actual history to what is already a fiction: the drama. Within the play world, we have no reason to believe that Cassius's and Antony's stories – save the example of Caesar's murder – are not in some way based in fact.
42. Meskill, 'The Tangled Thread of Authorship', 87–8.
43. Plutarch includes the mixed reception of Brutus's speeches but not the speeches themselves.
44. North, trans., *The lives of the noble Grecians and Romanes*, p. 1065.
45. Lorna Hutson, 'Introduction', in Ben Jonson, *Volpone and Other Plays* (London: Penguin Books, 1998), p. xxiv.
46. Parmelee, 'Neostoicism', pp. 3–19, pp. 3, 6.
47. Lipsius, *Two bookes of constancie*, sig. C^r (emphasis in the original). All further references will be made in the text.
48. Montaigne, 'An apology for Raymond Sebond', in *The Complete Essays*, II:12, p. 652; cf. 'Parmelee, 'Neostoicism', pp. 6–8.
49. Montaigne, 'An apology for Raymond Sebond', in *The Complete Essays*, II:12, p. 653, but see also his discussion from pp. 652–3.
50. Ben Jonson, *Sejanus His Fall*, ed. Tom Cain in *The Cambridge Edition of the Works of Ben Jonson*, ed. David Bevington, Martin Butler and Ian Donaldson, vol. 2, 1601–6 (Cambridge: Cambridge University Press, 2012), 1.64–5. All further citations will be made in the text.
51. Paul Daniel Menzer, 'The Olympic Bluff: Jonson's *Sejanus* and the Vanishing Point', *The Ben Jonson Journal*, 11 (2004), 41–66, 48–9.
52. Peter Gibbard citing Tacitus in Gibbard, 'Ben Jonson's *Sejanus*', p. 309.
53. Blair Worden, 'Classical Republicanism and the Puritan Revolution', in *History and Imagination: Essays in Honour of H. R. Trevor-Roper*, ed. Hugh Lloyd-Jones, Valerie Pearl and Blair Worden (London: Gerald Duckworth & Co, 1981), p. 186.
54. Cain, ed., 'Introduction', in Jonson, *Sejanus his Fall*, pp. 202, 205, and Donaldson, *Ben Jonson*, p. 192.
55. Arruntius seems to echo Cassius when the former states that Cato 'had power, / As not to live his slave, to die his [own] master', 1.91–2; cf. *Julius Caesar*, 1.2.97–8, 1.3.95–9.
56. That praise of Cassius reverberates dramatically and historically: Arruntius cites Cordus, the historian who will soon be sent to prison for this epideictic rhetoric. This phrase is also a citation of Brutus in the final act of *Julius Caesar*: 'the last of all the Romans, fare thee well', Brutus laments over the body of his friend (5.3.99), echoing Plutarch and, ultimately, Tacitus, who writes that Cordus was brought before the Senate on the 'novel and till then

unheard-of charge of publishing a history, eulogizing Brutus, and styling Cassius the last of the Romans', *Annals*, IV.xxxiv.
57. Barton, *Ben Jonson*, p. 101.
58. Cassius is notably absent from this list. This perfect mix of character suggests Antony's description of Brutus as 'the noblest Roman of them all', see discussion above, pp. 147–8.
59. Barton, *Ben Jonson*, p. 100, and cf. pp. 92–105 for her discussion of *Sejanus*.
60. Afer's assertion expresses the same anxiety about access to knowledge held by counter-Reformers, that an increased knowledge of scripture increased the opportunities for its misinterpretation.
61. Jonson is cited in Barton, *Ben Jonson*, p. 103.
62. Cain, ed., 'Introduction', in Jonson, *Sejanus his Fall*, p. 209, and p. 203, citing Holland.
63. See Chapter 2, pp. 77–8.
64. Daniell observes that '*Julius Caesar* is one of the plays of Shakespeare most referred to in the early seventeenth century', as lines from the play were cited and reworked in plays and poems of the time, including Jonson's own *Every Man Out of his Humour*, Daniell, ed., 'Introduction', in *Julius Caesar*, p. 14, but cf. pp. 14–15.
65. Cain, ed., in Jonson, *Sejanus His Fall*, p. 328 n.

Conclusion: Resisting Nostalgia

Starting from a critical position that questions how we understand nostalgia in early modernity, this book has argued that Shakespeare's Elizabethan histories stage nostalgia's power as a future-oriented, ambivalent, political rhetoric. By dramatising nostalgia as a rhetoric available to those in and out of power, Shakespeare marks nostalgia as a suspect practice as he reveals how accessible, and therefore how unstable, the language of the idealised past and its attendant promises of a better future are. Using the familiar idealising discourses of his time – of a merry world, of hospitality, of ancient Rome – Shakespeare emphasises nostalgia as rhetoric, rather than strictly a process of cultural memorialising. By situating nostalgia in that moral and political realm of rhetoric, I have not focused exclusively on what happens in the idealising process of nostalgia – what is remembered, what is forgotten, what is invented – but on how that idealisation is used. Shakespeare shows how quotidian such a process is; it happens in proverbs, in laments for long-waning social customs, in learned comparisons with ancient Rome. He then stages this discourse as consistently successful and reliably untrustworthy, thereby destabilising discourses familiar both on stage and off stage and insisting on the fictiveness of the idealised past. That there are multiple golden ages signifies that there never was one, but their image of perfection, he insists, is tantalising.

While contemporary attitudes to nostalgia reject its perceived futile sentimentality and impulse to reify the past, early modern English disapproval of nostalgia emerges from religious and political concerns. The suspicion of nostalgia staged by Shakespeare's dramaturgy expands and nuances a resistance to nostalgia evident in a range of sixteenth-century texts. Significantly, Shakespeare translates his contemporaries' qualms about nostalgia into a broader reflection on why the longing for an ideal past possesses such persuasive power, as he binds dramatic nostalgic rhetoric to the hope for a better future. By insisting on nostalgia's availability and by presenting nostalgia as a political tool – a political weapon, even – Shakespeare illustrates once more his interest in drama's capacity to challenge his audience's habits of mind and to shape civic political thought.

His mistrust of the idealised past links Shakespeare to those dramatists who influenced him and who he in turn influenced: the Queen's Men's playwrights, Marlowe, and Jonson. This study's close attention to the dramatic contexts of Shakespeare's nostalgic rhetoric has urged the importance of recognising that how Shakespeare employs nostalgia does not emerge from a dramatic-political vacuum. Rather, in the Queen's Men and Marlowe, as in the authors of Tudor interludes, he saw playwrights sceptical of the past, suggesting (as in *Famous Victories*) an ethical problem tied to the impulse of idealising what has gone before. This dramatic association of temporal consciousness with a moral or ethical value provides a new insight not only into the development of nostalgia, but the values associated with time itself. Early modernists have recognised the moral implications of using time wisely or idling, but the ethics of looking forward to the future or back to the (distant) past has remained largely undiscussed.

Reflecting on Shakespeare's use of the idealised past in his Elizabethan histories inevitably raises the question of where this dramaturgical strategy might surface in his Jacobean history plays. His Elizabethan uses of nostalgia insist on the past's instability and the persuasive force of idealising time, and these manifest in *Antony and Cleopatra* (1606), which stages a resistance to the idealised past not only through the lovers' vision of themselves but through the play's insistent examination of historical narratives more generally. Recent critical accounts have located in Shakespeare's Jacobean plays and particularly in *Antony and Cleopatra* an engagement with the politics of nostalgically representing Elizabeth in James's reign and Shakespeare's staging of the limits of such nostalgia. Arguing that Antony and Cleopatra reproduce the Elizabethan symbolism of chivalric romance and oceanic domination, Yuichi Tsukada concludes that their 'military defeat confirms that their idealistic self-styled roles are, after all, objects of nostalgia, objects with no power to alter the course of history'.[1] But as this book has argued, Shakespeare's Elizabethan histories stage precisely that danger of nostalgia: that it can alter the course of history, as it directs political currents and motivates rebellion.

These are not lovers who long for a bygone age: that past would preclude their origin as 'such a mutual pair', as Antony and Cleopatra.[2] Together the lovers embody the present's perfection, and consequently they reject that object of desire so ubiquitous in contemporary nostalgia; they reject youth. Cleopatra dismisses her own girlish behaviour, famously describing the time she loved and praised Julius Caesar as 'My salad days, / When I was green in judgement, cold in blood, / To say as I said then' (1.5.76–8). She may recall that she 'was a morsel for a monarch', but that recollection hardly reads as a longing still so to be, since she is no longer an easily edible 'morsel' but paradoxically rather 'makes hungry / Where most she satisfies' (1.5.32, 2.2.247–8). Similarly, Antony's constant disparaging of Caesar's youth – Octavius himself knows 'He calls me boy' (4.1.1) – registers not as longing or jealousy, but disdain. These lovers of their prime imagine not a perfect past, but a more perfect union after death, one that will apotheosise them in the manner they attempt in life, for 'Dido and her Aeneas shall want troops, / And all the haunt be ours', as Antony declares (4.14.54–5).[3] The lovers' glory, celebrated by themselves and those they leave behind, can manifest anew in the future – in the afterlife, the space of Cleopatra's 'immortal longings' (5.2.280). Where in *Julius Caesar* death, specifically Caesar's death, stages dramaturgical rupture and creation, for Cleopatra Antony's death signifies historical rupture and decline. After the event, the 'dull world [. . .] is / No better than a sty' (4.15.63–4). Death speedily enables a hagiography of Antony, who praises himself as 'the greatest prince o'th'world, / The noblest' and sets himself alongside Julius Caesar and Brutus. Octavius and his generals echo him: Agrippa declares 'A rarer spirit never / Did steer humanity' (5.1.31–2). Cleopatra famously eulogises him as a colossus, his voice the music of the spheres (5.2.81–3). But when she asks, 'Think you there was or might be such a man / As this I dreamt of?', Dolabella voices the play's refusal to rewrite the tragic hero's faults as the audience has seen them play out: 'Gentle madam, no' (5.2.93). Shakespeare stages the idealising process as a human response to grief, rendering the hope of that ideal's future immortal existence tenuous. Such an ideal could never have existed in the first place.

Throughout the play, Shakespeare displaces any confident image of the past, rather crafting it as a source of anxiety and instability. In the repeated references to Julius Caesar's death and to Brutus and Cassius, we are reminded not only of the peaceful triumvirate with which Shakespeare's last Roman tragedy concludes, but also with how the narrative of events since then has changed. Lepidus pleads with the quarrelling Antony and Octavius, 'That which combined us was most great, and let not / A leaner action rend us' (2.2.19–20). The men's memories fail, and marriage appears as the only means to unify them since they cannot recall the post-Caesar days that united them nor identify a shared political inheritance between them. As if in a Queen's Men play, history is attenuated. To create the future, Maecenas argues, the past cannot be debated or longed for; it must be forgotten:

> If it might please you to enforce no further
> The griefs between ye; to forget them quite
> Were to remember that the present need
> Speaks to atone you. (2.2.105–8)

In the moments of dramatic political crisis that this book has examined, it is the idealised past, not its erasure, that becomes the necessary model for 'present need'. Maecenas may argue here that to forget the past is 'to remember [. . .] the present', but Shakespeare maintains Brutus and Cassius as a binary lodestar in the present. Pompey glorifies the conspirators in his defence of his own actions, asking

> What was't
> That moved pale Cassius to conspire? And what
> Made the all-honoured, honest Roman, Brutus,
> With the armed rest, courtiers of beauteous freedom,
> To drench the Capitol, but that they would
> Have one man but a man? (2.6.14–19)

This political inheritance – the abolition of a tyrant – has not delivered the promised future, for as Pompey argues, 'that is it' which has brought him to war against the triumvirate (2.6.19). Moreover, audience members with good memories would have noted the irony of Antony's revisionary history; he falsifies and exaggerates what he did at Philippi, claiming that he 'struck / The lean and wrinkled Cassius, and 'twas I / That the mad Brutus ended' (3.11.36–8). In this epithet, Antony even seems to confuse his Roman history, conflating Brutus with his ancestor who feigned madness before driving the Tarquins from Rome. Perhaps the most obvious structural insistence on the evasiveness of historical truth comes through Scenes 2 to 4 of Act 2, where Shakespeare stages Antony's version of events to Octavia, Eros and Enobarbus's version, and finally Caesar's, without providing a settled narrative.

The future in language, as in the Elizabethan plays, becomes a place of unfulfilled promise in this tragedy. Almost as soon as Antony promises Octavia, 'I have not kept my square, but that to come / Shall all be done by th'rule' (2.3.6–7), the Soothsayer arrives to undermine that pledge, suggesting that despite what Antony might say, his fate is bound to Egypt. The instability of a mortal future suggested by this promise-breaking persists even through Caesar's confident anticipation that 'The time of universal peace is near. / Prove this a prosp'rous day, the three-nooked world / Shall bear the olive freely' (4.6.5–7). While some audience members would know that the *pax Romana* did manifest eventually, Antony's unexpected victory delays Caesar's triumph and his imperial rule. As some spectators would also have likely known, 'the *pax Romana* was said to be a fulfilment of the prophecies both of Isaiah (2:4) and of Virgil's fourth Eclogue', the latter announcing the return of the Golden Age.[4] Shakespeare thus delays and ultimately questions the good of such a peace by making the calculating, ambitious 'boy' its engine (3.13.17, 4.12.48).

Throughout his Elizabethan and his Jacobean histories, Shakespeare's dramaturgy undermines the notion of an idealised past, a Golden Age on which Elizabeth I traded throughout her reign to perform her authority and justness as a ruler. Simultaneously, that dramaturgy attends to the instability of narratives of the past and their promises for the future. As a result, Shakespeare argues implicitly against anticipating better or other leaders, even as he suggests that the desire for change is inevitable and politically important.

Shakespeare's Elizabethan suspicion of nostalgia persists into the Stuart period with *Henry VIII (All is True)* (1613). Scholars have noted how Stuart nostalgia emphasised the invocation of 'Good Queen Bess' in various forms to critique James's or Charles's respective reigns and governments, but nostalgic images of 'merry England' and the returned Golden Age were also – as in Elizabethan England – used as affirmatory symbols of the Stuart monarchs' peaceful and plentiful reign.[5] With *Henry VIII*, Shakespeare and John Fletcher seem superficially interested in whetting Jacobean appetites for a glimpse of Good Queen Bess's origin story and in satiating spectators' desires for the proximate past, and the play seems to deliver by providing 'nostalgic spectacle'.[6] However, this history seems to revise again the Queen's Men's model of future-focused temporality. Any longing inspired by such 'spectacle' is tempered by the play's staging of origin points and political prophecy, which establish a dramatic anticipation of the drama's own present and recent, known past. From its Prologue, the play declares itself uninterested in 'nostalgic fun', demanding that the audience 'Be sad, as we would make ye'.[7] Rather than staging the series of social-political ruptures that happen *to* sovereign figures in *2 Henry VI*, *Richard II* and *Julius Caesar* or elsewhere in the plays, Shakespeare and Fletcher stage a king who himself creates and weathers a schism, as his double divorce from Wolsey and Katherine show. With that schism, the playwrights dramatise a crucial origin point of Stuart England, thereby establishing nostalgia within the play itself, just as Shakespeare staged in *Richard II* and *Julius Caesar*. Katherine and Wolsey, from whom we might expect a murmur of lament for what seemed a golden age, utter nothing in praise of the past. Katherine's insistence on her innocence offers rather temporal continuity, bringing the past into the present and, she hopes, into the future. She asks her gentlewoman Patience,

> [. . .] When I am dead [. . .]
>   Strew me over
> With maiden flowers, that all the world may know
> I was a chaste wife to my grave.   (4.2.167–70)

The fallen queen and her cardinal nemesis are more invested in crafting their futures than rewriting their pasts, and as a result they 'suffer from the illusion of agency' created by the play's tantalising suggestions of action and choice and the resistance to historical determination.[8] In this way, Katherine and the cardinal recall Jonson's Germanicans, suggesting that there is no idealised past that can inspire or alter the course of the future.

Even in the unjust circumstances of Henry VIII's reign, the past appears not as decline, but progress. As Buckingham bitterly relates, 'I had my trial, / And must needs say a noble one; which makes me / A little happier than my wretched father', who suffered under Richard III (2.1.118–20). This connection between the tyrant Richard and Henry is significant, but the circumstances and questions surrounding Buckingham's fall temper outright critiques, producing instead a scepticism that likewise emerges from Cranmer's prophecy of Elizabeth. The Tudor genre of political prophecy is 'carefully updated' here, but it 'is both legitimized and problematized by its incorporation into a history play, enabling the audience to verify the events which have already taken place and thus presume the accuracy of those events which have not'.[9] The idealising claims of the prophecy, that 'every man shall eat in safety / Under his own vine what he plants, and sing / The merry songs of peace to all his neighbours' (5.4.33–5), demand judgement from the audience, whose participation in the prophecy is inevitable.[10] That judgement's outcome has the power to invalidate the play's performative claims of the past, present and future even as the act of judgement itself does more than in any other Shakespearean history to collapse historical distance and establish an illusion of temporal continuity.[11] The audience's inclusion in the prophecy could represent nostalgic satiety: their desire for connection with the past is gratified as they become part of the play's past-present. *Henry VIII*'s epilogue, however, recognises the impossibility of meeting all spectators' demands and desires – ''Tis ten to one this play can never please / All that are here' (Epi.1–2). The play's dramaturgy maintains that suspicion of nostalgia that characterises Shakespeare's Elizabethan histories as the dramatists stage the origin of origins, suggest history's progress, and use what had been an idealised past – the beginning of the 'true church' – as a source of dramatic 'misery' (Pro.30).

By complicating the idea of nostalgia that has fixed its orientation consistently to the past as a refuge against the future's inevitable decline, this book has argued that the idealised past possesses rhetorical force because it turns the nostalgic towards the future. Despite his love of Ovid, Shakespeare has short shrift with his favourite poet's degenerative history of humankind and the notion that there is a past preferable to the present. Shakespeare stages the power of praising the old ways, not the ways themselves, as there is little reason to believe their idyll ever existed.

Notes

1. Tsukada, *Shakespeare and the Politics of Nostalgia*, p. 84.
2. William Shakespeare, *Antony and Cleopatra*, ed. John Wilders, Arden Third Series (London: Routledge, 1995), 1.1.38. All further references will be made in the text.
3. Cf. John Garrison, *Shakespeare and the Afterlife* (Oxford: Oxford University Press, 2018), pp. 60–7.
4. Wilders, ed., *Antony and Cleopatra*, p. 237 n.
5. See the Introduction, p. 27, n 6, and Leah S. Marcus, *The Politics of Mirth: Jonson, Herrick, Milton, Marvell, and the Defense of Old Holiday Pastimes* (Chicago and London: University of Chicago Press, 1986), esp. pp. 106–39; Graham Parry, 'A Troubled Arcadia', in *Literature and the English Civil War*, ed. Thomas Healy and Jonathan Sawday (Cambridge: Cambridge University Press, 1990), pp. 38–55; Raymond A. Anselment, *Loyalist Resolve: Patient Fortitude in the English Civil War* (Cranbury, NJ and London: Associated University Presses, 1988), pp. 73–4 for a discussion of the images of Stuart prosperity owing their creative debt to the idea of 'blest Eliza' and royalist poet George Daniel's belief in Charles I as the 'the new "Charlemaine"'.
6. Karremann, 'Nostalgic Spectacle and the Politics of Memory in *Henry VIII*', 180–90, 181 and *passim*.
7. Sherman, *Skepticism and Memory*, p. 123; William Shakespeare and John Fletcher, *King Henry VIII (All is True)*, ed. Gordon McMullan, Arden Third Series (London: Arden Shakespeare, 2000), Pro.25. All future references will be made in the text.
8. Sherman, *Skepticism and Memory*, p. 151, but see pp. 121–52. Sherman draws a connection between the prologues of *Sejanus* and *All is True*.
9. McMullan, ed., *King Henry VIII (All is True)*, pp. 438–9 n.
10. On 'prophetic community', see D. L. Keegan, 'Performing Prophecy: More Life on the Shakespearean Scene', *Shakespeare Quarterly*, 62:3 (2011), 420–33, esp. 426–8.
11. Sherman, *Skepticism and Memory*, pp. 149–50.

Bibliography

Primary Sources

Anon, *Chronographia. A description of time, from the beginning of the world, unto the yeare of our Lord, 137. Divided into six periodes. Wherein the several histories, both of the Old and New Testament are briefly comprised, and placed in their due order of yeares. Collected out of sundrie authors, but for the greatest part, abridged and translated out of Laurentius Codomannus his Annales sacræ scripturæ*, 2nd edn (London, 1590).
—— *The famous victories of Henry the fifth containing the honourable Battell of Agin-court: as it was plaide by thc [sic] Queenes Majesties Players* (London, 1598).
—— *The life and death of Jack Straw, a notable rebell in England who was kild in Smithfield by the Lord Maior of London* (London, 1594).
—— [Nicholas Udall?], *Respublica* (1553), in *Tudor Interludes*, ed. Peter Happé (Harmondsworth: Penguin Books, 1972).
—— *Three sermons, or Homelies, to moove compassion towards the poore and needie in these times* (London, 1596).
—— *The True Chronicle History of King Leir, and his three daughters, Gonorill, Ragan, and Cordella* (London, 1605).
Baker, Richard, *A chronicle of the Kings of England, from the time of the Romans goverment [sic] unto the raigne of our soveraigne lord, King Charles containing all passages of state or church, with all other observations proper for a chronicle* (London, 1643).
Blundeville, Thomas, *The true order and Methode of wryting and reading hystories, according to the precepts of Francisco Patricio and Accontio Tridentino, two Italian writers, no lesse plainly than briefly, set forth in our vulgar speach, to the great profite and commoditye of all those that delight in Hystories* (London, 1574).
Burton, Robert, *The Anatomy of Melancholy* (London, 1621).
Burton, William, *Ten sermons upon the first, second, third and fourth verses of the sixt of Matthew containing diverse necessary and profitable treatises, viz. a preservative against the poyson of vaine-glory in the 1 & 2, the reward of sincerity in the 3, the uncasing of the hypocrite in the 4, 5 and 6, the reward of hypocrisie in the 7 and 8, an admonition to left-handed Christians in the 9 and 10: whereunto is annexed another treatise called The anatomie of Belial,*

set foorth in ten sermons upon the 12, 13, 14, 15 verses of the 6 chapter of the Proverbs of Salomon (London, 1602).

Caius, John, *A boke, or counseill against the disease commonly called the sweate, or sweatyng sicknesse* (London, 1552).

Calvin, John, *De Scandalis* (1550), in *Joannis Calvini Opera Selecta, vol. II: Scripta Calvini ab 1542 usque ad annum 1564 editos continens*, ed. Petrus Barth and Guilelmus Niesel (Eugene, OR: Wipf & Stock, 2011).

—— *Little booke of John Calvines concernynge offences whereby at this daye divers are feared, and many also quight withdrawen from the pure doctrine of the Gospell, a woorke very needefull and profitable*, trans. Arthur Golding (London, 1567).

Carr, John, *The ruinous fal of prodigalitie with the notable examples of the best aprooved aucthours which hath bin written of the same* (London, 1573).

Cox, Leonard, *The art or crafte of rhetoryke* (London, 1532).

Demosthenes, *The three orations of Demosthenes*, trans. Thomas Wilson (London, 1570).

England and Wales, *By the Queene. A proclamation for the dearth of corne*, vol. 2 (London, 1596).

England and Wales, *By the Queene. The Queenes Majesties proclamation, 1. For observation of former orders against ingrossers, [and] regraters of corne 2. And to see the markets furnished with corne. 3. And also against the carrying of corne out of the realme. 4. And a prohibition to men of hospitalitie from remooving from their habitation in the time of dearth. 5. And finally a strait commandement to all officers having charge of forts to reside thereon personally, and no inhabitant to depart from the sea coast* (London, 1596)

England and Wales, Privy Council, *A new charge given by the Queenes commandement, to all justices of peace, and all maiors, shiriffes, and all principall officers of cities, boroughs, and townes corporate, for execution of sundry orders published the last yeere for staie of dearth of graine, with certaine additions nowe this present yeere to be well observed and executed* (London, 1595).

England and Wales, Privy Council, *The renewing of certaine orders devised by the speciall commandement of the Queenes Majestie, for the reliefe and stay of the present dearth of graine within the realme: in the yeere of our Lord 1586. Nowe to bee againe executed this present yere 1594. upon like occasions as were seene the former yere. With an addition of some other particular orders for reformation of the great abuses in ale-houses and such like* (London, 1594).

Erasmus, Desiderus, *Proverbes or adagies with newe addicions gathered out of the Chiliades of Erasmus*, trans. Richard Taverner (London, 1539).

Farrant, Richard, *The warres of Cyrus King of Persia, against Antiochus King of Assyria with the tragicall ende of Panthaea* (London, 1594).

Fielde, John, *A caveat for Parsons Howlet concerning his untimely flighte, and seriching in the cleare day lighte of the Gospell, necessarie for him and all the rest of that darke broode, and uncleane cage of papistes, who with their untimely bookes, seeke the discredite of the trueth, and the disquiet of this Church of England* (London, 1581).

Foxe, John, *Actes and monuments of matters most speciall and memorable, happenyng in the Church with an uniuersall history of the same, wherein is set forth at large the whole race and course of the Church, from the primitive age to these latter tymes of ours, with the bloudy times, horrible troubles, and great persecutions agaynst the true martyrs of Christ, sought and wrought as well by heathen emperours, as nowe lately practised by Romish prelates, especially in this realme of England and Scotland. Newly revised and recognised, partly also augmented, and now the fourth time agayne published and recommended to the studious reader (London, 1583).

Froissart, Jean, *Here begynneth the first volum of sir Johan Froyssart of the cronycles of Englande, Fraunce, Spayne, Portyngale, Scotlande, Bretayne, Flau[n]ders: and other places adioynynge. Tra[n]slated out of frenche into our maternall englysshe tonge, by Johan Bourchier knight lorde Berners* [. . .] (London, 1523).

Greene, Robert, *A Maidens Dreame upon the Death of the Right Honorable Sir Christopher Hatton* (London, 1591).

—— *A quip for an upstart courtier: or, A quaint dispute betvveen velvet breeches and cloth breeches Wherein is plainely set downe the disorders in all estates and trades* (London, 1592).

Hall, Edward, *The union of the two noble and illustre famelies of Lancastre [and] Yorke, beyng long In continuall discension for the croune of this noble realme with al the actes done in both the tymes of the princes, both of the one linage [and] of the other, beginnyng at the tyme of kyng Henry the fowerth, the first aucthor of this devision, and so successiuely proceadi[n]g to ye reigne of the high and prudent prince kyng Henry the eyght, the indubitate flower and very heire of both the saied linages. Whereunto is added to every kyng a severall table* (London, 1550).

Harding, Thomas, *A confutation of a booke intituled An apologie of the Church of England* (Antwerp, 1565).

Heywood, John, *The workes of John Heiwood newlie imprinted. Namelie, a dialogue, wherein are pleasantlie contriued the number of all the effectuall proverbs in our English tongue: compact in a matter concerning two maner of mariages. Together with three hundred epigrammes vpon three hundred proverbes. Also a fourth, fifth and sixth hundreth of Other very pleasant, pithie and ingenious epigrammes* (London, 1598).

Hofer, Johannes, *Dissertatio Medica de Nostalgia, oder Heimwehe* (Basel: Jacobus Bertschius, 1688).

Holinshed, Raphael, *The Third Volume of Chronicles, beginning at duke William the Norman, commonlie called the Conqueror; and descending by degrees of yeeres to all the kings and queenes of England in their orderlie successions* (London, 1586).

—— *The first and second volumes of Chronicles comprising 1 The description and historie of England, 2 The description and historie of Ireland, 3 The description and historie of Scotland: first collected and published by Raphaell Holinshed, William Harrison, and others: now newlie augmented and continued (with manifold matters of singular note and worthie memorie) to the yeare 1586. by John Hooker aliàs Vowell Gent and others. With convenient tables at the end of these volumes* (London, 1587).

Jewel, John, *A defence of the Apologie of the Churche of Englande conteininge an answeare to a certaine booke lately set foorthe by M. Hardinge, and entituled, A confutation of &c.* (London, 1567).

—— *The second tome of homilees of such matters as were promised, and intituled in the former part of homilees. Set out by the aucthoritie of the Queenes Majestie: and to be read in every parishe church agreeably* (London, 1571).

Jonson, Ben, *The workes of Benjamin Jonson* (London, 1616).

Latimer, Hugh, *Fruitfull sermons preached by the right Reverend Father, and constant martyr of Jesus Christ, Master Hugh Latimer, to the edifying of all which will dispose themselves to the reading of the same*, 2nd edn (London, 1596).

Lever, Thomas, *Three fruitfull sermo[n]s, made by Thomas Leuer. Anno domini. 1550* (London, 1550).

Lipsius, Justus, *Politicorum, sive, Civilis doctrinae libri sex, qui ad principatum maximè spectant* (London, 1590)

—— *Sixe bookes of politickes or civil doctrine*, trans. William Jones (London, 1594).

—— *Two bookes of constancie. Written in Latine, by Justus Lipsius. Containing, principallie, A comfortable conference, in common calamities. And will serve for a singular consolation to all that are privately distressed, of afflicted, either in body or mind*, trans. John Stradling (London, 1595).

Lok, Henry, *Ecclesiastes, otherwise called The preacher Containing Salomons sermons or commentaries (as it may probably be collected) upon the 49. Psalme of David his father. Compendiously abridged, and also paraphrastically dilated in English poesie, according to the analogie of Scripture, and consent of the most approved writer thereof. Composed by H. L. Gentleman. Whereunto are annexed sundrie Sonets of Christian Passions heretofore printed, and now corrected and augmented, with other affectionate Sonets of a feeling conscience of the same authors* (London, 1597).

Luther, Martin, *An exposition of Salomons booke, called Ecclesiastes or the Preacher* (London, 1573).

Lyly, John, *Euphues and his England containing his voyage and adventures, myxed with sundry pretie discourses of honest love, the discription of the countrey, the court, and the manners of that isle: delightful to be read, and nothing hurtfull to be regarded, wherein there is small offence by lightnesse given to the wise, and lesse occasion of loosenes proffered to the wanton* (London, 1580).

Marlowe, Christopher, *Tamburlaine the Great Who, from a Scythian shephearde, by his rare and woonderfull conquests, became a most puissant and mightye monarque. And (for his tyranny, and terrour in warre) was tearmed, the scourge of God* (London, 1590).

Menewe, Gracious, *A plaine subversyon or turnyng up syde down of all the argumentes, that the Popecatholykes can make for the maintenaunce of auricular confession with a moste wholsome doctryne touchyng the due obedience, that we owe unto civill magistrates, made dialogue wyse betwene the prentyse and the priest* (Wesel, 1555).

Merbury, Charles, *Briefe discourse of royall monarchie, Whereunto is added by the same gen. a collection of Italian proverbes, in benefite of such as are studious of that language* (London, 1581).

Milton, John, *The readie and easie way to establish a free commonwealth and the excellence therof compar'd with the inconveniences and dangers of readmitting kingship in this nation* (London, 1660).

Montaigne, Michel de, *Essais* (Paris: A. l'Angelier, 1595).
Norton, Thomas, Letter to Francis Mylles, 31 August 1581, Folger Shakespeare Library, MS X.c.62.
Ovid, *Metamorphoses*, Books I–XIII, trans. Frank Justus Miller, rev. G. P. Goold, 2nd edn (Cambridge, MA and London: Harvard University Press, 1984).
Peacham, Henry, *The Garden of Eloquence conteyning the figures of grammer and rhetorick, from whence maye bee gathered all manner of flowers, coulors, ornaments, exornations, formes and fashions of speech, very profitable for all those that be studious of eloquence, and that reade most eloquent poets and orators, and also helpeth much for the better understanding of the holy Scriptures* (London, 1577).
Peele, George, *Descensus astraeae* (London, 1591).
—— *The famous chronicle of king Edward the first, sirnamed Edward Longshankes with his returne from the holy land. Also the life of Lleuellen rebell in Wales. Lastly, the sinking of Queene Elinor, who sunck at Charingcrosse, and rose againe at Pottershith, now named Queenehith* (London, 1593).
—— *The Troublesome Reign of John, King of England*, ed. Charles Forker, The Revels Plays series (Manchester: Manchester University Press, 2011/2016).
Plutarch, *The lives of the noble Grecians and Romanes, compared together by that grave learned philosopher and historiographer, Plutarke of Chaeronea: translated out of Greeke into French by James Amiot, abbot of Bellozane, Bishop of Auxerre, one of the Kings privie counsell, and great Amner of France, and out of French into English, by Thomas North*, trans. Thomas North (London, 1595).
Polybius, *The hystories of the most famous and worthy cronographer Polybius discoursing of the warres betwixt the Romanes & Carthaginenses, a riche and goodly worke, conteining holsome counsels & wonderfull devises against the incombrances of fickle fortune*, trans. Christopher Watson (London, 1568).
Prestion, Thomas, *A lamentable tragedie, mixed full of plesant mirth, containing the life of Cambises king of Percia from the beginning of his kingdome, unto his death, his one good deed of execution, after that many wicked deedes and tyrannous murders, committed by and through him, and last of all, his odious death by Gods justice appointed. Done in such order as followeth* (London, 1595).
Public Record Office, *Calendar of State Papers: Domestic Series of the Reign of Elizabeth 1598–1601* (London: Longman, Brown, Green, Longmans & Roberts, 1856–).
Puttenham, George, *The arte of English poesie Contrived into three bookes: the first of poets and poesie, the second of proportion, the third of ornament* (London, 1589).
—— *The Art of English Poesy by George Puttenham: A Critical Edition*, ed. Frank Whigham and Wayne A. Rebhorn (Ithaca, NY and London: Cornell University Press, 2007).
Rainolde, Richard, *A booke called the Foundacion of rhetorike because all other partes of rhetorike are grounded thereupon, every parte sette forthe in an oracion upon questions* (London, 1563).
de Serres, Jean, *A Godlie and learned comentarie*, trans. John Stockwood (London, 1585).

Shakespeare, William, *Mr William Shakespeares Comedies, Histories, & Tragedies* (London, 1623).
Sherry, Richard, *A Treatise of Schemes and Tropes* (London, 1550).
Sidney, Sir Phillip, *The defence of poesie* (London, 1595).
Smith, Henry, *A fruitfull sermon upon part of the 5. chapter of the first epistle of Saint Paule to the Thessalonians* (London, 1591).
Smith, Sir Thomas, *De Republica Anglorum [1583]*, ed. Mary Dewar (Cambridge, 1982).
Speed, John, *The history of Great Britaine under the conquests of ye Romans, Saxons, Danes and Normans* (London, 1611).
Stow, John, *The Annales of England* (London, 1592).
—— *The Survey of London* (London, 1603).
Tacitus, *The Annals: books I–III*, trans. John Jackson (London: Heinemann, 1931).
—— *Tacitus: in five volumes/III, The Histories: books IV–V*, trans. Clifford H. Moore (Cambridge, MA: Harvard University Press, 1931).
Tarlton, Richard, *Tarltons jests Drawne into these three parts. 1 His court-wittie jests 2 His sound cittie jests. 3 His country prettie jests. Full of delight, wit, and honest myrth* (London, 1613).
Thomas, William, *A speech of William Thomas, Esquire, in Parliament, in May, 1641, being A short view and examination of the actions of bishops in Parliament from Anno Dom. 1116 to this present of 1641* (London, 1641).
Trollope, Rev. William, *A History of the Royal Foundation of Christ's Hospital. With an account of the plan of education, the internal economy of the institution, and memoirs of eminent blues: preceded by a narrative of the rise, progress, and suppression of the convent of the grey friars in London* (London: William Pickering, 1834).
Wever, R., *An enterlude called lusty Juventus* (London, 1550).
Wilson, Thomas, *The arte of rhetorique for the use of all suche as are studious of eloquence* (London, 1553).
—— 'The bounding of Greecelande according to Ptolomeus', in Demosthenes, *The three orations of Demosthenes*, trans. Thomas Wilson (London, 1570).

Modern Editions

Alexander, Gavin, ed., *Sidney's 'The Defence of Poesy' and Selected Renaissance Literary Criticism* (London: Penguin Books, 2004).
Anon, *The Famous Victories of Henry the Fifth*, ed. Chiaki Hanabusa. The Malone Society Reprints, Vol. 171 2006 (2007).
—— *The First Part of the Reign of King Richard the Second or Thomas of Woodstock*, ed. Wilhelmina Frijlinck (London: the Malone Society, 1929).
—— *The life and death of Jack Straw: 1594*, prep. Kenneth Muir and F. P. Wilson (Oxford: the Malone Society, 1957).
—— *Rhetorica ad Herennium*, trans. Harry Caplan (Cambridge, MA and London: Harvard University Press, 1954; repr. 1999).
—— *Rites of Durham: being a description or brief declaration of all the ancient*

monuments, rites, & customs belonging or being within the monastical church of Durham before the suppression (1593), ed. J. T. Fowler (Durham: for the Society by Andrews & co., 1903).
—— *Thomas of Woodstock, or the First Part of Richard II*, ed. Peter Corbin and Douglas Sedge (Manchester: Manchester University Press/New York: Palgrave, 2002).
—— *A Tragedy of King Richard the Second, Concluding with The Murder of the Duke of Gloucester at Calais*, ed. J. O. Halliwell (London: T. Richards, 1870).
—— *The Tragical Reign of Selimus: 1594*, prep. W. Bang (London: the Malone Society, 1909).
—— *The True Tragedy of Richard the Third*, ed. John Johnson, gen. ed. W. W. Greg (Oxford: Oxford University Press for the Malone Society, 1929).
—— *York Mystery Plays: A Selection in Modern Spelling*, ed. Richard Beadle and Pamela M. King (Oxford: Clarendon Press, 1984).
Arber, Edward, ed., *A Transcript of the registers of the Company of Stationers of London, 1554–1640*, vol. II (London, 1875–84).
Aristotle, *The Nicomachean Ethics*, trans. H. Rackham. Loeb Classical Library 73 (Cambridge, MA: Harvard University Press, 1926).
Barker, William, ed., *A Selection from Erasmus's Adages* (Toronto and London: University of Toronto Press, 2001).
Bevington, David, and Lars Engle, Katherine Eisaman Maus and Eric Rasmussen, eds., *English Renaissance Drama: A Norton Anthology* (New York: W. W. Norton & Co Ltd, 2002).
Cicero, Marcus Tullus, *De inventione: De optimo genere oratorum*, trans. H. M. Hubbell (London: William Heinemann Ltd/Cambridge, MA: Harvard University Press, 1949).
—— *De oratore*, Books I–II, trans. E. W. Sutton, intro. and compl. H. Rackham (Cambridge, MA and London: Harvard University Press, 1942).
Erasmus, Desiderus, *Adages*, in *Collected Works of Erasmus*, vol. 32, trans. R. A. B. Mynors (Toronto, Buffalo, London: University of Toronto Press, 1989).
—— *The Ciceronian: A Dialogue on the Ideal Latin Style*, in *Collected Works*, vol. 28, ed. A. H. T. Levi, intro. and trans. Betty I. Knott (Toronto, Buffalo, London: University of Toronto Press, 1986).
Foakes, R. A., ed., *Henslowe's Diary*, 2nd edn (Cambridge and New York: Cambridge University Press, 2002).
Greene, Robert, *Friar Bacon and Friar Bungay*, prep. W. W. Greg (Oxford: Oxford University Press for the Malone Society, 1926).
—— *Friar Bacon and Friar Bungay*, ed. Daniel Seltzer (London: Edward Arnold, 1963).
Hofer, Johannes, 'Dissertatio Medica de Nostalgia, oder Heimweh', 'Medical Dissertation on Nostalgia' trans. Carolyn Kiser Anspach, *Bulletin of the Institute of the History of Medicine*, 2 (1934), 376–91.
Jonson, Ben, *Epicene or The Silent Woman*, in *The Alchemist and Other Plays*, ed. Gordon Campbell (Oxford: Oxford University Press, 1995/2008).
—— *Poetaster*, ed. C. H. Herford and Percy Simpson, in *Ben Jonson*, 11 vols (Oxford: Clarendon Press, 1925–52), IV (1932).

—— *Sejanus his fall* (London, 1605).
—— *Sejanus His Fall*, ed. Phillip J. Ayres (Manchester: Manchester University Press, 1990).
—— *Sejanus His Fall*, ed. Jonas Barish (New Haven, CT and London: Yale University Press, 1965).
—— *Sejanus His Fall*, ed. Tom Cain in *The Cambridge Edition of the Works of Ben Jonson*, ed. David Bevington, Martin Butler and Ian Donaldson, vol. 2, 1601–6 (Cambridge: Cambridge University Press, 2012).
—— *Sejanus His Fall*, ed. C. H. Herford and Percy Simpson, in *Ben Jonson*, 11 vols (Oxford: Clarendon Press, 1925–52), IV (1932).
—— *Volpone and Other Plays*, ed. Lorna Hutson (London: Penguin Books, 1998).
Kyd, Thomas, *The Spanish Tragedy*, in *English Renaissance Drama: A Norton Anthology*, ed. David Bevington, Lars Engle, Katherine Eisamun Maus and Eric Rasmussen (New York: W. W. Norton & Co Ltd, 2002).
Marlowe, Christopher, *Edward II*, in *English Renaissance Drama: A Norton Anthology*, ed. David Bevington, Lars Engle, Katherine Eisamun Maus and Eric Rasmussen (New York: W. W. Norton & Co Ltd, 2002).
—— *Tamburlaine the Great, Part One*, in *English Renaissance Drama: A Norton Anthology*, ed. David Bevington, Lars Engle, Katherine Eisamun Maus and Eric Rasmussen (New York: W. W. Norton & Co Ltd, 2002).
—— *Tamburlaine the Great: Parts One and Two*, ed. Anthony Dawson (London: A & C Black, 2005).
Marx, Karl, *The Eighteenth Brumaire of Louis Bonaparte*, in *The Marx-Engels Reader*, ed. Robert C. Tucker, 2nd edn (New York: Norton, 1978).
Montaigne, Michel de, *The Complete Essays*, trans. M. A. Screech (London: Penguin Books, 1987, repr. 2003).
Nashe, Thomas, *Pierce Penilesse, his supplication to the Devil*, in *The Works of Thomas Nashe*, ed. R. B. McKerrow, corr. F. P. Wilson, 5 vols (Oxford: Basil Blackwell, 1958), I (1958).
—— *Summers last will and testament*, in *The Works of Thomas Nashe*, ed. R. B. McKerrow, corr. F. P. Wilson, 5 vols (Oxford: Basil Blackwell, 1958), I (1958).
Polybius, *The Histories*, trans and ed. W. R. Paton, 6 vols (London: William Heinemann Ltd/Cambridge, MA: Harvard University Press, 1922–7; repr. 1922/1954), vol. I.
Quintilian, *Institutio oratoria*, trans. H. E. Butler, 4 vols (Cambridge, MA and London: Harvard University Press and William Heinemann Ltd, 1920), I (repr. 1969).
Ralegh, Sir Walter, *The History of the World*, ed. C. A. Patrides (London and Basingstoke: Macmillan Press Ltd, 1971).
Seneca, *His Tenne Tragedies*, ed. Thomas Newton [1581], intro. T. S. Eliot (London: Constable and Co. Ltd/NY: Alfred A Knopf, 1927).
Shakespeare, William, *Antony and Cleopatra*, ed. John Wilders, Arden Third Series (London: Routledge/The Arden Shakespeare, 1995).
—— *The First Part of the Contention: 1594*, prep. William Montgomery (Oxford: Oxford University Press, 1985).
—— *Julius Caesar*, ed. David Daniell, Arden Third Series (London: Thompson Learning, repr. 2006).

—— *Julius Caesar*, ed. T. S. Dorsch, Arden Two Series (London: Methuen and Co., 1955).
—— *Julius Caesar*, ed. Sarah Neville, in *The New Oxford Shakespeare: Modern Critical Edition* (Oxford: Oxford University Press, 2017).
—— *Julius Caesar*, ed. Marvin Spevack (Cambridge: Cambridge University Press, 1988).
—— *King Henry V*, ed. T. W. Craik, Arden Third Series (London: Routledge/The Arden Shakespeare, 1995).
—— *King Henry VI Part 1*, ed. Edward Burns, Arden Third Series (Walton-on-Thames: Thomas Nelson Ltd, 1999).
—— *King Henry VI Part 2*, ed. Ronald Knowles, Arden Third Series (Walton-on-Thames: Thomas Nelson Ltd, 2000).
—— *King Henry VI Part 3*, ed. John Cox and Eric Rasmussen, Arden Third Series (Walton-on-Thames: Thomas Nelson Ltd, 2001).
—— *1 Henry VI*, ed. Sarah Neville, in *The New Oxford Shakespeare: The Complete Works, Critical Reference Edition*, vol. 2, p. gen. eds Gary Taylor, John Jowett, Terri Bourus and Gabriel Egan (Oxford: Oxford University Press, 2017).
—— *King John*, eds Jesse M. Lander and J. J. M. Tobin, Arden Third Series (London: Bloomsbury, 2018).
—— *The Life and Death of King John*, ed. Ivor B. John (London, 1907).
—— *The Oxford Complete Works*, gen. eds Stanley Wells and Gary Taylor (Oxford: Clarendon Press, 1988; reissued 1998).
—— *Richard II*, ed. Charles R. Forker, Arden Third Series (Walton-on-Thames: Thomas Nelson Ltd, 2002).
—— *Titus Andronicus*, ed. Jonathan Bate, Arden Third Series (London: Routledge/The Arden Shakespeare, 1995).
—— and John Fletcher, *King Henry VIII (All is True)*, ed. Gordon McMullan, Arden Third Series (London: Arden Shakespeare, 2000).
—— and Ben Jonson, 'The Tragedie of Seianus', ed. Gary Taylor, *The New Oxford Complete Works, Critical Reference Edition*, vol. 1 (Oxford: Oxford University Press, 2017).
——, Marlowe and others, *2 Henry VI*, ed. Rory Loughnane, in *The New Oxford Shakespeare*, gen. eds Gary Taylor et al. (Oxford: Oxford University Press, 2017).
—— and others, *The Book of Sir Thomas More*, ed. W. W. Greg. The Malone Society Reprints, with revised material by Harold Jenkins (Oxford: 1911, 1961, 1990).
Stow, John, *A Survey of London*, ed. Charles Lethbridge Kingsford (Oxford: Clarendon Press; repr. 1971).
Tacitus, Cornelius, *Annals*, trans. John Jackson (London: William Heinemann Ltd, 1937).
—— *The Annals of Imperial Rome*, trans. and intro. Michael Grant (London: Penguin Books, 1989, rev. edn).
Virgil, *Eclogues, Georgics, Aeneid* I–VI, trans. H. Rushton Fairclough, rev. G. P. Goold (Cambridge, MA and London: Harvard University Press, 1999).
Wever, R., *An Enterlude Called Lusty Juventus*, prep. J. M. Nosworthy (London: for the Malone Society, 1971).

Young, R. V., ed., *Justus Lipsius' Concerning Constancy. Medieval and Renaissance texts and studies 389* (Tempe: ACMRS (Arizona Center for Medieval and Renaissance Studies), 2011).

Secondary Sources

Allen, Percy, *Shakespeare, Jonson, and Wilkins as Borrowers: A Study in Elizabethan Dramatic Origins and Imitations* (London: Cecil Palmer, 1928).
Altman, Joel, *The Tudor Play of Mind* (Berkeley and London: University of California Press, 1978).
Anderson, Benedict, *Imagined Communities: Reflections on the Origin and Spread of Nationalism*, rev. edn (London and New York: Verso, 1991).
Anderson, Judith H. 'Wonder and Nostalgia in *Hamlet*', *SEL*, 58:2 (2018), 353–72.
Anselment, Raymond A., *Loyalist Resolve: Patient Fortitude in the English Civil War* (Cranbury, NJ and London: Associated University Presses, 1988).
Archer, Ian, 'The Nostalgia of John Stow', in *The Theatrical City: Culture, Theatre and Politics in London, 1576–1649*, ed. David L. Smith, Richard Strier and David Bevington (Cambridge: Cambridge University Press, 1995).
Archer, Jayne Elisabeth, Elizabeth Goldring and Sarah Knight, eds., *The Progresses, Pageants, and Entertainments of Queen Elizabeth I* (Oxford: Oxford University Press, 2007).
Arnold, Oliver, *The Third Citizen: Shakespeare's Theater and the Early Modern House of Commons*, Parallax series (Baltimore, MD: The Johns Hopkins University Press, 2007).
Aston, Margaret, 'English Ruins and English History: The Dissolution and the Sense of the Past', *Journal of the Warburg and Courtauld Institutes*, 36 (1973), 231–55.
Atia, Nadia and Jeremy Davies, 'Editorial: Nostalgia and the Shapes of History', *Memory Studies*, 3:3 (2010), 181–6.
—— eds, *Memory Studies*, 3:3 (2010).
Auden, W. H., *Lectures on Shakespeare*, reconstr. and ed. Arthur Kirsch (London: Faber and Faber, 2000).
Austin, J. L., *How to Do Things with Words*, ed. J. O. Urmson and Marina Sbisa, 2nd edn (Oxford: Oxford University Press, 1975).
Austin, Linda M., *Nostalgia in Transition, 1780–1917* (Charlottesville and London: University of Virginia Press, 2007).
Baldo, Jonathan., *Memory in Shakespeare's Histories: Stages of Forgetting in Early Modern England* (New York: Routledge, 2012).
Barret, J. K., *Untold Futures: Time and Literary Culture in Renaissance England* (Ithaca, NY: Cornell University Press, 2016).
Barton, Anne, *Ben Jonson, Dramatist* (Cambridge: Cambridge University Press, 1984).
Bate, Jonathan, *Shakespeare and Ovid* (Oxford: Oxford University Press, 1993).
Becker, Tobias, ed., 'Historical Forum' on Nostalgia in *History and Theory*, 57:2 (2018).
—— 'The Meanings of Nostalgia: Genealogy and Critique', *History and Theory*, 57:2 (2018), 234–50.

Beecher, Donald, 'Nostalgia and the Renaissance Romance', *Philosophy and Literature*, 34:2 (2010), 281–301.
Ben-Amos, Ilana Krausman, *The Culture of Giving: Informal Support and Gift-Exchange in Early Modern England*, Cambridge Social and Cultural Histories series, ed. Margot C. Finn, Colin Jones and Keith Wrightson (Cambridge: Cambridge University Press, 2008).
Benario, Hebert, 'Tacitus, Germanicus, and Henry V', *Notes and Queries*, 57: 3 (2010), 372–3.
Bennett, Susan, *Performing Nostalgia: Shifting Shakespeare and the Contemporary Past* (London and New York: Routledge, 1996).
Berger, Jr., Harry, *Second World and Green World: Studies in Renaissance Fiction-Making*, sel., arr., intro. John Patrick Lynch (Berkeley and London: University of California Press, 1988).
Bergeron, David M., '"Richard II" and Carnival Politics', *Shakespeare Quarterly*, 42:1 (1991), 33–43.
Bernthal, Craig A., 'Jack Cade's Legal Carnival', *Studies in English Literature 1500–1900*, 42:2 (2002), 259–74.
Bevington, David, *From Mankind to Marlowe: Growth of Structure in the Popular Drama of Tudor England* (Cambridge, MA: Harvard University Press, 1962).
Bhabha, Homi K., ed., *Nation and Narration* (London and New York: Routledge, 1990).
Birney, Alice Lotvin, *Satiric Catharsis in Shakespeare: A Theory of Dramatic Structure* (Berkeley and London: University of California Press, 1973).
Bland, Mark, 'Ben Jonson and the Legacies of the Past', *Huntington Library Quarterly*, 67:3 (2004), 371–400.
Boggs, R. S., 'Proverb Lore', *South Atlantic Bulletin*, 3:4 (1938), 1, 7.
Boughner, Daniel, 'Jonson's Use of Lipsius in *Sejanus*', *Modern Language Notes*, 73:4 (1958), 247–55.
—— '*Sejanus* and Machiavelli', *Studies in English Literature, 1500–1900*, 1:2 (1961), 81–100.
Boulukos, Athanasios, 'The Cobbler and the Tribunes in Julius Caesar', *MLN*, 5 (2004), 1083–9.
Boutcher, Warren, 'Humanism and Literature in Late Tudor England: Translation, the Continental Book and the Case of Montaigne's *Essais*', in *Reassessing Tudor Humanism*, ed. Jonathan Woolfson (Basingstoke and New York: Palgrave Macmillan, 2002), pp. 246–64.
Bowling, William Glasgow, 'The Wild Prince Hal in Legend and Literature', Washington University Studies Vol. XII, Humanistic Series, No. 2 (1926), pp. 305–34.
Boym, Svetlana, *The Future of Nostalgia* (New York: Basic Books, 2001).
Brooks, Douglas A., 'Sejanus, His Fall', *The Ben Jonson Journal*, 12 (2005), 175–80.
Bullough, Geoffrey, *The Narrative and Dramatic Sources of Shakespeare*, 8 vols (London and New York: Routledge and Kegan Paul, 1957–75), III and IV.
Burke, Peter, *The Renaissance Sense of the Past* (London: Edward Arnold, 1969).
—— 'A Survey of the Popularity of Ancient Historians, 1450–1700', *History and Theory*, (1966), 135–52.

—— 'Tacitism', in *Tacitus*, ed. T. A. Dorey (London: Routledge and Kegan Paul, 1969), pp. 149–71.
—— 'Tacitism, Scepticism, and Reason of State', in *The Cambridge History of Political Thought*, ed. J. H. Burns (Cambridge: Cambridge University Press, 1991), pp. 479–98.
Burt, Richard, *Licensed by Authority: Ben Jonson and the Discourses of Censorship* (Ithaca, NY and London: Cornell University Press, 1993).
Butler, Judith, *Excitable Speech* (New York and London: Routledge, 1997).
Butler, Martin, ed., *Re-Presenting Ben Jonson* (London: Macmillan Press Ltd, 1999).
—— *Theatre and Crisis: 1632–1642* (Cambridge: Cambridge University Press, 1984).
Cambell, Lily B., *Shakesepeare's Histories: Mirrors of Elizabethan Policy* (London: Methuen, 1964).
Campana, Joseph, 'The Child's Two Bodies: Shakespeare, Sovereignty, and the End of Succession', *ELH*, 81:3 (2014), 811–39.
Carpi, Daniela, 'Law and Sedition in *Julius Caesar*', in *Shakespeare and the Law*, ed. Daniela Carpi (Ravenna, Italy: Longo Editore, 2003), pp. 103–15.
Carr, Virginia, 'The Power of Grief in *Richard II*', *Études Anglaises*, 31:2 (1978), 145–51.
Carrol, Peter N., *Keeping Time: Memory, Nostalgia, and the Art of History* (Athens: University of Georgia Press, 1990).
Carroll, Clare, 'Humanism and English Literature in the Fifteenth and Sixteenth Centuries', in *The Cambridge Companion to Renaissance Humanism*, ed. Jill Kraye (Cambridge: Cambridge University Press, 1996).
Cartelli, Thomas, 'Jack Cade in the Garden: Class Consciousness and Class Conflict in *2 Henry VI*', in *Enclosure Acts: Sexuality, Property, and Culture in Early Modern England*, ed. Richard Burt and John Michael Archer (Ithaca, NY and London: Cornell University Press, 1994), pp. 48–67.
Cavanagh, Dermot, *Language and Politics in the Sixteenth-Century History Play* (New York and Basingstoke: Palgrave Macmillan, 2003).
Cave, Terence, *The Cornucopian Text* (Oxford: Clarendon Press, 1979).
—— *Recognitions* (Oxford: Clarendon Press, 1988).
Chambers, E. K., *The Elizabethan Stage*, 4 vols (Oxford: Oxford University Press, 1923, reiss. 2009).
Champion, Larry S., '"What Prerogatives Meanes": Perspective and Political Ideology in "The Famous Victories of Henry V"', *South Atlantic Review*, 53:4 (1988), 1–19.
Chapman, Alison A., 'Whose St Crispin's Day Is It?: Shoemaking, Holiday Making, and the Politics of Memory in Early Modern England', *Renaissance Quarterly*, 54 (2001), 1467–94.
Charnes, Linda, 'Anticipating Nostalgia: Finding Temporal Logic in a Textual Anomaly', *Textual Cultures*, 4:1 (2009), 72–83.
—— 'Reading for the Wormholes: Micro-periods from the Future', in *Early Modern Culture: An Electronic Seminar*, ed. Jonathan Gil-Harris, issue 6. http://eserver.org/emc/1-6/charnes.html
—— 'Shakespeare, and Belief, in the Future', in *Presentist Shakespeares*, ed.

Hugh Grady and Terence Hawkes (London and New York: Routledge, 2007).

Chase, Malcolm and Christopher Shaw, eds., 'The Dimensions of Nostalgia', in *The Imagined Past: History and Nostalgia* (Manchester and New York: Manchester University Press, 1989).

Chernaik, Warren, *The Myth of Rome in Shakespeare and his Contemporaries* (Cambridge: Cambridge University Press, 2011).

Clare, Janet, *Art Made Tongue Tied By Authority*, Revels Plays series, gen. eds E. A. Honigmann et al. (Manchester and New York: Manchester University Press, 1990).

Clemen, Wolfgang, *English Tragedy before Shakespeare*, trans. T. S. Dorsch (London: Methuen & Co, 1961).

Cohen, Simona, *Transformations of Time and Temporality in Medieval and Renaissance Art* (Leiden: Brill, 2014).

Cohen, Stephen, 'Introduction', in *Shakespeare and Historical Formalism*, ed. Stephen Cohen (Routledge, 2007), pp. 1–30.

Colclough, David, *Freedom of Speech in Early Stuart England*, Ideas in Context series, gen. ed. Quentin Skinner (Cambridge: Cambridge University Press, 2005).

Collinson, Patrick, *The Birthpangs of Protestant England* (Houndmills and London: Macmillan Press Ltd, 1988).

—— *Elizabethan Essays* (London and Rio Grande: The Hambledon Press, 1994).

—— 'Field, John (1544/5?–1588)', *Oxford Dictionary of National Biography* (Oxford University Press, September 2004; online edition January 2008).

—— *The Religion of Protestants: The Church in English Society 1559–1625* (Oxford: Clarendon Press, 1982).

Condren, Conal, 'Shakespeare's *Richard II*: The Ethics of Office, Scepticism, Tyranny and the Symbolism of the Garden' (unpublished article, 2009).

Conley, Thomas M., *Rhetoric in the European Tradition* (Chicago and London: University of Chicago Press, 1990).

Cook, Ann-Jennalie, 'Audiences: Investigation, Interpretation, Invention', in *A New History of English Drama*, ed. David Scott Kastan and John Cox (New York: Columbia University Press, 1997), pp. 305–20.

Corbin, Peter and Douglas Sedge, eds., *The Oldcastle Controversy: Sir John Oldcastle Part 1 and The Famous Victories of Henry V* (Manchester: Manchester University Press, 1991).

Cormack, Bradin, 'Shakespeare Possessed: Legal Affect and the Time of Holding', in *Shakespeare and the Law*, ed. Paul Raffield and Gary Watt (Oxford and Portland, OR: Hart Publishing, 2008), pp. 83–100.

Craig, Hugh, 'The Three Parts of *Henry VI*' in *Shakespeare, Computers, and the Mystery of Authorship* (New York: Cambridge University Press, 2009), pp. 40–77.

Cressy, David, *Literacy and the Social Order: Reading and Writing in Tudor and Stuart England* (Cambridge: Cambridge University Press, 1980).

Cromartie, Alan, *The Constitutionalist Revolution: An Essay on the History of England, 1450–1642* (Cambridge: Cambridge University Press, 2006).

Dames, Nicholas, *Amnesiac Selves: Nostalgia, Forgetting, and British Fiction, 1810–1870* (Oxford: Oxford University Press, 2001).

—— 'Response: Nostalgia and Its Disciplines', *Memory Studies*, 3:3 (2010), 269–75.
Davis, Alex, 'Coming Home Again: Johannes Hofer, Edmund Spenser, and Premodern Nostalgia', in Approaches to Early Modern Nostalgia special issue, ed. Kristine Johanson, *Parergon*, 33:2 (2016), 17–38.
Davis, Fred, *Yearning for Yesterday: A Sociology of Nostalgia* (New York and London: The Free Press and Collier Macmillan Publishers, 1979).
Dawson, Anthony B., 'The Arithmetic of Memory: Shakespeare's Theatre and The National Past', *Shakespeare Survey*, 52 (1999), 54–67.
Dean, Paul, 'Tudor Humanism and the Roman Past: A Background to Shakespeare', *Renaissance Quarterly*, 41:1 (1988), 84–111.
Dell, Helen, 'Nostalgia and Medievalism: Conversations, Constructions, Impasses', *postmedieval: a journal of medieval cultural studies*, 2 (2011), 115–26.
—— ed., *postmedieval: a journal of medieval cultural studies*, 2 (2011).
Deneault, Benjamin, '"The World Runs on Wheeles": John Stow's Indescribable London', *ELH*, 78:2 (2011), 337–58.
Dent, R. W., *Shakespeare's Proverbial Language: An Index* (Berkeley and London: University of California Press, 1981).
Dewar, Mary, ed., *A Discourse of the Common Weal of this Realm of England* (Washington, DC: Folger Shakespeare Library, 1969).
Dillon, Janette, *Shakespeare and the Staging of English History*, Oxford Topics in Shakespeare (Oxford: Oxford University Press, 2012).
Doebler, John, 'Beaumont's *The Knight of the Burning Pestle* and the Prodigal Son Plays', Elizabethan and Jacobean Drama, *Studies in English Literature, 1500–1900*, 5:2 (1965), 333–44.
Dohrn-van Rossum, Gerhard, *History of the Hour: Clocks and Modern Temporal Orders*, trans. Thomas Dunlap (Chicago and London: University of Chicago Press, 1996).
Dollimore, Jonathan, *Radical Tragedy: Religion, Ideology, and Power in the Drama of Shakespeare and his Contemporaries* (Brighton: The Harvester Press, 1984).
Donaldson, Ian, *Ben Jonson: A Life* (Oxford: Oxford University Press, 2011).
—— '"Misconstruing Everything": *Julius Caesar* and *Sejanus*', in *Shakespeare Performed: Essays in Honour of R. A. Foakes*, ed. Grace Ioppolo (London: Associated University Presses, 2000), pp. 88–107.
Donker, Marjorie and George M. Muldrow, *Dictionary of Literary-Rhetorical Conventions of the English Renaissance* (Westport, CT and London: Greenwood Press, 1982).
Doran, Susan and Thomas S. Freeman, eds., *The Myth of Elizabeth* (Basingstoke: Palgrave Macmillan, 2003).
Doty, Jeffrey S. 'Shakespeare's *Richard II*, "Popularity", and the Early Modern Public Sphere', *Shakespeare Quarterly*, 61:2 (2010), 183–205.
—— *Shakespeare, Popularity, and the Public Sphere* (Cambridge: Cambridge University Press, 2017).
Duffy, Eamon, *The Stripping of the Altars: Traditional Religion in England 1400–1580*, 2nd edn (New Haven, CT and London: Yale University Press, 2005).
Dutton, Richard, '*The Famous Victories* and the 1600 Quarto of *Henry V*', in

Ostovich et al., *Locating the Queen's Men, 1583–1603: Material Practices and Conditions of Playing* (London and New York: Routledge, 2016), pp. 135–46.

Eastman, Richard M., 'Political Values in Henry IV, Part One: A Demonstration of Liberal Humanism', *College English*, 33:8 (1972), 901–7.

Eggert, Katherine, 'Nostalgia and the Not Yet Late Queen: Refusing Female Rule in *Henry V*', *ELH*, 61:3 (1994), 523–50.

Elam, Keir, *The Semiotics of Theatre and Drama*, New Accents Series, gen. ed. Terence Hawkes (London and New York: Methuen, 1980).

Evans, Robert C., *Habits of Mind: Evidence and Effects of Ben Jonson's Reading* (Lewisburg, PA and London: Bucknell University Press/Associated University Presses, 1995).

Fitter, Chris, 'Historicising Shakespeare's *Richard II*: Current Events, Dating, and the Sabotage of Essex', *Early Modern Literary Studies*, 11:2 (2005), 1.1–47.

—— 'Introduction: Rethinking Shakespeare in the Social Depth of Politics', in *Shakespeare & the Politics of Commoners: Digesting the New Social History*, ed. C. Fitter (Oxford: Oxford University Press, 2017).

Forker, Charles, 'Marlowe's *Edward II* and its Shakespearean Relatives: The Emergence of a Genre', in *Shakespeare's English Histories: A Quest for Form and Genre*, ed. John W. Velz (Tempe, AZ: Medieval & Renaissance Texts and Studies, 1997), pp. 55–89.

Fowler, W. Warde, *Roman Essays and Interpretations* (Oxford: Clarendon Press, 1920).

Freebury-Jones, Darren, 'Did Shakespeare Really Co-Write 2 Henry VI with Marlowe?', *ANQ: A Quarterly Journal of Short Articles, Notes and Reviews*, 30:3 (2017), 137–41.

Frey, David L., *The First Tetralogy: Shakespeare's Scrutiny of the Tudor Myth* (The Hague and Paris: Mouton, 1976).

Frisch, Andrea, 'French Tragedy and the Civil Wars', *Modern Language Quarterly*, 67:3 (2006), 287–312.

Fritzsche, Peter, 'Specters of History: On Nostalgia, Exile, and Modernity', *American Historical Review* (2001), 1587–1618.

Frye, Northrop, *Fools of Time: Studies in Shakespearean Tragedy* (Toronto: University of Toronto Press, 1967).

Gadaleto, Michael, 'Shakespeare's Bastard Nation: Skepticism and the English Isle in King John', *Shakespeare Quarterly*, 69:1 (2018), 3–34.

Gallagher, Lowell, '"This seal'd-up Oracle": Ambivalent Nostalgia in *The Winter's Tale*', *Exemplaria: A Journal of Theory in Medieval and Renaissance Studies*, (1995), 465–98.

Garrison, John, *Shakespeare and the Afterlife* (Oxford: Oxford University Press, 2018).

Gasquet, Francis Aidan (Cardinal), *Monastic Life in the Middle Ages with a Note on Great Britain and the Holy See (1792–1806)* (Freeport, NY: Books for Libraries Press, 1922; repr. 1970).

Gibbard, Peter, 'Ben Jonson's *Sejanus* and the Middle Way of Annals 1–6', *Studies in English Literature, 1500–1900*, 56:2 (2016), 307–25.

—— *Republicanism, Tacitism and Style in English Drama: 1585–1608*, PhD dissertation, The University of Sydney, 2014.

Gilbert, Felix, *Machiavelli and Guicciardini: Politics and History in Sixteenth-Century Florence* (Princeton, NJ: Princeton University Press, 1965).

Goodman, Kevis, 'Romantic Poetry and the Science of Nostalgia', in *The Cambridge Companion to British Romantic Poetry*, eds James Chandler and Maureen N. McLane (Cambridge: Cambridge University Press, 2008), pp. 195–216.

—— '"Uncertain disease": Nostalgia, Pathologies of Motion, Practices of Reading', *Studies in Romanticism*, 49:2 (2010), 197–227.

Gopen, George D., 'Private Grief into Public Action: The Rhetoric of John of Gaunt in "Richard II"', *Studies in Philology*, 84:3 (1987), 338–62.

Goy-Blanquet, Dominique, *Shakespeare's Early History Plays: From Chronicle to Stage* (Oxford: Oxford University Press, 2003).

Grady, Hugh, 'Shakespeare's Links to Machiavelli and Montaigne: Constructing Intellectual Modernity in Early Modern Europe', *Comparative Literature*, 52:2 (2000), 119–42.

—— and Terence Hawkes, eds., *Presentist Shakespeares* (London and New York: Routledge, 2007).

Grafton, Anthony and Lisa Jardine, *From Humanism to the Humanities: Education and the Liberal Arts in Fifteenth- and Sixteenth-Century Europe* (London: Duckworth, 1986).

de Grazia, Margreta, 'The Modern Divide: From Either Side', *Journal of Medieval and Early Modern Studies*, 37:3 (2007), 453–67.

Greenblatt, Stephen, 'Murdering Peasants: Status, Genre, and the Representation of Rebellion', *Representations*, 1 (1983), 1–29.

—— *Renaissance Self-Fashioning* (Chicago and London: University of Chicago Press, 1980).

Greene, Thomas M., *The Light in Troy* (New Haven, CT and London: Yale University Press, 1982).

Grell, Ole Peter, 'The Protestant Imperative of Christian Care and Neighborly Love', in *Health Care and Poor Relief in Protestant Europe 1500–1700*, eds Andrew Cunningham and Ole Peter Grell, Studies in the Social History of Medicine (London: Routledge, 1997), pp. 42–63.

Griffin, Benjamin, *Playing the Past: Approaches to English Historical Drama, 1385–1600* (London: DS Brewer, 2001).

Groves, Beatrice, 'Memory, Composition, and the Relationship of *King John* to *The Troublesome Raigne of King John*', *Comparative Drama*, 38:2, 3 (2004), 277–90.

Gurr, Andrew, *Playgoing in Shakespeare's London* (Cambridge: Cambridge University Press, 1987).

Guy, John, *Tudor England* (Oxford: Oxford University Press, 1988).

Hackel, Heidi Brayman, '"Rowme" of Its Own: Printed Drama in Early Libraries', in *A New History of English Drama*, ed. David Scott Kastan and John Cox (New York: Columbia University Press, 1997), pp. 113–32.

Hadfield, Andrew, 'Jonson and Shakespeare in an Age of Lying', *The Ben Jonson Journal*, 23:1 (2016), 52–74.

—— *Shakespeare and Renaissance Politics* (London: Thomson Learning, 2004).

—— *Shakespeare and Republicanism* (Cambridge: Cambridge University Press, 2005).

Halkett, Samuel and John Laing, *Dictionary of Anonymous and Pseudonymous*

English Literature, rev. and enlarg. edn (Edinburgh and London: Oliver & Boyd, 1926–62).
Hall, William Keith, 'The Topography of Time: Historical Narration in John Stow's Survey of London', *Studies in Philology*, 88:1 (1991), 1–16.
Halliwell, J. O., gen. ed., *The Works of Shakespeare Illustrated* (London and New York: John Tallis and Company, 1830).
Halpern, Richard, *Shakespeare Among the Moderns* (Ithaca, NY and London: Cornell University Press, 1997).
Hamlin, Hannibal, *The Bible in Shakespeare* (Oxford: Oxford University Press, 2013).
Hampton-Reeves, Stuart and Carol Chillington Rutter, eds., *The Henry VI Plays*, Shakespeare in Performance Series, gen. ed. James C. Bulman and Carol Chillington Rutter (Manchester and New York: Manchester University Press, 2006).
Harlan, Susan E., *Memories of War in Early Modern England: Armor and Militant Nostalgia in Marlowe, Sidney, and Shakespeare* (Basingstoke: Palgrave Macmillan, 2016).
Harris, Jonathan Gil, *Untimely Matter in the Time of Shakespeare* (Philadelphia: University of Pennsylvania Press, 2009).
—— 'Untimely Mediations', in *Early Modern Culture: An Electronic Seminar*, ed. Jonathan Gil Harris, issue 6. http://eserver.org/emc/1-6/harris.html
Hayes, Douglas W., *Rhetorical Subversion in Early English Drama*, Studies in the Humanities: Literature–Politics–Society Series, gen. ed. Guy Mermier (New York: Peter Lang Press, 2004).
Heal, Felicity, 'The Crown, the Gentry and London: The Enforcement of Proclamation, 1596–1640', in *Law and Government Under the Tudors: Essays Presented to Sir Geoffrey Elton*, ed. Claire Cross, David Loades and J. J. Scarisbrick (Cambridge: Cambridge University Press, 1988), pp. 211–26.
—— *Hospitality in Early Modern England* (Oxford: Clarendon Press, 1990).
Helgerson, Richard, 'Shakespeare and Contemporary Dramatists of History', in *A Companion to Shakespeare's Works, Volume II: The Histories*, ed. Richard Dutton and Jean Howard (Oxford and Malden, MA: Blackwell Publishing, 2003), pp. 26–47.
Henderson, John, 'Jonson's Too Roman Plays: From *Julius Caesar* to *Sejanus* and *Catiline*', in *Tragedy in Transition*, ed. Sarah Annes Brown and Catherine Silverstone (Oxford: Blackwell Publishing, 2007), pp. 103–22.
Hillman, Richard, *Intertextuality and Romance in Renaissance Drama: The Staging of Nostalgia* (Basingstoke: Macmillan, 1992).
Hindle, Steve, *The Birthpangs of Welfare: Poor Relief and Parish Governance in Seventeenth-Century Warwickshire* (Stratford-upon-Avon: Dugdale Society in association with the Shakespeare Birthplace Trust, 2000).
—— 'Dearth, Fasting and Alms: The Campaign for General Hospitality in Late Elizabethan England', *Past and Present*, 172:1 (2001), 44–86.
Hirsh, James, ed., *New Perspectives on Ben Jonson* (London: Associated University Presses, 1997).
Hockey, Dorothy C., 'A World of Rhetoric in *Richard II*', *Shakespeare Quarterly*, 15:3 (1964), 179–91.
Hopkins, Lisa, 'The King's Melting Body: Richard II', in *Shakespeare's Works*.

Vol. II: The Histories, ed. Jean Howard and Richard Dutton (Oxford: Blackwell Publishing, 2003), pp. 395–411.
House, Seymour Baker, 'Becon, Thomas (1512/13–1567)', *Oxford Dictionary of National Biography* (Oxford: Oxford University Press, 2004; online edition October 2009).
Howard, Jean, *Shakespeare's Art of Orchestration* (Urbana and Chicago: University of Illinois Press, 1984).
—— *The Stage and Social Struggle in Early Modern England* (London and New York: Routledge, 1994).
—— and Scott Cutler Shershow, 'Introduction', in *Marxist Shakespeares*, ed. Jean Howard and Scott Cutler Shershow (New York: Routledge, 2001).
Hunt, Maurice, 'Cobbling Souls in Shakespeare's *Julius Caesar*', *Cahiers Elisabethains*, 64 (2003), 19–28.
—— 'Jonson vs. Shakespeare: The Roman Plays', in *The Ben Jonson Journal*, 23:1 (2016), 75–100.
Hunter, G. K., 'Rhetoric and Renaissance Drama', in *Renaissance Rhetoric*, ed. Peter Mack (Basingstoke: Palgrave Macmillan, 1994), pp. 103–18, p. 111ff.
Hutcheon, Linda, 'Irony, Nostalgia, and the Postmodern', *Methods for the Study of Literature as Cultural Memory, Studies in Comparative Literature*, 30 (2000), 189–207.
Hutchings, Mark, 'The "Turk Phenomenon" and the Repertory of the Late Elizabethan Playhouse', *Early Modern Literary Studies* Special Issue 16 (2007), 10.1–39. http://purl.oclc.org/emls/si-16/hutcturk.htm
Hutson, Lorna, 'Chivalry for Merchants; or, Knights of Temperance in the Realms of Gold', *The Journal of Medieval and Early Modern Studies*, 26:1 (1996), 29–59.
—— *The Invention of Suspicion* (Oxford: Oxford University Press, 2007).
—— 'Noises Off: Participatory Justice in *2 Henry VI*', in *The Law in Shakespeare*, ed. Constance Jordan and Karen Cunningham (New York and Basingstoke: Palgrave Macmillan, 2007), pp. 143–66.
—— *Thomas Nashe in Context* (Oxford: Clarendon, 1989).
Hutton, Ronald, *The Rise and Fall of Merry England: The Ritual Year, 1400–1700* (Oxford: Oxford University Press, 1994).
Illbruck, Helmut, *Nostalgia: Origins and Ends of an Unenlightened Disease* (Chicago: Northwestern University Press, 2012).
Iser, Wolfgang, 'The Reality of Fiction: A Functionalist Approach to Literature', *New Literary History*, 7:1 (1975), 7–38.
Jackson, Macdonald P., 'By Anon?', *TLS*, 9 April 2008.
—— 'The Date and Authorship of *Thomas of Woodstock*: Evidence and Its Interpretation', *Research Opportunities in English Renaissance Drama*, 46 (2007), 67–100.
—— 'Shakespeare's *Richard II* and the Anonymous *Thomas of Woodstock*', *Medieval and Renaissance Drama in England*, 14 (2001), 17–65.
Jacobsen, Michael Hviid, 'Introduction', in *Nostalgia Now: Cross-Disciplinary Perspectives on the Past in the Present*, ed. Michael Hviid Jacobsen (London: Routledge, 2020 [Vital Source Bookshelf], n.p.).
Jacquot, Jean, 'Ralegh's "Hellish Verses" and the "Tragicall Raigne of Selimus"', *The Modern Language Review*, 48:1 (1953), 1–9.

Jameson, Frederic, *Marxism and Form* (Princeton, NJ: Princeton University Press, 1971).
—— *Postmodernism: Or, The Cultural Logic of Late Capitalism* (Durham, NC: Duke University Press, 1991).
Jenkins, Gary W., 'Smith, Henry (c.1560–1591)', *Oxford Dictionary of National Biography* (Oxford: Oxford University Press, 2004).
Johanson, Kristine, ed., Approaches to Early Modern Nostalgia special issue of *Parergon*, 33:2 (2016).
—— '"Our brains beguiled": Ecclesiastes and Sonnet 59's Poetics of Temporal Instability', in *The Sonnets: State of Play*, ed. Hannah Crawforth, Elizabeth Scott-Baumann and Clare Whitehead (London: Bloomsbury, 2017), pp. 55–76.
—— 'Regulating Time and the Self in Shakespearean Drama', in *Staged Normality in Shakespeare's* England, ed. Rory Loughnane and Edel Semple (Basingstoke: Palgrave Macmillan, 2019), pp. 89–108.
Jones, Emrys, *The Origins of Shakespeare* (Oxford: Oxford University Press, 1977).
Jones-Davies, M. T., 'Historical Consciousness and Convention in Shakespeare's First Tetralogy', in *Shakespeare's Universe: Renaissance Ideas and Conventions: Essays in Honour of W. R. Elton*, ed. John M. Mucciolo, with the assistance of Steven J. Doloff and Edward A. Rauchut (Aldershot: Scolar Press, 1996), pp. 52–9.
Kahn, Coppélia, *Roman Shakespeare: Warriors, Wounds and Women*, Feminist Readings of Shakespeare Series (New York and London: Routledge, 1997).
Kahn, Victoria, *Machiavellian Rhetoric: From the Counter-Reformation to Milton* (Princeton, NJ: Princeton University Press, 1994).
—— *Rhetoric, Prudence, and Skepticism in the Renaissance* (Ithaca, NY and London: Cornell University Press, 1985).
Kantorowicz, Ernst H., *The King's Two Bodies: A study in Medieval Political Theology*, 2nd edn (Princeton, NJ: Princeton University Press, 1997).
Karremann, Isabel, *The Drama of Memory in Shakespeare's History Plays* (Cambridge: Cambridge University Press, 2015).
—— 'Nostalgic Spectacle and the Politics of Memory in *Henry VIII*', *Shakespeare Survey*, 67 (2014), 180–90.
Kastan, David Scott, 'The Shape of Time: Form and Value in the Shakespearean History Play', *Comparative Drama*, 7 (1973), 259–77.
—— and John D. Cox, eds, *A New History of English Drama* (London and New York: Columbia University Press, 1997).
Keegan, D. L., 'Performing Prophecy: More Life on the Shakespearean Scene', *Shakespeare Quarterly*, 62:3 (2011), 420–33.
Keilen, Sean, 'English Literature in its Golden Age', in *The Forms of Renaissance Thought: New Essays in Literature*, ed. Leonard Barkan, Bradin Cormack and Sean Keilen (Basingstoke: Palgrave Macmillan, 2009), pp. 46–74.
Keller, James R., 'Arden's Land Acquisitions and the Dissolution of the Monasteries', *ELN*, 30 (1993), 20–3.
Kennedy, William J., *Rhetorical Norms in Renaissance Literature* (New Haven, CT and London: Yale University Press, 1978).
Kewes, Paulina, 'History and Its Uses', in *The Uses of History in Early Modern England*, ed. Pauina Kewes (San Marino, CA: Huntington Library, 2006).

Kiefer, Frederick, 'The Conflation of Fortuna and Occasio in Renaissance Thought and Iconography', *Journal of Medieval and Renaissance Studies*, 9 (1979), 1–27.
King, Pamela M., 'Minority Plays: Two Interludes for Edward VI', *Medieval English Theatre*, 15 (1993), 87–102.
Knapp, Jeffrey, 'Preachers and Players in Shakespeare's England', *Representations*, 44 (1993), 29–59.
—— *Shakespeare's Tribe* (Chicago and London: University of Chicago Press, 2002).
Knowles, David, *Bare Ruined Choirs: The Dissolution of the Monasteries* (Cambridge: Cambridge University Press, 1976).
Knowles, James, '"In the purest times of peerless Queen Elizabeth": Nostalgia, Politics, and Jonson's Use of the 1575 Kenilworth Entertainments', in *The Progresses, Pageants, and Entertainments of Queen Elizabeth I*, ed. J. E. Archer, Elizabeth Goldring and Sarah Knight (Oxford: Oxford University Press, 2007), pp. 247–67.
Knutson, Roslyn, 'The Start of Something Big', in Ostovich et al., *Locating the Queen's Men, 1583–1603: Material Practices and Conditions of Playing* (London and New York: Routledge, 2016), pp. 99–108.
Korda, Natasha, '"The Sign of the Last": Gender, Material Culture, and Artisanal Nostalgia in The Shoemaker's Holiday', *Journal of Medieval and Early Modern Studies*, 43:3 (2013), 573–97.
Kreps, Barbara, 'Bad Memories of Margaret? Memorial Reconstruction versus Revision in *The First Part of the Contention* and 2 *Henry VI*', *Shakespeare Quarterly*, 51:2 (2000), 154–80.
Kuskin, William, 'Recursive Origins: Print History and Shakespeare's 2 *Henry VI*', in *Shakespeare and the Middle Ages*, ed. Curtis Perry and John Watkins (Oxford: Oxford University Press, 2009), pp. 126–50.
Ladino, Jennifer K., *Reclaiming Nostalgia: Longing for Nature in American Literature* (Charlottesville and London: University of Virginia Press, 2012).
Lake, Peter, *How Shakespeare Put Politics on Stage* (New Haven, CT: Yale University Press, 2016).
—— and Steve Pincus, 'Rethinking the Public Sphere in Early Modern England', *Journal of British Studies*, 45 (2006), 270–92.
Lancashire, Ian, ed., *Two Tudor Interludes: The Interlude of Youth and Hick Scorner* (Manchester: Manchester University Press/Baltimore, MD: Johns Hopkins University Press, 1980).
Landwehr, Achim, 'Nostalgia and the Turbulence of Times', *History and Theory*, 57:2 (2018), 251–68.
Laslett, Peter, *The World We Have Lost*, 2nd edn (London: Methuen, 1970).
Lees-Jeffries, Hester, *England's Helicon: Fountains in Early Modern Literature and Culture* (Oxford, 2007).
—— 'Location as Metaphor in Queen Elizabeth's Coronation Entry (1559): *Veritas Temporis Filia*', in *The Progresses, Pageants, and Entertainments of Queen Elizabeth I*, ed. Jayne Elisabeth Archer, Elizabeth Goldring and Sarah Knight (Oxford: Oxford University Press, 2007).
LeGoff, Jacques, *Time, Work, & Culture in the Middle Ages*, trans. Arthur Goldhammer (Chicago: University of Chicago Press, 1980).

Lemon, Rebecca, *Treason by Words* (Ithaca, NY and London: Cornell University Press, 2006).
Lerner, Laurence, *The Uses of Nostalgia: Studies in Pastoral Poetry* (London: Chatto and Windus, 1972).
Lesser, Zachary, 'Typographic Nostalgia: Play-Reading, Popularity, and the Black Letter', in *The Book of the Play: Playwrights, Stationers, and Readers in Early Modern England*, ed. Marta Straznicky (Amherst and Boston: University of Massachusetts Press, 2006), pp. 99–126.
Levin, Harry, *The Myth of the Golden Age in the Renaissance* (Bloomington and London: Indiana University Press, 1969).
—— 'Sitting upon the Ground (*Richard II*, IV, i)', in *Shakespeare's Universe: Renaissance Ideas and Conventions: Essays in Honour of W. R. Elton*, ed. John M. Mucciolo, with the assistance of Steven J. Doloff and Edward A. Rauchut (Aldershot: Scolar Press, 1996), pp. 3–20.
Lievsay, John L., '"Silver-Tongued Smith", Paragon of Elizabethan Preachers' *The Huntington Library Quarterly*, 11:1 (1947), 13–36.
Lopez, Jeremy, *Theatrical Convention and Audience Response in Early Modern Drama* (Cambridge: Cambridge University Press, 2003).
Love, Harold, *Scribal Publication in Seventeenth-Century England* (Oxford: Clarendon Press, 1993).
Lowenthal, David, *The Past is a Foreign Country* (Cambridge: Cambridge University Press, 1985).
Luis-Martínez, Zenón, 'Shakespeare's Historical Drama as "Trauerspiel: Richard II": And After', *ELH*, 75:3 (2008), 673–705.
Lupton, Julia Reinhard, 'The Affordances of Hospitality: Shakespearean Drama between Historicism and Phenomenology', *Poetics Today*, 35:4 (2014), 615–33.
—— 'Macbeth's Martlets: Shakespearean Phenomenologies of Hospitality', *Criticism*, 54:3 (2012), 365–76.
—— 'Making Room, Affording Hospitality: Environments of Entertainment in *Romeo and Juliet*', *Journal of Medieval and Early Modern Studies*, 43:1 (2013), 145–72.
McAlindon, Thomas, '"Tamburlaine the Great" and "The Spanish Tragedy": The Genesis of a Tradition', *The Huntington Library Quarterly*, 45:1 (1982), 59–81.
McCabe, Richard A., 'Elizabethan Satire and the Bishops' Ban of 1599', *The Yearbook of English Studies*, Literature and Its Audience, II Special Number, vol. 11 (1981), 188–92.
McCrea, Adriana, *Constant Minds: Political Virtue and the Lipsian Paradigm in England, 1584–1650* (Toronto: University of Toronto Press, 1997).
McDonald, Russ, *Shakespeare and Jonson/Jonson and Shakespeare* (Lincoln and London: University of Nebraska Press, 1988).
McGowan, Margaret, 'Caesar's Cloak: Diversion as an Art of Persuasion in Sixteenth-Century Writing', *Renaissance Studies*, 18:3 (2004), 437–8.
Mack, Peter, *Elizabethan Rhetoric: Theory and Practice*, Ideas in Context Series, gen. ed. Quentin Skinner (Cambridge: Cambridge University Press, 2002).
McLaren, A. N., *Political Culture in the Reign of Elizabeth I: Queen and Commonwealth 1558–1585*, Ideas in Context Series, gen. ed. Quentin Skinner (Cambridge: Cambridge University Press, 1999).

McMillin, Scott and Sally-Beth MacLean, *The Queen's Men: Their Plays* (Cambridge and New York: Cambridge University Press, 1998).
McRae, Andrew, *God Speed the Plough: The Representation of Agrarian England, 1500–1660* (Cambridge: Cambridge University Press, 1996).
Magnusson, Lynne, 'Shakespearean Tragedy and the Language of Lament', in *The Oxford Handbook of Shakespearean Tragedy*, ed. Michael Neill and David Schalkwyk (Oxford: Oxford University Press, 2016).
Maguire, Laurie, *Shakespearean Suspect Texts* (Cambridge: Cambridge University Press, 1996).
Manley, Lawrence, 'From Strange's Men to Pembroke's Men: *2 Henry VI* and *The First Part of the Contention*', *Shakespeare Quarterly*, 54:3 (2003), 253–87.
Marcus, Leah S., *The Politics of Mirth: Jonson, Herrick, Milton, Marvell, and the Defense of Old Holiday Pastimes* (Chicago and London: The University of Chicago Press, 1986).
Maus, Katherine Eisaman, 'Proof and Consequences: Inwardness and its Exposure in the English Renaissance', *Representations*, 34 (1991), 29–52.
Mazzaro, Jerome, 'Shakespeare's "Books of Memory": *1* and *2 Henry VI*', *Comparative Drama*, (2001/2002), 393–414.
Mebane, John S., *Renaissance Magic and the Return of the Golden Age: The Occult Tradition and Marlowe, Jonson, and Shakespeare* (Lincoln and London: University of Nebraska Press, 1989).
Menzer, Paul Daniel, *Crowd Control: The Corporate Body on the Renaissance Stage*, unpublished PhD thesis from the University of Virginia, 2001.
—— 'The Olympic Bluff: Jonson's *Sejanus* and the Vanishing Point', *The Ben Jonson Journal*, 11 (2004), 41–66.
Meskill, Lynn S., 'The Tangled Thread of Authorship: Shakespeare's *Julius Caesar* and Jonson's *Sejanus, His Fall*', in *Medieval and Early Modern Authorship*, SPELL: Swiss Papers in English Language and Literature 25, eds Guillemette Bolens and Lukas Erne (Tübingen: Narr Verlag, 2011), pp. 75–91.
Miles, Gary B., 'The Cycle of Roman History in Livy's First Pentad', *The American Journal of Philology*, 107:1 (1986), 1–33.
Miller, Anthony, 'The Roman State in *Julius Caesar* and *Sejanus*', in *Jonson and Shakespeare*, ed. Ian Donaldson (London: Macmillan in association with Humanities Research Centre, Australian National University, 1983), pp. 179–201.
Miola, Robert S., '*Julius Caesar* and The Tyrannicide Debate', *Renaissance Quarterly*, 38 (1985), 271–89.
Moisan, Thomas, '"Knock Me Here Soundly": Comic Misprision and Class Consciousness in Shakespeare', *Shakespeare Quarterly*, 42:3 (1991), 276–90.
Mossmann, Judith, '*Henry V* and Plutarch's *Alexander*', *Shakespeare Quarterly*, 45:1 (1994), 57–73.
Mott, Lewis, 'Foreign Politics in an Old Play', *Modern Philology*, 19 (1921), 65–71.
Mozley, James Frederic, *Coverdale and His Bibles* (London: Lutterworth Press, 1953).
Mukerji, Subha, *Law and Representation in Early Modern Drama* (Cambridge: Cambridge University Press, 2006).

Mulryan, John, 'Tradition and the Individual Talent: Shakespeare's and Jonson's Appropriation of the Classics', *Ben Jonson Journal: Literary Contexts in the Age of Elizabeth, James and Charles*, 10 (2003), 117–37.
Munro, Ian, *The Figure of the Crowd in Early Modern London: The City and Its Double* (New York: Palgrave Macmillan, 2005).
Munro, Lucy, *Archaic Style in English Literature, 1590–1674* (Cambridge: Cambridge University Press, 2014).
Nance, John V., '"We, John Cade": Shakespeare, Marlowe, and the Authorship of 4.2.33–189 2 Henry VI', *Shakespeare*, 13:1 (2017), 30–51.
Natali, Marcos Piason, 'History and the Politics of Nostalgia', *Iowa Journal of Cultural Studies*, 5 (2004), 10–25.
Neale, J. E., *Queen Elizabeth I* (London: Cape, 1938).
Norbrook, David, 'A Liberal Tongue: Language and Rebellion in *Richard II*', in *Shakespeare's Universe: Renaissance Ideas and Conventions: Essays in Honour of W. R. Elton*, ed. John M. Mucciolo, with the assistance of Steven J. Doloff and Edward A. Rauchut (Aldershot: Scolar Press, 1996), pp. 37–51.
—— *Poetry and Politics in the English Renaissance* (London: Routledge & Kegan Paul, 1984).
Nutton, Vivian, 'Caius, John (1510–1573)', *Oxford Dictionary of National Biography* (Oxford: Oxford University Press, 2004).
Obelkevich, James, 'Proverbs and Social History', in *The Social History of Language*, ed. Peter Burke and Roy Porter, Cambridge Studies in Oral and Literate Culture Series, vol. 12 (Cambridge: Cambridge University Press, 1997), pp. 43–72.
Oberer, Karen, 'Appropriations of the Popular Tradition in *The Famous Victories of Henry V* and *The Troublesome Raigne of King John*', in *Locating the Queen's Men 1583–1603: Material pPractices and Conditions of Playing*, ed. Helen Ostovich, Holger Schott Syme and Andrew Griffin, (London and New York: Routledge, 2016), pp. 171–82.
—— 'Charles R. Forker (ed.), The Troublesome Reign of John, King of England', *Early Theatre*, 16:1 (2013), p. 185ff. Literature Resource Center. https://link.gale.com/apps/doc/A335292882/LitRC?u=amst&sid=LitRC&xid=8dd4045c
Orgel, Stephen, 'Prologue: "I am Richard II"', in *Representations of Elizabeth I in Early Modern Culture*, ed. Alessandra Petrina and Laura Tosi (New York: Palgrave Macmillan, 2011).
Ostovich, Helen, Holger Schott Syme and Andrew Griffin, eds., *Locating the Queen's Men, 1583–1603: Material Practices and Conditions of Playing* (London and New York: Routledge, 2016).
O'Sullivan, Lisa, 'The Time and Place of Nostalgia: Re-situating a French Disease', *Journal of the History of Medicine and Allied Sciences*, 67:4 (2011), 626–49.
Palmer, Daryl W., *Hospitable Performances: Dramatic Genre and Cultural Practices in Early Modern England* (West Lafayette, IN: Purdue University Press, 1992).
Panofsky, Erwin, *Renaissance and Renascences in Western Art* (New York, Hagerstown, San Francisco and London: Harper and Row, 1972).
Parker, Barbara L., 'From Monarchy to Tyranny: *Julius Caesar* Among

Shakespeare's Roman Works', in *Julius Caesar: New Critical Essays*, ed. Horst Zander (New York and London: Routledge, 2005), pp. 111–26.
Parmelee, Lisa Ferraro, 'Neostoicism and Absolutism in Late Elizabethan England', in *Politics, Ideology and the Law in Early Modern Europe*, ed. Adrianna E. Bakos (Rochester, NY: University of Rochester Press, 1994), pp. 3–19.
Parry, Graham, 'A Troubled Arcadia', in *Literature and the English Civil War*, ed. Thomas Healy and Jonathan Sawday (Cambridge: Cambridge University Press, 1990).
Parvini, Neema, *Shakespeare's History Plays: Rethinking Historicism* (Edinburgh: Edinburgh Unviersity Press, 2012).
Patriquin, Larry, 'The Agrarian Origins of the Industrial Revolution in England', *Review of Radical Politics*, 36:2 (2004), 196–216, 210.
Patterson, Annabel, *Censorship and Interpretation* (Madison and London: University of Wisconsin Press, 1984).
—— *Reading Holinshed's Chronicles* (Chicago and London: University of Chicago Press, 1994).
—— *Shakespeare and the Popular Voice* (Cambridge, MA: Basil Blackwell, 1989).
Paul, Joanne, 'The Use of *Kairos* in Renaissance Political Philosophy', *Renaissance Quarterly*, 67:1 (2014), 43–78.
Pechter, Edward, '*Julius Caesar* and *Sejanus*: Roman Politics, Inner Selves and the Powers of the Theatre', in *Shakespeare and his Contemporaries: Essays in Comparison*, ed. E. A. J. Honigmann (Manchester and Dover, NH: Manchester University Press, 1986), pp. 60–78.
Peltonen, Markku, *Classical Humanism and Republicanism in English Political Thought 1570–1640*, Ideas in Context Series, gen. ed. Quentin Skinner (Cambridge: Cambridge University Press, 1995).
—— 'Rhetoric and Citizenship in the Monarchical Republic of Queen Elizabeth', in *The Monarchical Republic of Early Modern England: Essays in Response to Patrick Collinson*, ed. John F. McDiarmid (Aldershot: Ashgate, 2007), pp. 109–27.
Pendleton, Thomas A., ed., *Henry VI: Critical Essays*, Shakespeare Criticism Series, gen. ed. Philip C. Kolin (New York and London: Routledge, 2001).
Perry, Curtis, 'The Citizen Politics of Nostalgia: Queen Elizabeth in Jacobean London', *Journal of Medieval and Renaissance Studies*, 23 (1993), 89–111.
Petrey, Sandy, *Speech Acts and Literary Theory* (New York and London: Routledge, 1990).
Pettegree, Jane, *Foreign and Native on the English Stage, 1588–1611: Metaphor and National Identity*, unpublished PhD thesis for the University of St Andrews, January 2009.
Phialas, Peter G., 'The Medieval in *Richard II*', *Shakespeare Quarterly*, 12:3 (1961), 305–10.
Phillips, Harriet, 'Late Falstaff, the Merry World, and The Merry Wives of Windsor', *Shakespeare*, 10:2 (2014), 111–37.
—— *Nostalgia in Print and Performance, 1510–1613: Merry Worlds* (Cambridge: Cambridge University Press, 2019).

Pickering, Jean and Suzanne Kehde, 'Introduction', in *Narratives of Nostalgia, Gender and Nationalism*, ed. Jean Pickering and Suzanne Kehde (Basingstoke and London: Macmillan Press Ltd, 1997), pp. 1–8.
Pinciss, G. M., 'Thomas Creede and the Repertory of the Queen's Men 1583–1592', *Modern Philology*, 67:4 (1970), 321–30.
Potter, Lois, 'The Swan Song of the Stage Historian', in *Re-Presenting Ben Jonson*, ed. Martin Butler (London: Macmillan Press Ltd, 1999), pp. 193–209.
Price, G. R., 'Henry V and Germanicus', *Shakespeare Quarterly*, xii (1961), 57–60.
Quinones, Ricardo, *The Renaissance Discovery of Time*, Harvard Studies in Comparative Literature, vol. 31 (Cambridge, MA: Harvard University Press, 1972).
Rackin, Phyllis, 'The Role of the Audience in Shakespeare's *Richard II*', *Shakespeare Quarterly*, 36:3 (1985), 262–81.
—— *Stages of History* (London: Routledge, 1990).
Radstone, Susannah, *The Sexual Politics of Time: Confession, Nostalgia, Memory* (London and New York: Routledge, 2007).
Richards, Jennifer, 'Assumed Simplicity and the Critique of Nobility: Or, How Castiglione Read Cicero', *Renaissance Quarterly*, 54:2 (2001), 460–86.
—— *Rhetoric and Courtliness in Early Modern Literature* (Cambridge: Cambridge University Press, 2003).
Riggs, David, *Shakespeare's Heroical Histories: Henry VI and Its Literary Tradition* (Cambridge, MA: Harvard University Press, 1971).
Roberts-Smith, Jennifer, '"What makes thou upon a stage?": Child Actors, Royalist Publicity, and the Space of the Nation in the Queen's Men's *True Tragedy of Richard the Third*', *Issue in Review: Making Theatrical Publics on the Early Modern Stage*, ed. Paul Yachnin, *Early Theatre*, 15:2 (2012), 192–205.
Rosaldo, Renato, 'Imperialist Nostalgia', *Representations*, 26 (1989), 107–22.
Rose, Jacqueline, *States of Fantasy* (Oxford: Clarendon Press, 1996).
Ruiter, David, 'Shakespeare and Hospitality: Opening *The Winter's Tale*', *Mediterranean Studies*, 16 (2007), 157–77.
Ryan, Kiernan, 'Measure for Measure: Marxism before Marx', in *Marxist Shakespeares*, ed. Jean E. Howard and Scott Cutler Shershow (New York: Routledge, 2001), pp. 227–44.
Rycroft, Eleanor, 'Morality, Theatricality, and Masculinity in The Interlude of Youth and Hick Scorner', in *The Oxford Handbook of Tudor Drama*, ed. Thomas Betteridge and Greg Walker (Oxford: Oxford University Press, 2012), pp. 465–81.
Sacks, Peter, 'Where Words Prevail Not: Grief, Revenge, and Language in Kyd and Shakespeare', *ELH*, 49:3 (1982), 576–601.
Sackton, Alexander H., *Rhetoric as a Dramatic Language in Ben Jonson* (London: Frank Cass & Co., 1967).
Sanders, Julie, *Ben Jonson's Theatrical Republics* (London: Macmillan Press, Ltd, 1998).
Schanzer, Ernest, *The Problem Plays of Shakespeare* (London: Routledge and Kegan Paul, Ltd, 1963).
Schell, Edgar T., 'Prince Hal's Second "Reformation"', *Shakespeare Quarterly*, 21:1 (1970), 11–16.

Schwyzer, Philip, *Archaeologies of the English Renaissance* (Oxford: Oxford University Press, 2007).
—— '"Late" Losses and the Temporality of Early Modern Nostalgia', in Approaches to Early Modern Nostalgia special issue, ed. Kristine Johanson, *Parergon*, 33:2 (2016), 97–114.
—— 'Lees and Moonshine: Remembering Richard III, 1485–1635', *Renaissance Quarterly*, 63 (2010), 850–83.
—— *Literature, Nationalism, and Memory in Early Modern England and Wales* (Cambridge: Cambridge University Press, 2004).
Scott, William O., 'Landholding, Leasing, and Inheritance in "Richard II"', *Studies in English Literature, 1500–1900*, 42:2 (2002), 275–92.
Sedikides, Constantine, Keynote Lecture 'Back to the Future: Nostalgia Fosters Optimism, Inspiration, and Creativity', German Historical Institute London, 1 October 2015.
—— et al., 'Nostalgia Motivates Pursuit of Important Goals by Increasing Meaning in Life: Nostalgia, Meaning, Motivation', *European Journal of Social Psychology*, 48:2 (2018), 209–16.
Segarra, Santiago, Mark Eisen, Gabriel Egan and Alejandro Ribeiro, 'Attributing the Authorship of the Henry VI Plays by Word Adjacency', *Shakespeare Quarterly*, 67:2 (2016), 232–56.
Serpieri, Alessandro, 'Shakespeare and Plutarch: Intertextuality in Action', in *Shakespeare, Italy, and Intertextuality*, ed. Michele Marrapodi (Manchester and New York: Manchester University Press, 2004), pp. 47–58.
Shapiro, H. A., *Myth into Art: Poet and Painter in Classical Greece* (London and New York: Routledge, 1994).
Sharp, Buchanan, *In Contempt of All Authority: Artisans and Riot in the West of England, 1586–1640* (Berkeley: University of California Press, 1980).
Sharpe, Kevin, *Reading Revolutions: The Politics of Reading in Early Modern England* (New Haven, CT and London: Yale University Press, 2000).
Shell, Alison, *Catholicism, Controversy and the English Literary Imagination, 1558–1660* (Cambridge: Cambridge University Press, 1999).
—— *Oral Culture and Catholicism in Early Modern England* (Cambridge: Cambridge University Press, 2007).
Sherman, Anita Gilman, *Skepticism and Memory in Shakespeare and Donne* (Basingstoke: Palgrave Macmillan, 2007).
Shrank, Cathy, *Writing the Nation in Reformation England, 1530–1580* (Oxford: Oxford University Press, 2004).
Sipiora, Phillip and James S. Baumlin, eds, *Rhetoric and Kairos: Essays in History, Theory, and Praxis* (Albany: State Univetsity of New York Press, 2002).
Skinner, Quentin, *Reason and Rhetoric in the Philosophy of Hobbes* (Cambridge: Cambridge University Press, 1996).
Slack, Paul, 'Dearth and Social Policy in Early Modern England', *Social History of Medicine*, 5:1 (1992), 1–17.
Slights, Camille, 'Time's Debt to Season: *The Comedy of Errors*, IV.ii.58', *ELN*, 24 (1986), 22–5.
Slights, William W. E., *Ben Jonson and The Art of Secrecy* (Toronto: University of Toronto Press, 1994).
Smith, Molly, 'Mutant Scenes and "Minor" Conflicts', in *Richard II: A Feminist*

Companion to Shakespeare, ed. Dympna Callaghan, 2nd edn (London: Wiley & Sons, 2000/2016).

Spencer, T. J. B., 'Shakespeare and the Elizabethan Romans', *Shakespeare Survey*, 10 (1957), 27–38.

Spevack, Martin, *A Complete and Systematic Concordance to the Works of Shakespeare*, 2 vols (Hildesheim: Georg Olms, 1968), vol. II.

Starobinski, Jean, 'The Idea of Nostalgia', trans. Will Kemp, *Diogenes*, 14 (1966), 81–103.

Stern, Tiffany, 'Time for Shakespeare: Hourglasses, Sundials, Clocks, and Early Modern Theatre', *Journal of the British Academy*, 3 (2015), 1–33.

Stewart, Susan, *On Longing: Narratives of the Miniature, the Gigantic, the Souvenir, the Collection* (Durham, NC and London: Duke University Press, 1993).

Stirling, Brents, 'Shakespeare's Mob Scenes: A Reinterpretation', *The Huntington Library Quarterly*, 8:3 (1945), 213–40.

Stober, Karen, *Later Medieval Monasteries and their Patrons: England and Wales, c. 1300–1540*, Studies in the History of Medieval Religion, vol. XXIX (Woodbridge: The Boydell Press, 2007).

Strohm, Paul, *Politique: Languages of Statecraft between Chaucer and Shakespeare* (Notre Dame, IN: University of Notre Dame, 2005).

Su, John J., *Ethics and Nostalgia in the Contemporary Novel* (Cambridge: Cambridge University Press, 2005).

Sullivan Jr., Garett A., *Memory and Forgetting in English Renaissance Drama*, Cambridge Studies in Renaissance Literature and Culture, gen. ed. Stephen Orgel (Cambridge: Cambridge University Press, 2005).

Taylor, Gary and Rory Loughnane, 'The Canon and Chronology', in *The New Oxford Authorship Companion*, eds Gary Taylor and Gabriel Egan (Oxford: Oxford University Press, 2017), pp. 417–602.

Taylor, Warren, *Tudor Figures of Rhetoric*, ed. Warren Shibles (Whitewater, WI: Language Press, 1972).

Thomas, Keith, *The Perception of the Past in Early Modern England*, The Creighton Trust Lecture (London: University of London, 1983).

Thomson, Peter, 'Tarlton, Richard (d. 1588)', *Oxford Dictionary of National Biography*, ed. H. C. G. Matthew and Brian Harrison (Oxford: Oxford University Press, 2004; online edition 2009).

Tigner, Amy L., *Literature and the Renaissance Garden from Elizabeth I to Charles II: England's Paradise* (Farnham: Ashgate, 2012).

Tilley, Morris Palmer, *Dictionary of the Proverbs in England in the Sixteenth and Seventeenth Centuries* (Ann Arbor: University of Michigan, 1950).

Tillyard, E. M. W., *Shakespeare's History Plays* (London: Chatto and Windus, 1944).

Todd, Margo, *Christian Humanism and the Puritan Social Order* (Cambridge: Cambridge University Press, 2003).

Trevor-Roper, Hugh, 'History and Imagination', in *History and Imagination: Essays in Honour of Hugh Trevor-Roper*, ed. Hugh Lloyd-Jones, Valerie Pearl and Blair Worden (London: Duckworth, 1981), pp. 356–69.

Trilling, Renée R., *The Aesthetics of Nostalgia: Historical Representation in Old English Verse* (Toronto: University of Toronto Press, 2009).

Tsukada, Yuichi, *Shakespeare and the Politics of Nostalgia: Negotiating the Memory of Elizabeth I on the Jacobean Stage* (London: Bloomsbury, 2019).

Tuck, Richard, *Philosophy and Government, 1572–1651*, Ideas in Context Series, gen. ed. Quentin Skinner (Cambridge: Cambridge University Press, 1993).

Tupper Jr., Frederick, 'The Shakespearean Mob', *PMLA*, 27:4 (1912), 486–523.

Ule, Louis, *A Concordance to the Works of Christopher Marlowe*, The Elizabethan Concordance Series, ed. Jean Jofen (Hildesheim and New York: Georg Olms, 1979).

Urkowitz, Steven, '"If I Mistake in Those Foundations Which I Build Upon": Peter Alexander's Textual Analysis of Henry VI Parts 2 and 3', *English Literary Renaissance*, 18 (1988), 230–56.

Van Es, Bart, 'In Brief', *TLS*, 15 February 2008.

Vaught, Jennifer C., *Masculinity and Emotion in Early Modern English Literature* (Aldershot: Ashgate, 2008).

Vendler, Helen, *The Art of Shakespeare's Sonnets* (Cambridge, MA: Harvard University Press, 1997).

Vickers, Brian, '*The Troublesome Reign*, George Peele, and the Date of *King John*', in *Words that Count: Essays on Early Modern Authorship in Honor of MacDonald P. Jackson*, ed. Brian Boyd (Newark: University of Delaware Press, 2004), pp. 78–116.

Walsh, Brian, 'Chantry, Chronicle, Cockpit: Henry V and the Forms of History', in *Shakespeare and the Middle Ages*, ed. Curtis Perry and John Watkins (Oxford: Oxford University Press, 2009), pp. 151–71.

—— *Shakespeare, the Queen's Men, and the Elizabethan Performance of History* (Cambridge: Cambridge University Press, 2009).

—— 'Theatrical Temporality and Historical Consciousness in *The Famous Victories of Henry V*', *Theatre Journal*, 59:1 (2007), 57–73.

Walsham, Alexandra, *Providence in Early Modern England* (Oxford: Oxford University Press, 1999).

—— *The Reformation of the Landscape: Religion, Memory, and Identity in Early Modern Britain and Ireland* (Oxford: Oxford University Press, 2011).

Ward, Bernard M., '*The Famous Victories of Henry V*: Its Place in Elizabethan Dramatic Literature', *The Review of English Studies*, 4 (1928), 270–94.

Warkentin, Germaine, ed., *The Queen's Majesty's Passage and Related Documents* (Toronto: Published by Centre for Reformation and Renaissance Studies, 2004).

Warley, Christopher, 'Shakespeare's Fickle-Fee Simple: A Lover's Complaint, Nostalgia, and the Transition from Feudalism to Capitalism', in *Shakespeare and the Middle Ages*, eds Curtis Perry and John Watkins (Oxford and New York: Oxford University Press, 2009), pp. 21–44.

Warren, Roger, 'The Quarto and Folio Texts of 2 *Henry VI*: A Reconsideration', *The Review of English Studies*, 51:202 (2000), 193–207.

Weiner, Carol Z., 'The Beleaguered Isle: A Study of Elizabethan and Early Jacobean Anti-Catholicism', *Past and Present*, 51 (1971), 27–62.

Wells, Robin Headlam, '*Julius Caesar*, Machiavelli, and The Uses of History', *Shakespeare Survey*, 55 (2002), 209–18.

Wells, Stanley and Gary Taylor et al., *William Shakespeare: A Textual Companion* (Oxford: Clarendon Press, 1986).

White, Hayden, 'The Value of Narrativity in the Representation of Reality', *Critical Inquiry*, 7:1 (1980), 5–27.
Williams, Raymond, *The Country and the City* (London: Chatto and Windus, 1973).
Wilson, J. Dover, 'Shakespeare's Richard III and The True Tragedy of Richard the Third, 1594', *Shakespeare Quarterly*, 3:4 (1952), 299–306.
Wilson, Luke, *Theaters of Intention: Drama and the Law in Early Modern England* (Stanford, CA: Stanford University Press, 2000).
Womersley, David, 'Sir Henry Savile's Translation of Tacitus and the Political Interpretation of Elizabethan Texts', *The Review of English Studies*, New Series, 42:167 (1991), 313–42.
Wood, David Houston, *Time, Narrative, and Emotion in Early Modern England* (Farnham: Ashgate, 2009).
Woods, Gillian, *Shakespeare's Unreformed Fictions* (Oxford: Oxford University Press, 2013).
Woolf, D. R., *The Idea of History in Early Stuart England* (Toronto, Buffalo, London: University of Toronto Press, 1990).
Worden, Blair, 'Classical Republicanism and the Puritan Revolution', in *History and Imagination: Essays in Honour of H. R. Trevor-Roper*, ed. Hugh Lloyd-Jones, Valerie Pearl and Blair Worden (London: Gerald Duckworth & Co, 1981), pp. 182–200.
—— 'Historians and Poets', *The Huntington Library Quarterly*, 68 (2005), 71–93.
—— *Literature and Politics in Cromwellian England: John Milton, Andrew Marvell, Marchamont Nedham* (Oxford: Oxford University Press, 2007).
—— 'Shakespeare and Politics', in *Shakespeare and Politics*, ed. Catherine M. S. Alexander (Cambridge: Cambridge University Press, 2004), pp. 22–43.
—— *The Sound of Virtue: Philip Sidney's Arcadia and Elizabethan Politics* (New Haven, CT and London: Yale University Press, 1996).
Yates, Frances A., *The Art of Memory* (London: Routledge & Kegan Paul, 1966).
—— *Astraea: The Imperial Theme in the Sixteenth Century* (London and Boston, MA: Routledge and Kegan Paul, 1975).
—— 'Queen Elizabeth as Astraea', *Journal of the Warburg and Courtauld Institutes*, 10 (1947), 27–82.

Index

absent hospitality, 96–131
Achilles, 49
Adam and Eve, 1, 83–4
Admiral's Men, 36
Alexander the Great, 22
Allen, Percy, 132–3
Allott, Richard, *England's Parnassus*, 115
ambivalence, 19–20, 31n, 79–89
'anticipatory nostalgia', 16
'anti-history' heroism, 53
Antony, Mark, 162–3n
argumentum in utramque partem, 26, 109
Aristotle, 14
Astraea, 54–5, 72
   Elizabeth I as, 9, 21–2, 54–5, 74

Baker, Sir Richard, *A chronicle of the Kings of England*, 76
Baldo, Jonathan, 4
Bale, John, *King Johan*, 58
Ball, John, 82–5, 94n
banishment, 8, 114–15
Banks, Joseph, 7, 29n
Barret, J. K. *see* 'anticipatory nostalgia'
Beacon, Richard, *Solon: his follie*, 14
Becon, Thomas, 73–4, 92n
Ben-Amos, Ilana Krausman, 100
Bible, 73–5, 92n
   Ecclesiastes, 19–20, 59, 76
   Gospel of Matthew, 103
Bishops' Ban 1599, 134
Black Prince, 2
Bloch, Ernst, 12

Boym, Svetlana, 12, 23
Burton, Robert, *Anatomy of Melancholy*, 7–9
Burton, William, 'The Anatomie of Belial', 75

Caesar, Julius 2
   Tower of London, 6
Cain, Tom, 156
Caius, John, 68, 89–90n
Calvin, John, 70–1, 91n
Cassirer, Ernst, 20
Catholicism, 58–9, 68–89, 92n, 105, 107, 117, 152
Chamberlain's Men, 36, 133
Charles V, 21
Chernaik, Warren, 142
chivalric code, 98
chorismos, 20
Cicero, *De inventione*, 21
'Common-weale', 48–9
commonwealth, failing, 123
constancy, 149–50
continuity, 17–23
counter-Reformation, 164n
Cromwell, Thomas, 104–5
cyclical history, 134–5, 139, 140–1

Daniell, David, 163n, 164n
Davis, Alex, 10
Davis, Fred, 10
dearth of corn, 99–102, 122
degeneration, 139, 141
Delisle, Jennifer, 12
Demosthenes, 18–19

Derrida, Jacques, *Of Hospitality*, 98
desire
  dramaturgy, 24
  Elizabeth I, 169–71
  embodied actor, 37
  Henry V, 1, 16–17, 41
  Jack Cade, 85–7
  Julius Caesar, 143–8
  Lord of Misrule, 64n
  'merry world,' 69, 75
  nostalgia, 3, 8–12, 15, 19
  nostalgic paroemia, 77
  Richard II, 97–9, 108, 118, 124
  Sejanus, 148–52
  Tamburlaine, 50, 52
Digges, Leonard, 132, 135–6
disease, nostalgia as, 6–7, 29n
Dissolution of the Monasteries, 25, 54, 76, 98, 103–4, 106–8
Donaldson, Ian, 133
Doty, Jeffrey, 98, 109
dramaturgy, 3–5
  Jonson, Ben, 26, 135, 158
  Queen's Men, 37–42, 46–7, 54, 56–7
  Shakespeare, William, 13–17, 23–4, 26, 36, 79–80, 83, 98, 109, 124, 135, 165, 169–70
Durham Cathedral, 107

Ecclesiastes (Bible), 19–20, 59, 76
Eden, 1, 55–6, 71, 83–4, 115, 125
Edward III, 2
Eggert, Katherine, 9
Elizabeth I, 49–50
  as Astraea, 9, 21–2, 54–5, 74
  'Good Queen Bess', 4, 169
  Stuart England's nostalgia for, 4
Elyot, Thomas, *The Book of the Governor*, 20
England as new Rome, 1–2
'England's inheritance', 69, 97, 119
equity, 82–9
Erasmus, 21
  Adagia, 19, 70
  Adagiorum chiliades, 70
  Ciceronianus, 19
  Collectanea, 70
Essex, Earl of, 97, 137

fasting days, 117–18
Fielde, John, 77–8, 85
  A caveat for Parsons Howlet, 74
Fletcher, John, 169
  King Henry VIII (All is True), 169–71
Fortune, 20, 45–7, 50–1, 53
Foxe, John, *Actes and monuments*, 58, 73–4
future
  anticipation of an unknown, 37–8
  imperative, 50–7
  inevitable decline, 10–11
  in language, 168–9
  longings, 38–45
  looking forward to, 35–67
  prophecies of the, 57–9, 61, 169–70
  as void, 11
future-focused history play, 39–40, 57

'garden of England', 48–9, 65n
Gibson, James C., 98
Golden Age, return of, 9, 21–2, 50, 54–7, 76, 169
Golding, Arthur, 54, 70–1
'Good Queen Bess', 4, 169
Gospel of Matthew (Bible), 103
'Gracious Menewe', 92n
  A plaine subversyon, 73–4
Grafton, Richard, *A Chronicle at Large*, 83
Great Revolt 1381, 82–4, 94n
Greene, Robert, 53–4
  A Maidens Dreame upon the Death of the Right Honorable Sir Christopher Hatton, 54
  A quip for an upstart courtier, 84, 94n
Greene, Thomas, 18
Greneway, Richard, 137
grief, 122–3, 131n

Harding, Thomas, *A confutation of a booke intituled An apologie of the Church of England*, 75–6
Heal, Felicity, 96, 102
Hector, 49, 59
Henry III, 58
Henry V, 162n

Henry VIII, 58, 76, 101, 104
'heroic world', 154–5
Hick Scorner, 71–3, 77, 79, 91n
historical consciousness, 37
historicising nostalgia, 5–13
historiography, 134–5, 137–8
history plays, 4, 11–12
Hofer, Johannes, 5
  Dissertatio Medica de Nostalgia, oder Heimwehe, 6–7
Holinshed, Raphael, *The Third Volume of Chronicles*, 83
Holland, Philemon, 156
Holy Roman Empire, 21–2
homesickness, 6–9, 29n
hope and political action, 12
hospitality, 47
  absent, 96–131
  inhospitable England, 108–18
  locating Elizabethan, 99–108
  'myth of hospitality', 96
humanism, 13–14, 18–20, 87, 138, 156
Humphreys, Arthur, 38
Hunt, Maurice, 143
Hutson, Lorna, 149

Illbruck, Helmut, 12
imitatio, 19
inhospitable England, 108–18
innovatio, 19
Iron Age, 21–2, 54, 60–1, 71–2

Jacobean history plays, 166
Jameson, Frederic, 12
Jewel, John, Bishop of Salisbury, 75–6
  A defence, 76
Jonson, Ben
  dramaturgy, 26, 135, 158
  Epicene or The Silent Woman, 132, 137
  Sejanus, 132–6, 139–40, 148–64
  and Shakespeare, 132–64
Justices of the Peace, 100, 113

Kahn, Coppélia, 143
Kahn, Victoria, 13
kairos, 119–20; see also *occasio*
Karremann, Isabel, 4
King, Pamela, 77

King's Men, 133
Korda, Natasha, 11

Lambarde, William, 98
language and political power, 14, 117–18
language manipulation, 134
Laslett, Peter, *The World We Have Lost*, 64n
Lassells, John (or Lascelles), 76
legitimacy crisis, 60
The life and death of Jack Straw, 83–5
Lipsius, Justus, 157
  Sixe bookes of politickes or civil doctrine, 137, 149–50
  Two bookes of constancie, 149–51, 153, 162n
longing
  for the future, 38–45
  nostalgia as, 3, 37
Lord of Misrule, 64n
Lupton, Julia Reinhard, 98
Lusty Juventus, 77–9, 157

Machiavelli, Niccolò, 120
MacLean, Sally-Beth, *The Queen's Men and their Plays*, 35
McMillin, Scott, *The Queen's Men and their Plays*, 35
McRae, Andrew, 103
Marlowe, Christopher, 3, 166
  Tamburlaine, 11, 35–8, 46, 50–7, 62
The Marriage of Wit and Wisdom, 79
Marx, Karl, *The Eighteenth Brumaire of Louis Bonaparte*, 10, 12
Marxism, 10
'mean season', 96–131, 126–7n
medieval dramatic traditions, 40
melancholy, 7–9
  and femininity and age, 9
memorial reconstruction, 40–1
memory, 19, 146, 156
'merry England', 39, 68–95, 169
Meskill, Lynn, 132
methixis, 20
modernity, 5–6, 12
  degenerate, 138–9
Montaigne, Michel de, 19, 150
Munro, Lucy, 11

Mylles, Francis, 107
myth of hospitality, 96
mythos of the republic, 143–5

Nashe, Thomas, *Pierce Penilesse*, 38–9
Neostoicism, 19, 134, 148–59
Nero, 59
New Historicism, 4–5, 10
Norfolk, Duke of
   Howard, Thomas, 76, 104
   Mowbray, Thomas, 104
Norton, Thomas, 107
nostalgia
   against, 35–67
   'anticipatory nostalgia', 16
   as catalyst for political action, 3
   as desire in time, 3
   as disease, 6–7, 29n
   engine of, 140–8
   future-focused, 3
   historicising, 5–13
   lessons of, 132–64
   as longing, 3, 37
   resisting, 165–71
   rethinking, 1–34
   rhetoric as means of persuasion, 2–3
   Stuart England's nostalgia for Elizabeth, 4
   'supernostalgia', 9
   suspicion of, 23, 25, 69, 79, 83, 88–9, 165, 169–71
'now', 51–2, 61, 116

Obelkevich, James, 70
occasio, 20–1, 119–20
Ovid, 56, 72, 131n, 139
   Metamorphoses, 54
Oxfordshire rising 1596, 82

paroemia, 68–95
past
   futility of the ideal, 69, 77, 80, 113, 148, 154, 157
   political convenience of an idealised, 2
   and present, 17–23, 37, 60
   rupture between past and present, 17–23, 51–2

Paul, Joanne, 119–20
Peele, George, 59, 66–7n
   Descensus astraeae, 55
   The Troublesome Reign of King John, 36, 57–62
Peltonen, Markku, 14
Persia, 51
Phillips, Harriet, 11, 68
pilgrimage, 114–15, 121–2, 125, 130n
Plutarch, 145, 148, 162–3n, 163n
polis, 15–16
political 'good' and action, 14–15
Polybius, 53, 139, 150, 161–2n
Poor Law 1536, 101, 103–5
poor relief, 99–102
present
   fantasy of a continuous present, 123–4
   and past, 17–23, 37, 60
   rupture between past and present, 17–23, 51–2
Privy Council, 99–101, 155
Privy Council Proclamation 1596, 97, 101–2, 108, 112–13
prophecies of the future, 57–9, 61, 124–5, 169–70
Protestantism, 58–9, 68–95, 105
proverbs, 70, 73–4, 84–5
Puttenham, George, *The arte of English poesie*, 19

Queen's Men, 3, 35–67, 167–8, 169
   dramaturgy, 37–42, 46–7, 54, 56–7
   The Famous Victories of Henry the Fifth, 35, 38–45, 63–4; king's death, 40–3, 64n
   Selimus, 35, 50–7; Golden Age speech, 54–6
   The True Chronicle History of King Leir, 36, 63n
   The Troublesome Reign of King John, 36, 57–62
   The True Tragedy of Richard the Third, 35, 45–50, 64n
Quinones, Ricardo, 18

reclamation, 22–3, 88, 97, 124, 139
Reformation, 68–95, 103
renovatio, 21–2, 49

Republic, Roman, 143–59
Respublica, 78, 157
rhetoric and politics, 13–17
Richard I, and Tarquin, 59
Richard II, 43–4
   Elizabeth as, 97–8
Rites of Durham, 107
ritual season, 68–95
Roman Empire, 48–9
Rome, 132–64
   England as new, 1–2
   Republic, 143–59
rupture, 17–23, 51–2

Savile, Sir Henry, 137, 156
scarcity of corn, 99–102, 122
scepticism, 20, 24
sensus communis, 42, 70, 146
Shakespeare, William
   Antony and Cleopatra, 166–9
   The Book of Sir Thomas More, 78–9
   Coriolanus, 8
   The First Part of the Contention Betwixt the Two Famous Houses of York and Lancaster, 69, 83, 87–8, 90n
   1 Henry IV, 38
   Henry V, 1–2, 9, 15–17, 21, 22, 43–4, 65n; Saint Crispin's Day speech, 15–16, 21
   1 Henry VI, 39, 89
   2 Henry VI, 3, 14–15, 68–70, 79–95, 90n, 134–5; Cockaigne speech, 81
   Henry VIII (All is True), 169–71
   Julius Caesar, 3, 15–17, 44, 53, 117, 132–64, 167
   King John, 57–62, 130n
   Othello, 135–6
   Richard II, 3, 8, 14, 21–2, 44, 61, 65n, 96–104, 108–31, 134–5; 'Sceptred isle' speech, 98, 115–18, 125
   Romeo and Juliet, 21
   Sonnet 64, 106
   Sonnet 73, 105–6
   Titus Andronicus, 105–6, 131n
   dramaturgy, 13–17, 23–4, 26, 36, 79–80, 83, 98, 109, 124, 135, 165, 169–70
   and Jonson, 132–64
Sharp, Buchanan, 82
The Shoemaker's Holiday, 11
similitudo temporum, 137–8, 150–1, 155–6
Smith, Henry, 75, 92n
Smith, Thomas, *A Discourse of the Common Weal of this Realm of England*, 112–13
sovereignty in time, 118–26
Starobinski, Jean, 5
Stationers' Register, 63–4n, 64–5n, 71
status conflict, 82–9
Stewart, Susan, 10–11
Stow, John, 83, 94n
   'old time,' 6
   Survey of London, 6, 106–8
Suffolk, Duke of, 76
suspects of history, 136–9
suspicion of nostalgia, 23, 25, 69, 79, 83, 88–9, 165, 169–71

Tacitus, 134, 136–9, 152, 155, 157, 159, 163n
   Annals, 138
Tarlton, Richard, 63n
Tarquin, 59
Taverner, Richard, 21
   Proverbes or adagies, 70
temporal
   collapse, 60
   consciousness, 24, 37–8, 41, 51, 54, 77, 166
   cycles, 59
   desire, 118, 124
   displacement, 84–5
   investments, 37
   as political, 37
Thomas, Sir William, 76
Thomas of Woodstock, 111–14, 117, 129–30n
   Pleshy, 111–14, 123
Three sermons, or Homelies to moove compassion towards the poore, 103
time-telling devices, 20–1
topicality, 4–5, 39, 60, 84

Trilling, Renée, 11
Tsukada, Yuichi 166
Tyler, Wat, 82–3
tyranny, 14, 25, 58, 99, 121, 125, 133, 136, 147, 151–8

Veritas Temporis Filia (Truth is the Daughter of Time), 54
Vespasian, 138
Virgil, *Fourth Eclogue*, 54, 169
Vogel, Ralph Augustus, 7

Walsh, Brian, 37
Walsham, Alexandra, 97, 106
Welshness, 22
Wever, R., *Lusty Juventus*, 77–9, 157
Williams, Raymond, 9
   The Country and the City, 96
Wilson, Thomas, 18–19
'world was never', 70–3, 94n

Yates, Frances, 49
   Astraea, 21–2

EU representative:
Easy Access System Europe
Mustamäe tee 50, 10621 Tallinn, Estonia
Gpsr.requests@easproject.com

www.ingramcontent.com/pod-product-compliance
Lightning Source LLC
Chambersburg PA
CBHW070354240426
43671CB00013BA/2491